HOW LUXURY
CONQUERED THE WORLD

BY ASTRID WENDLANDT

Au bord du monde, une vagabonde dans le Grand Nord sibérien,
Robert Laffont, 2010.

L'Oural en plein cœur, des steppes à la taïga sibérienne,
Albin Michel, 2014.

Astrid Wendlandt

HOW LUXURY
CONQUERED THE WORLD

The inside story of its pioneers

Foreword by Sylvain Tesson

MISS
TWEED
Publishing

ISBN 978-2-9569335-1-9.

D.L. : October 2019.

Cover illustration: © Claire Laude, www.clairelaude.com

Cover design: Claire Laude.

Illustrations inside the book: © Claire Laude.

Copyright © 2019 Miss Tweed Publishing.

Published by Miss Tweed Publishing, 28, rue de Poissy, 75005 Paris, France.

http://www.misstweed.com

To my father, Hans–Christian Wendlandt.

Edited by Tom Heneghan, a former Reuters colleague.

Contents

The Earth is chic! by Sylvain Tesson   13

On secrecy and economic might   17

Eternal Karl   27

The Magnificent Six.   41
     Pioneers.   43

Alain-Dominique the conqueror   51
     Antiques dealer   55
     The *"Les Must"* adventure   56
     Belle Époque   61
     "Big Bang" Parties   64
     The ADP way   66
     Moving on.   70
     Cartier Foundation for Contemporary Art.   72
     What about Cartier today?   75

Jean-Louis the artist   79
     Soft power.   81
     Hermès: the story   85
     The Hermès way   90

Discovering the world 92

Family business............................. 97

Old money 98

Leila Menchari.............................. 100

The workshops.............................. 102

Advertising 104

Running the business 107

After Jean-Louis............................. 109

Yves the geostrategist 115

The world is my oyster....................... 119

The diplomat............................... 121

From sponges to handbags 123

Racamier's heritage 126

Building blocks 128

Conquering the world 130

Image makers 133

Branching out into fashion................... 135

Always everywhere.......................... 138

Dark days................................. 140

Louis Vuitton after Carcelle.................. 145

Good leadership............................. 149

The value of access.......................... 154

What is more precious than a job?.............. 157

More Gypsies please......................... 160

The reality behind the dream 162

José the revolutionary........................ 169

Working together........................... 174

Internet refuseniks 178

Meditating leader........................... 181

Geek turns entrepreneur...................... 182

Building Farfetch 186

José the deal-maker 190

Lion's share 192

Farfetch visit 193

Focus on values   195
Store of the future   198
Tomorrow's challenges   204

Ralph the coach   209
The Toledano clan   214
Karl Lagerfeld Inc.   218
Designer whisperer.   221
The Chloé adventure   227
The Puig period.   235
Victoria Beckham   240
Where is fashion going?   242

Jacques the Cossack.   247
The watch factory   256
The Raketa story   260
Miss World.   264
BRIC luxury.   266

Origins and spirituality of luxury.   271
Symbolism.   280

The future of luxury.   283

Bibliography.   291

Index   295

The Earth is chic!

PERHAPS ONE DAY LONG AGO, DEEP IN THE AFRICAN Savannah, a hominid took a bird's feather, planted it in his hair and returned to his fellow men who were slicing up a warthog. They looked at him with surprise, they envied him, they imitated him. Other members of the group started hunting for feathers that were rarer and more beautiful. The idea of luxury, that is to say of beauty, adornment and exclusivity was born. Some planted more feathers in their hair: it was the luxury of abundance. Others found some that were very rare: it was the luxury of distinction. Some discovered the biggest feathers: it became the luxury of magnificence. Suddenly, something changed in the clan: the head of the tribe adorned himself with all the best feathers. Luxury had become the emblem of power.

A few million years later, people are snatching up Louis Vuitton bags in Shanghai and Cartier declares that a trinket is a *Must*. Ultimately, man has not changed that much. *Homo sapiens* is a species that never really reinvented itself. It has only made some progress in the art of arranging diamonds and engraving platinum. And if we no longer eat raw hyena liver, we still desire things that shine, embellish and stand out. Hence any writer who reflects on the "idea of luxury" ends up in the field of philosophy. One should not treat Astrid Wendlandt's book as a purely journalistic investigation into the luxury industry. Admittedly, the author does come from the world of journalism. At Reuters and for international newspapers, she practiced the art of the interview, conducted investigations and crafted stories.

It is one thing to reveal the dealings of great industrial empires, to meet their captains and drill through their mysteries. It is quite another to capture the essence of the meaning of luxury. A luxury object signifies more than what it is, is worth more than what it costs and weighs more than its mass in metal. In *How Luxury Conquered the World*, Astrid Wendlandt reflects on the very idea of luxury as she paints the portrait of its greatest promotors. As the book progresses, one gets a sense of man's strange propensity to spend considerable amounts of energy on the possession of an object that will be of no use to him. It will not allow him to hammer in a nail or hunt an antelope. It will provoke the envy of his neighbors and sarcasm among his friends, and it will call for care regarding theft and degradation. Luxury, in short, is what triggers a sort of fever of greed that will only be appeased through acquisition. It is actually the epitome of commerce: a pathology and its remedy. The object delightfully traps both suitor and owner.

With each passing chapter, the reader will discover personalities more or less famous, more or less intense.

Many know Alain-Dominique Perrin, demiurge of the global luxury industry, everyone admires Karl Lagerfeld, Field-Marshall of the order of chic, and associates Ralph Toledano with the world championship of elegance. Most people have heard of Jean-Louis Dumas, the man who had more than one trick in his bag, and Yves Carcelle, Louis Vuitton's prophet. No-one ignores the youth of a Hermès fragrance, the silhouette of a Chanel little black dress or the hieroglyph of a Vuitton bag. Fewer people have crossed the path of José Neves and Jacques von Polier. But these great experts of what is useless and desirable, superfluous and excellent, each in his own way underscore the same idea, so well expressed by Paul Valéry: "What is deepest in man is his skin."

In other words, one cannot do without what we don't need. We don't realize that the accessory is crucial. So, Cartier was right to call a *Must* what we thought we could describe as "not needed." Perhaps, it is specific to humans to want to turn a useless item into an object of conquest. Astrid Wendlandt reminds us that it would be a mistake to reduce one's eagerness to sell beautiful clothes to a simple ploy aimed at stoking vanities. No, there is a greater motive behind the race for luxury. Reality is not enough for us. Religion being too rigorous and art too elitist, one had to invent a means of escape within the reach of all desires. Luxury stems from religion and art. It takes from the former its irrational side, from the latter its style.

One will discover that the strategists that have carved up the luxury market among themselves lead consortiums endowed with considerable power. The revenues are gigantic, the stakes are worthy of arms contracts and the negotiations have the allure of state secrets. What a strange world this is of lightness and ornaments, governed by the laws of superpowers. But this paradox does not frighten Astrid Wendlandt, accustomed to reconciling opposites. Ten years ago, she traipsed across the Arctic tundra and the Urals. She followed nomadic tribes migrating behind their reindeer herds, climbed peaks with Russian adventurers, slept under the stars, dined on a bear shank and jumped onto the Trans-Siberian train. None of which predisposed her to become a luxury world specialist. None of which really? One should not be so sure. After all, admiring the northern lights at sunset on a summer evening in front of the Kara Sea is a luxury. At least, it is a permanent quest for splendor (minus the desire to acquire its object).

The author readily admits it: one finds in luxury craftsmanship an endeavor to prolong, to embody and celebrate the world's beauty.

Just think, though—nature does not need to make such effort.

Sylvain Tesson.

On secrecy and economic might

LITERATURE EXISTS "BECAUSE LIFE IS NOT ENOUGH," writes Portuguese poet Fernando Pessoa. He could have said the same thing of luxury. Extreme sports, travel, gastronomy, art and luxury objects are among the last areas in which we can let our imagination run free. In a disenchanted and frightened world, hamstrung by political correctness and technocratic processes, we long for fresh air, for adventure, for new horizons. For our own Ultima Thule.

Luxury is about escapism. It promises a break from the daily grind. It makes us believe that we are worth more than we are. Vanity of vanities, all is vanity. Luxury, whether it is about fashion, jewelry or travel, simply would not exist if we did not nurture irrational needs. Objectively, a Hermès scarf serves no purpose. But some women believe they need it as much as their husband's love.

We define ourselves by the objects, experiences and memories we acquire. We're not talking here about things we need to subsist but about what fulfils our quest for beauty, gives meaning to our lives and brings us pleasure and social recognition. *Cogito ergo sum* (I think therefore I am) are the famous words declared by French philosopher René Descartes in his *Discourse on the Method* published in the mid-17th century. Transplanting this concept in our consumerist 21st century, it morphs into *I spend therefore I am*. If I spend, I must therefore exist. Some of us live by our special moments and purchases, and by what others will say about them, offline and online, via social networks such as Instagram, Facebook and Weibo.

If we are what we spend, the luxury goods industry helps Europe exist both economically and culturally. Ralph Toledano, president of the French Federation of Fashion and Haute Couture, sums it up well: "What do you think? Do people know about France thanks to Airbus or thanks to Chanel, Dior and Saint Laurent?" Fashion helps remind the world France exists.

In France, the luxury industry represents more than a million jobs and generates in excess of 150 billion euros in annual sales, which is more than the automobile and aerospace industries combined. In 2018, total sales generated by LVMH, the world's biggest luxury group with more than 70 brands including Dior, Celine, Fendi and Louis Vuitton, came to 46.8 billion euros. In 2019, the group's revenues were on track to reach more than 50 billion euros or five times France's annual budget for culture and the arts.

The luxury goods sector, which barely existed four decades ago, has become a major pillar of the global economy. It is one of the few industries that still grows and creates jobs. Many countries including the United States, South Korea, Russia, Japan and China are fast building their own luxury brands and the sector has become an important contributor to their economic and cultural development.

However, luxury is not only about expensive flagships. Think of farmers cultivating patchouli plants in Indonesia for Guerlain perfumes, embroiderers and stonecutters in India toiling for Hermès, Chanel and Cartier. The luxury business represents a gigantic ecosystem of traders, artisans, models, photographers, designers, retailers, marketing gurus, head-hunters and consultants who together make up a workforce of millions. They are the faces behind the perfumes, cosmetics, jewelry, watches, gastronomy, high-end hotels and ready-to-wear that generate huge revenues for luxury brands.

However, few journalists enjoy the "luxury" of writing freely about this powerful and secretive industry. Many media rely on fashion and luxury brands' advertising budgets to make ends meet. It is not easy to bite the hand that feeds you. Officially, most editors-in-chief say their reporters write whatever they want but in reality, they censor themselves. They need to preserve good relations with brands. Otherwise, that precious ad budget might not be renewed. Luxury brands expect journalists to write the story they want them to write—and no other. They do not want you to know their little secrets and how they build the dream.

Image is a luxury brand's raison d'être. It should be protected and defended at all costs. Toilers of the luxury industry know it is strictly forbidden to talk to the press about what they do. They are only allowed to discourse on the beauty and superior quality of their products.

One man who embodies this culture of secrecy is Bernard Arnault, the boss and controlling shareholder of LVMH. One can understand him. Rivals (and journalists) have big ears. Confidentiality is an obsession for Arnault. He makes sure every LVMH employee understands that control of information is paramount. Most people who work for the group, headquartered on the fashionable Avenue Montaigne in Paris, sign non-disclosure agreements that prevent them revealing anything that goes on internally. Such practice is found in many other luxury *maisons*, including arch-rival Chanel, notorious for its secrecy.

If Arnault will not reveal much about his own affairs, he likes to know what goes on elsewhere. The world's second-wealthiest man behind Amazon's Jeff Bezos in 2019 has relied on private investigation consultants for many years. According to the media, Arnault had retained the services of Bernard Squarcini, former head of France's domestic intelligence unit, officially to handle issues related to counterfeiting. When Squarcini ran into judicial troubles in 2016, Arnault let him go.[1]

Sometimes, one comes across inconsistencies. Kering is one of France's most high-profile groups, controlled by the Pinault family. It owns many big luxury brands including Gucci, Saint Laurent, Balenciaga and Bottega Veneta. In 2019, Kering announced a tax settlement of 1.25 billion euros, the highest ever agreed with Italian

---

[1] "L'affaire Squarcini ravive les tensions entre LVMH et Hermès," *Le Monde*, Simon Pièle, November 19, 2016.

authorities, following their investigation into the group's Swiss transit and logistical platform for its luxury goods. If it was so worried about its image, why didn't Kering think about it before setting up such "tax optimization" scheme in Switzerland? The exemplary image Kering seeks to project through its laudable initiatives to help preserve the environment and improve women's lives would have resonated more and been more credible had it started by paying its taxes first. There were numerous press reports[1] about the investigation into Kering's alleged tax fraud but they had no impact whatsoever on the group's sales. In 2018, they reached record levels again and continued to grow nicely in 2019. A tax fraud involving well-heeled managers and a luxury group apparently does not surprise or shock anyone, and certainly not luxury customers—they themselves do what they can to pay as little tax as possible.

Most of Kering's customers do not read the French press anyway since they live abroad. But luxury brands will not give up control easily. The authoritative French media group *Les Échos-Le Parisien* still belongs to LVMH. The French weekly *Le Point* is still part of the Pinault family's Artemis holding company. Artemis and LVMH representatives have signed documents in which they pledged not to interfere with the editorial content of their media. But have we ever read scoops or investigative stories about the luxury business in the pages of *Le Point, Le Parisien* or *Les Échos*?

---

[1] The investigation was first revealed in 2018 by the French news website *Mediapart*, which worked with the Italian weekly *Espresso* and Germany's *Handelsblatt* newspaper under the aegis of the European Investigative Collaborations (EIC) association.

Centuries ago, monarchs and churchmen sponsored many forms of artistic creativity. Without their backing, no ambitious project got off the ground. Today, the generosity of princes and cardinals has been replaced by the largesse of Chanel, Prada, Cartier, Prada, Hermès and others. Nearly every successful artist, designer, filmmaker, architect, dancer or sculptor is backed in some shape or form by a luxury group or brand. If one published a *Who's Who* of all the creative minds sponsored by the luxury industry, it would fill several big volumes. And every major luxury or fashion brand has an art gallery or a foundation thanks to which it can tell the world about how much support it gives artists and the arts in general.

On top of journalists and artists, the luxury industry also helps artisans and precious know-how survive. Chanel and Hermès have been at the forefront of a vast rescue operation in the past two decades, injecting cash and taking stakes in their suppliers specialized in areas such as leather tanning, silk, lace and embroidery. The luxury industry has also stepped up to take the place of cash-strapped states that can ill afford the necessary and expensive renovations of monuments and artworks. Culture has become an expensive luxury for poor Europe. The fierce fire that devastated Notre-Dame cathedral in Paris on April 15, 2019 was hardly put out before François-Henri Pinault, the CEO of Kering, promised 100 million euros to finance its reconstruction and Bernard Arnault pledged another 200 million euros a few hours later.

It is telling that the first to raise their hands and offer money were the country's two luxury magnates. Paris owes much to luxury groups that have done much to preserve its appeal and heritage. LVMH has financed the reconstruction of several landmarks, including the palace of Versailles and its adjacent properties. Elsewhere in Europe, luxury brands also play an important role in terms of preserving culturally important sites and institutions. In Italy, Fendi infused new life into the Trevi fountain in Rome, celebrated in the 1960 film *La Dolce Vita*, while Tod's financed the renovations of Rome's Coliseum. And the list goes on.

But luxury and fashion brands' interest in ancient stones and old paintings is nothing compared with their enthusiasm for young designers and their training grounds in fashion and business schools. All big groups and brands fund universities and young designer prizes through institutions such as the ANDAM (Association Nationale de Développement des Arts de la Mode), of which Pierre Bergé, Yves Saint Laurent's business partner, was the first president. Another important event is the International Fashion, Accessories and Photography Festival in Hyères, in the south of France. In 2014, LVMH created a prize for young designers supervised by Bernard Arnault's daughter Delphine, a member of the group's executive committee and No.2 at Louis Vuitton. Other prominent prizes include those granted by the Council of Fashion Designers of America (CFDA) and the British Fashion Council.

Since 1991, LVMH has funded a department at the French business school ESSEC and the group has set up its own luxury crafts and know-how training programs under its Institut des Métiers d'Excellence. Kering sponsors HEC, one of France's top business schools and François-Henri Pinault's *alma mater*. In 2003, the Richemont group, owner of brands such as Cartier, Chloé and Van Cleef & Arpels, founded the Creative Academy in Milan specialized in jewelry and watchmaking. Meanwhile, Hermès has signed partnerships with several professional lycées and schools, including La Fabrique in Paris and leather goods specialists such as Boudard in Franche-Comté, in eastern France.

Fashion and luxury brands finance cultural events, museums and institutions without which tourists would not come and visit luxury boutiques. Sometimes they sponsor a place or a field with which they have long been associated. Chanel, for example, has pledged some 25 million euros to renovate the Grand Palais in Paris where it stages its shows. French jeweler Van Cleef & Arpels, which created numerous collections around ballet, sponsors the winter ball of the School of American Ballet in New York as well as many other initiatives in the field.

But fashion and luxury are not only about money, economic might and who finances whom. The sector would not exist without those who invent fabulous stories, without those talents who capture the spirit of the day and give a pertinent and subtle reading of the world. For the 20th century German philosopher and art critic Walter Benjamin, fashion designers are crystal-ball readers. "Each fashion season, with its latest creations, yields secret signals of things to come. Whoever could read them would find out ahead of time not only about new art movements but also about laws, wars and revolutions."[1]

---

[1] *Les Grands Textes de la mode*, commented by Émilie Hammen and Benjamin Simmenauer, Éditions IFM-Regard, 2017, pp.39-41.

However, could it be that fashion is not a mirror of our society but rather the instigator of our mood changes? Pippa Malmgren, a former economic advisor to U.S. President George W. Bush and now a strategist for large corporations, argues that the sector carries significant social responsibility not only in terms of jobs but also in terms of inspiration. "Everyone follows the lead of the luxury goods world," she told me.[1] "So, if it is worried, or depressed or uncertain, then the whole of society tends to become the same. If the luxury goods world is confident and bold in its vision, then everybody will follow."[2]

---

[1] At the Conde Nast International luxury conference in Muscat, Oman, in 2017.

[2] See *Signals, how everyday signs can help us navigate the world's turbulent economy*, Dr. Pippa Malmgren, Grosvenor House Publishing, 2015.

Eternal Karl

THE MAN WHO UNDERSTOOD EVERYTHING ABOUT luxury was Karl Lagerfeld. Before he died on February 19th, 2019,[1] Lagerfeld was the last of the great couturiers still at work.[2] For most people, the more they age, the less they want to work. For Lagerfeld, it was the opposite. Toward the end of his life, he was running out of time. He still had so much to say and so many things to create, so every year his output increased. By 2018, he was designing 17 collections a year, of which 10 were for Chanel and the rest for Fendi and his own eponymous brand. Karl was one of the last, if not the last couturier who drew everything himself. Another species on the verge of extinction. His fashion shows were jaw-dropping, breathtaking events. Karl asked for the impossible and got it. "Anyway, if someone tells me it is too expensive, then

---

[1] Note the esthetics of the date: 19.02.2019.
[2] One would have liked to add Jean-Paul Gaultier, who contributed a lot to fashion, but now only produces two haute couture collections a year. There is also Azzedine Alaïa, who left us too quickly in 2017.

I answer that I do not work for poor people," Lagerfeld told me in a long interview on which this chapter is based. At his fashion shows in the Grand Palais in the heart of Paris, Lagerfeld transported us into fantasy worlds ranging from the Chanel cruise ship and Chanel space rocket to the North Sea island of Sylt, complete with vista, white sand and lapping waves. He never stopped raising the bar in terms of strong impressions. In the luxury world, there was Karl and the rest. His shows put pressure on rivals such as Louis Vuitton, Gucci and Dior to up their ante and stage fashion extravaganzas just as spectacular as his.

Chanel was able to surprise without changing designers. Other brands, which did not have Karl's equivalent at hand, constantly had to hire new blood to awe buyers and the media. "You know, if you change designers every three days, it is difficult. Me, I guess I am a little bit more consistent. I do nothing vis-à-vis others," Lagerfeld told me. "But there are times when I find myself *nul* (lame), lazy, sometimes I even have to pay back my client because it is so disgusting what I have just done... I do not have a discourse on ready-to-wear. I am less dramatic. I have done this job all my life. It preoccupies me, it stimulates me and worries me. I do not have a very intellectual discourse. Sometimes, when you listen to designers talk about their collection, I have no idea where they saw that. Their inspiration, where do they take it from? It is all in the mind, right?" he adds with a touch of irony.

The Hamburg-born designer spent some thirty-six years at Chanel and in parallel more than half a century at Fendi. Prior to Chanel, he honed his skills at Chloé, and before that at Jean Patou and Pierre Balmain. He turned Fendi into a respected fashion house by reinventing its use of fur and bringing a touch of humor and impertinence to its classic Roman style. Karl Lagerfeld built Chanel into the world's second-largest luxury brand in terms of sales behind Louis Vuitton. He also designed for his eponymous brand founded in 1984, which he described in the last years of his life as a sort of caricature of himself. Commercially, the Karl Lagerfeld *maison* has been through its ups and downs and has never enjoyed the success of Chanel and Fendi. One day, a fortune-teller told him: "For you, it starts when it ends for others," he recalled. "I have left a few people along on the road. I did what had to be done at that moment, me, I saw further ahead."

Nobody really knew Lagerfeld's age. His brand's website says he was born in 1938 but other sources cite 1933 and 1935. When he died, people said he was 85 but how can one be so sure? Karl Lagerfeld would have never been Karl Lagerfeld if one knew everything about him. The mystery around his age was part of the myth. In 2018, the couturier surprised the fashion world by appearing publicly with a beard, which, with hindsight, aptly cloaked his age and illness, complemented by his Michael Jackson-style leather gloves and high collars.

But his beard actually made him look like a modern Zeus. Karl Lagerfeld was the spiritual leader of the fashion crowd. He captured better than anybody else the spirit of the day and the moods of tomorrow. He chose the theme of each collection, wowing the audience every time. He drew and took photos with ease. He seemed to make no mistakes—or at least nobody remembered him doing it.

Karl's eye saw everything. Like Zeus, Karl Lagerfeld watched over his progeny—his colleagues and friends. People worked alongside him for decades, a sign they were well-looked after and enjoyed the challenge. "One doesn't leave Chanel, one dies at Chanel," people often said about the fashion house. Caroline Lebar, his head of communications and member of his first circle, worked with him for more than 30 years.

What will Chanel become after Karl in the long term? That is the most asked question in the luxury business to which Chanel does not really give a clear answer. Many potential replacements have been mentioned. Some people zeroed in on Phoebe Philo, who was at Celine before Hedi Slimane took the helm in 2018. The Wertheimer brothers Alain and Gérard, who own Chanel, also need to think about their own succession. It is not yet certain whether their children will pick up the baton.

The future of Chanel rests on the answers to these two questions about succession, from a creative and a management point of view. Alain Wertheimer gave the creative reins to Virginie Viard, head of the Chanel studio, "to prolong the work and heritage of Gabrielle Chanel and of Karl Lagerfeld," Chanel said in a statement after its longtime designer passed away. Viard worked with the Kaiser for more than three decades and is well placed to ensure continuity. Surely, she is talented. But will she have the energy to shine and awe the crowds for many years? Chanel got over the exit of Coco—more than a decade after its founder's death. Is Karl Lagerfeld replaceable? Probably but not right away. It is very likely that Chanel will want to cultivate the memory of Karl Lagerfeld for years and will not hurry into hiring a new designer. And another question lies on the horizon. How far can a *maison* expand when it already makes 12 billion dollars in revenues and runs stores on every beautiful street and avenue of the planet? The key for long-term success in luxury is preserving the allure of being small and exclusive while attracting a growing number of customers.

On a cold November evening in 2017, I found refuge in Lagerfeld's warm office for this interview. His workplace was hidden behind the 7L bookstore in the 7th arrondissement in Paris, not far from Serge Gainsbourg's house on rue de Verneuil. The 7L bookstore is sober, calm and elegant, with a quality selection of design and coffee-table books. It's a place where you want to buy almost everything, from the Finnish black-and-white bird album to a gigantic encyclopedia of textiles. A few years ago, I was browsing books here alongside Diego Della Valle, chairman and controlling shareholder of Tod's, who regularly visited the place. Lagerfeld had often said about collecting books: "It is a disease for which there exists no remedy."

Next to the cashier, a thick metal and opaque glass door stood firmly closed. The world of Karl Lagerfeld was hidden behind and there was no point pushing it without being invited. The managers of the bookstore followed strict rules. They would not provide any information about Lagerfeld or the bookstore. I stayed there for about an hour before being allowed to pass through the mysterious door, giving me ample time to enjoy Karl's bookstore, the best waiting room in the world.

The moment finally arrives and I enter what looks like a dining room. It is a white open space with bar-height tables and chairs. Fresh salads, fruit and cheese assortments are displayed. Each plate is accompanied by a little white card that describes its contents, out of courtesy for those with allergies or intolerances. A cook in a white toque agitates his hands behind his kitchen's pass-through. A waltz of orders comes from various assistants and models. A stout man, bald and tattooed, walks up to him and says: "It will just be the scallops for me thanks." People speak French, English or Italian and eat dinner together without really dining together. This is not a restaurant but a refueling station. People take what they need and leave.

I had often heard that Karl worked only under the best conditions. Now I understand better what that meant. Three towering graces wearing flower wreaths and rose pastel tweed costumes float through the dining room, laughing out loud. They are getting ready to seduce the camera by exchanging jokes. A voice shouts: "Karl, we are ready for the photo when you are!"

I follow the models' footsteps and enter a room as big as a gymnasium, its walls covered from top to bottom with books. I have never seen so many books in one single room in my entire life. Surely, there are enough to open several bookstores. I think about all those that closed on Boulevard Saint-Germain in Paris such as La Hune, which was known for its well-endowed philosophy section, or the Geography Bookstore. They've been replaced by Louis Vuitton and Poiray jewelers respectively. Maybe their books found shelter here? Lagerfeld's library is not only an incredible monument to bibliophilia. In my imagination, it is a Noah's Ark for all the books chased away by luxury boutiques in the Latin Quarter.

A spiral staircase serves as the mast of the boat, linking up to a balcony with a balustrade that gives access to those books situated at higher levels. On the floor, long taupe grey sofas invite you to sit and enjoy the collection. Like Zeus, Lagerfeld speaks nearly every language, well almost every language. He reads English, French, German, Italian, Spanish and Latin. He is unbeatable in art history, northern European literature, design, photography and philosophy. In a corner of this gigantic library, a creamy white background paper several meters long lies unfolded like a tongue. That is where Lagerfeld takes his photos. Projectors and spotlights of all sizes await their prey. I am told I need to leave. Strangers are not allowed to stay while Karl works.

A few minutes later, the master accepts to see me in an adjacent room. I find him sitting at a table under a large white parasol that emanates a strange blue light. Lagerfeld wears a grey jacket over his traditional white shirt with a high starched collar and a black silk tie, on which is pinned a silver motif of his blue-eyed Burmese cat Choupette. Around his neck are long necklaces of pearls in various shades of grey. They match his silver leather gloves cut half-way. As he greets me, he takes off his sunglasses. The gesture takes me by surprise. Karl Lagerfeld never shows his eyes. He is over 80 but I find his gaze young, fresh and alert. His eyes mirror the vivacity of his mind. They also express a genuine kindness, which perhaps is something he sought to hide for fear it could be interpreted as a form of weakness.

Lagerfeld has accepted to see me to talk about Ralph Toledano, the first person who ran his eponymous brand from the mid-1980s to the mid-1990s. Lagerfeld has a lot of affection for Toledano. "Ralph has human qualities very few others have," is the first thing he tells me. Then, as the interview progresses, the designer makes unexpected remarks about the Darwinian evolution of fashion. "No but you know, the 1980s for fashion, it is prehistory!," he says with his trademark German accent, rolling the "r." When I mention fashion brands such as Guy Laroche, which Toledano managed after he left Lagerfeld, Karl asks me sarcastically: "Does this brand still exist?"

Kaiser Karl says what he thinks, which many don't do anymore in our ultra-controlled and paranoid world. For the couturier, political correctness was the ultimate expression of boredom. One must avoid at all costs these *Gutmenschen* who keep talking about all the good things they do. Karl attacked the limits placed on freedom of speech. "Now, you are still responsible for what you said 40 years ago. Everything is forbidden! Back in the days [in 1968,] it was forbidden to forbid. And we are surprised by the rise of populists! It is because they actually say something."

Lagerfeld flees normality. He will do anything to stand out and be different, which is why the world of luxury and fashion suits him so well. He is in his element. Lagerfeld is endowed with a natural class, an innate sense of artistic harmony. A true esthete, he goes so far as to ban words from his vocabulary. "I hate the word unisex! Everybody has arms and legs. And for the rest—that can be arranged!" he adds tongue-in-cheek.

Chanel gave Karl free rein for many decades but the *maison* started getting a little nervous about what the old couturier could say publicly in the last few years before his death. In 2018, Lagerfeld barely gave any interviews after his shows. In May that year, he sparked controversy—yet again—by threatening to give up his German citizenship. He declared that he did not want to be a member of this "club of neo-Nazis" that let extreme rightists become members of parliament. He blamed Chancellor Angela Merkel's lax immigration policy—she suddenly let in large numbers of people from the Middle East fleeing war and oppression in the summer of 2015—for Germany's subsequent turn toward the right wing.

At the end of the October 2018 fashion show, where a décor inspired by Sylt Island in the North Sea was installed in the Grand Palais, I saw Alain Wertheimer and Bruno Pavlovsky, head of fashion at Chanel, run towards Lagerfeld right after the last model disappeared. It looked as if they wanted to make sure he would not speak to any media. Lagerfeld had saluted the crowd much longer this time. Under a thunder of applause, he had left and come back again, battling to stand straight on the deck built over the artificial beach. It was obvious he did not want to leave. He probably knew that he was making his last bow to the general public.[1]

A few months later, in January 2019, for the first time, Lagerfeld would not salute the audience after his haute

---

[1] He would salute at his last *Défilé des Métiers d'Art* for Chanel in December 2018 in New York, a show generally attended by a much smaller audience than the 2,600 guests present at Paris Fashion Week events.

couture show for Chanel. He had pancreatic cancer. Yet right until the end, his entourage would tell people asking about his health: "Mr. Lagerfeld is doing very well. He works a lot." Secrecy at all costs.

The couturier died suddenly, some two weeks before his last show scheduled on March 5, 2019 at the end of Paris Fashion Week. Lagerfeld wanted to recreate the atmosphere of a glorious winter day in the Alps, with rows of snow-covered chalets built for the occasion, surrounded by evergreens and vistas of rocky mountains. Black lacquered Chanel skis were planted in the fake powdery snow. The show started with a radio broadcast of an interview during which Karl Lagerfeld remembered Queen Elizabeth's reaction to one of his shows on which "we spent fortunes on flowers." "Oh, it is like walking into a painting," he recalled her saying. Then there was a minute's silence. Everyone who counted in fashion's eco-system was there, mournful and sad, hands joined, heads down. Some closed their eyes, others allowed tears to flow. The sound of tinkling bells filled the cold air like music from a fairy tale, bringing an unexpected softness to a tragic moment. The models came out, one by one, led by star model Cara Delevingne, whose sense of humor Lagerfeld appreciated. All of his favorite girls were there, either on the front-row or strutting in the snowy alleys, wearing fedoras and large floating tweed coats. David Bowie's song *Heroes* accompanied the finale, when all the models marched together, many of them holding hands. Even the most cold-blooded fashion critics could not hold back their tears. With Lagerfeld's death, a chapter of their lives had disappeared. "For sure, without him, it will never be the same again," I heard one of them saying with regret.

Karl Lagerfeld hated conformism and strived to never give a banal answer. To the rather banal question of what made him happy, the designer had told me: "That is a much too ambitious question I do not ask myself. You know, I am in a very good position. I have life-long contracts with Fendi and Chanel, I do what I want, when I want, where I want. It is very reassuring. Actually, firing me would cost more money than keeping me, so... And I do not have an oversized ego. I am easy to work with." Having done his job for such a long time, he knew exactly what worked and what did not. When he was younger, he admitted, he had a big ego. After a certain age — we will never know when — he said he became humbler.

One of the key elements of success in luxury, tested and approved by Karl Lagerfeld, is the perpetual renewal of the same idea. Since his arrival at Chanel in 1983, the designer has always stayed true to Gabrielle Chanel's sensibility and universe while giving it a contemporary interpretation. Striking the right balance between heritage and relevance is a form of art. For Yves Saint Laurent, fashion is "not really an art but it needs an artist to exist."

Coco Chanel thought that creativity meant living in harmony with one's times and anticipating those to come. For Chanel, creativity was a form of "collaboration between the designer and her time. Fashion does not only exist in dresses. Fashion is in the air. The wind brings it, one foresees it, one breathes it, it is in the sky and on the street, it is everywhere. It comes from ideas, from mores and events."[1]

---

[1] Émilie Hammen and Benjamin Simmenauer, *op. cit.*, p.54.

The early 20th-century couturier Paul Poiret thought fashion played a predominant role in society. "A couturier-creator is used to look ahead and must guess the trends that will inspire future epochs," he wrote in his autobiography published in 1930.[1] Poiret freed women from corsets and created extravagant outfits for them featuring ample, richly adorned coats and kimonos. The couturier embodied the extraordinary era that was Paris at the dawn of the 20th century, when it was becoming an international city opening itself up to foreign cultures. The city throbbed with new energy. It was a refuge to all artists and sensitive souls, wherever they came from.

For Lagerfeld, nothing was impossible. He always aimed high. Everything had to meet his own norms, which were beyond anyone else's norms. "Karl says that we must do unimaginable things," said Hubert Barrère, a professional corset-maker and creative director of Maison Lesage, a specialist embroiderer that belongs to Chanel.[2]

Lagerfeld always refused to write his memoirs or take part in retrospectives about his life or his work. He published many books of photos and drawings with German publisher Steidl and released a best-seller dedicated to Choupette.[3]

Lagerfeld was only interested in the present and in what would happen tomorrow. "You know I am not very good at delving into my past," he told me. "Especially

[1] *En habillant l'époque*, Paul Poiret, Éditions Grasset, p. 188.
[2] "From oranges to outfits. Fashion's interest in alternative fabrics continues to grow," *The New York Times*, Astrid Wendlandt, 13 November 2017.
[3] *Choupette: The private life of a high-flying fashion cat*, Thames & Hudson, 2014.

not my own past. I am in the here and now. I know others' stories better than my own. Mine—I never think about them. When you start talking about the good old days, I leave. *Quelle horreur!*"

Whether Lagerfeld liked it or not, many books have been written about him and other fashion designers. Bookstores and libraries are filled with biographies of designers from Britain's Charles Frederick Worth, the first great couturier in Paris, to Yves Saint Laurent, Alexander McQueen and John Galliano. Their work and life stories are well documented.

However, few books exist on the business masterminds of luxury, on the entrepreneurs who made a lasting impact on this industry. The story behind big brands such as Cartier, Hermès and Louis Vuitton is one of visionaries who like Microsoft's Bill Gates and Amazon's Jeff Bezos built empires and created tens of thousands of jobs. Without these men, the luxury industry would not have grown into the powerhouse it is today. Their life was an adventure, full of passion and drama.

"Follow the money," the saying goes. One learns as much, if not more, about the luxury business by talking to entrepreneurs than by listening to designers. The latter make us dream while the former tell us how the dream was built. To find out what is really happening, start by knocking on the boss' door.

The Magnificent Six

TIGHTROPE WALKERS ON THE EDGE OF THE ABYSS, adventurers love life and do not fear losing it. Thumbing their noses at destiny gives them strength. The bigger the risk, the happier they feel. Comfort and routine are an insult to who they are and what they stand for. To make it in the luxury business, one needs to be an adventurer with the sensitivity of an artist. "Left brain and right brain," as they say in the trade. The inside story of the industry's pioneers shines a light on a world that is as enchanting as it is brutal. It is a constant play between light and darkness. And it is the co-existence of these opposites that makes it so interesting. Through the prism of luxury, one explores all aspects of human nature. Luxury is about extremes and excess. It brings out the best and the worst.

Job uncertainty and a climate of war plague many human enterprises. But in this business, such violence troubles us since luxury is an invitation to happiness and easy life. Luxury responds to our most irrational needs.

But it happens that the ideal it sells us is worlds away from the daily grind of those who craft it. One does not expect to find a battlefield behind the facade of a palace.

The luxury industry relies on creative minds and sensitive souls ill-equipped to counter the brutality of the modern system. They sometimes let themselves be destroyed by it.[1] Behind the glamorous and powerful images brands project, everyone—from the anonymous embroiderers known as the *petites mains* (little hands) to high-profile managers—is at risk of suffering from abuse, manipulation and humiliation. Some go through depression and burnout. Others are sacked or go on autopilot and hide. They internalize the pressure piled on them. This is just one of the many sinister sides of the luxury business. Behind the glitter operates a tyranny of beauty, a force that dopes the ego and stifles the heart by covering it with gold. Fashion is a mirage that can lead to a fall. The secret face of luxury is as dark as its smile is bright.

No-one dares evoke the issue. Yet, it is costing the industry dear as young people are starting to rebel against it. There are yoga and meditation teachers specialized in mending luxury's wounded. They help them heal and regain a minimum level of internal peace and self-confidence to function normally. Fashion and luxury CEOs are among the most exposed to the industry's heartlessness. The CEO of a major luxury brand in France—whose name I cannot divulge as I have been threatened by lawyers if I did—was sacked a few years

---

[1] Examples include designers such as Christophe Decarnin, who revamped Balmain and left abruptly in 2011 after sinking into depression. The list is very long.

ago simply because somebody in the company wanted his head. It was a battle of egos. His forced exit had nothing to do with the brand's performance. Actually, it was improving back then. The CEO in question, a sensitive person, took years to get over it. Naturally, that kind of situation happens all the time, in every industry, not just in fashion. However, the contrast between the brutality of rapports and the magical world of fashion seems stronger than in any other industry. When one talks about high levels of stress and burnouts, one tends to think more about investment bankers, lawyers and emergency doctors than about fashion and luxury managers.

Oblivious to the sector's ruthlessness, young graduates continue to throw themselves at the first jobs on offer. In 2019 in France, LVMH, L'Oréal, Chanel and Hermès were among the most wanted employers, according to a LinkedIn survey. In terms of attraction, they were up there with Google, Apple, Facebook and Amazon. Yet, in the 1990s, it was unusual for graduates to look for a job in the luxury business. Back then, it was the preserve of esthetes, homosexuals, aristocrats and other minorities. It was not regarded as a promising sector for ambitious young entrepreneurs.

Pioneers

Many industry leaders, who for the most part did not know anything about luxury before they started, have been replaced by professionally trained individuals who seem to share one important characteristic: they are all obsessed with financial performance. Handsome and brilliant, they are so focused on results that they tend to forget about the well-being and motivation of their teams. In the worst-case scenario, they also lack charisma and a certain luxury sensibility. These are qualities one cannot pick up at a school. You either have them or you don't.

Beyond their accomplishments, the pioneers portrayed in this book embody one of the brightest aspects of the luxury business. There is always a temptation to think that things were better in the past, but while I conducted my research, I was taken aback by how much positive energy these entrepreneurs brought and by how little of it was left in the industry today.

Patrick Thomas, the affable executive who replaced Jean-Louis Dumas at the helm of Hermès, once told me: "Actually, the only real luxury one should worry about is having beautiful relations with people." He was right, but most people do not think in those terms. Thomas drew inspiration from writer and adventurer Antoine de Saint-Exupéry, who famously said: "The greatness of a profession probably rests, before everything else, in how it unites men, but there is only one real luxury and it is that of human relationships."

Luxury today is found everywhere but in human relationships. It is never easy to remain elegant when one fights for survival. Managers struggle with the sector's digital transformation. They do not know where it will lead them and how they should adapt. They are also worried about the rising power of artificial intelligence and social media, which they cannot control. Before the Internet, the men who led brands such as Cartier, Louis Vuitton and Hermès were not only pioneers but mercenaries of beauty, die-hard romantics who dreamed of changing the world. They had access to government ministers, socialized with celebrities and built ties with the decision-makers of all the countries in which they invested. They were "influencers" before their time. To travel through the history of Cartier, Hermès and Louis Vuitton is to relive some of the greatest and most creative sagas of the late 20th and early 21st centuries.

Alain-Dominique Perrin turned Cartier into the world's biggest jeweler and democratized luxury with *Les Must* in the 1970s and 1980s. ADP, as many call him, has this magnetic power men born to lead naturally have. I will call him Alain-Dominique *the conqueror*. Perrin built Cartier with lots of fun and wild parties, attended by what he described himself as "trainloads of celebrities." After Perrin, the fun disappeared. Appetite for risk was sacrificed on the altar of financial performance. And those who came after him decided that Cartier should become a serious, ultra-luxurious, high-end manufacturer that offered watches with complications and other extra features that cost more than an S-Class Mercedes sedan.

Jean-Louis Dumas earns the title *the artist* for turning dreaming into a profession and Hermès into a trademark synonymous with elegance and style. Through his drawings and photos, he brought a lightness and a distinct sense of humor that are behind Hermès' success today. Under Dumas and long after him, Hermès' spirit remained traditionally French in the best sense of the term, a corporate culture his nephew Axel Dumas, in charge of the venerable *maison* since 2014, has been trying to change and modernize. But Axel Dumas is a victim of Hermès' popularity and of the banes that plague every big name in luxury—dehumanization and paralysis stemming from having given too much authority and importance to corporate processes.

Yves Carcelle, who led Louis Vuitton for more than 20 years, was a luxury missionary. He spread its gospel to the four corners of the planet and preached truth, good and beauty according to Louis Vuitton. A tireless traveler, Carcelle constantly looked for the blank spots on the world map of luxury. He was the industry's leading geostrategist. The Louis Vuitton brand was nearly always the first to arrive in the best streets in Asia, Europe or America. The story of Yves Carcelle gives precious insight into the ultra-competitive world of LVMH. Against his own will, he harbored a strange rivalry with his boss, Bernard Arnault. His story is that of a loyal captain who gave his life to a brand, to a group and to a man, only to be brutally sacked by him after more than 20 years of good and loyal service.

At the end of this first series of portraits, we will mark a pause, as if we were in a gallery of portraits to reflect on the following question: what does it take to succeed in this industry and be a good leader? More answers will be found in some of the following portraits of contemporary chiefs. There is, for example, José Neves, founder of Internet fashion and luxury marketplace Farfetch. José — let's call him *the revolutionary* — constantly projects himself into the future. Thanks to him, one understands better the extent to which most players in fashion and luxury, be they brands, boutiques or suppliers, are constantly at war with each other. Farfetch forced many of these warring people to cooperate, triggering a genuine revolution in this traditionally bellicose and complacent milieu. The Internet changed the luxury

industry forever. It compelled brands to question themselves and make genuine efforts to embrace the new
digital order.

Next comes Ralph Toledano, a veteran who knows
everything about fashion and has led many brands including Chloé and Karl Lagerfeld. Today, he is the non-executive chairman of the Victoria Beckham label and of
the French Federation of Fashion and Haute Couture.
Ralph deserves to be called *the coach* for he is good at
spotting talent and at getting the best out of designers.
His story provides insight into what a brand needs to
take off. Toledano's brutal sacking in 2010 is also a good
example of the kind of thing that happens behind closed
doors at luxury *maisons*.

After that comes Russia, where we meet Jacques von
Polier, a Frenchman exiled in Moscow who has sacrificed his youth to resuscitate Raketa, the country's oldest
watch brand. Polier has revamped and developed Raketa
with little money and tonnes of audacity. Thanks to his
talent for improvisation, Jacques *the Cossack* has managed
to get out of strange situations one only finds in Russia,
land of the unexpected. Polier always finds his way. His
connections range from a brothel owner in Moscow to
Russia's industry minister himself. The story of Raketa
is one of success against the odds. Its sales figures remain
modest but it is probably one of the most impressive
turnaround stories in the former Soviet bloc. His tale
also leads one to think that the great names in the luxury
business of tomorrow will not only come from Europe
but also from the likes of so-called BRIC countries — Brazil, Russia, India and China.

The tour ends with a close-up take on the origins and spirituality of luxury. What did luxury mean for prehistoric man? What is the relationship between luxury and our inner quest for beauty? Why are symbols so important to us? Then we look into the future of luxury, from the idea itself to its material expression. The definition of luxury changes constantly and there are as many expressions of it as there are people living on this planet. Luxury is not necessarily an object. It can be a precious moment, a trip, maybe an adventure one will want to post photos of on social networks to generate buzz and flatter one's ego.

What will become of the business of fashion? In addition to all its internal problems, the industry ranks as one of the most destructive for the environment after oil and gas. The sector struggles to live up to its responsibilities towards the planet as the natural resources it needs become scarcer every day. Serious and profound change in our political, social and economic systems and in our values could be on the cards if the world continues as it has been going. Money will not be worth much if we go ahead and destroy nature.

Unfortunately, all the pioneers in this book—aside from José Neves—are French. I would have liked to include Italians such as Diego Della Valle, Tod's chairman and controlling shareholder, as well as Giorgio Armani or Patrizio Bertelli, Muccia Prada's business partner and Prada CEO. But they all declined to be interviewed. I wanted also to include Bruno Pavlovsky but my project was ill-suited to Chanel's culture of secrecy. A portrait of Angela Ahrendts, another luxury veteran who led Burberry for more than eight years, would have added at least one woman to this gallery and explained what she did at Apple as its retail maestro. But the Silicon Valley giant vetoed her participation. Natalie Massenet, founder of fashion Internet retailer Net-a-Porter, also politely declined to participate.

Bernard Arnault, François-Henri Pinault and Johann Rupert were purposely left out of this portrait gallery as their lawyers and spin doctors would have tried to alter the tone and content of this book. It was better and more realistic to talk about them through their captains instead. Carcelle and Dumas, whom I met personally, are no longer of this world. I did not have to ask for their permission to write their portrait but their entourage agreed to co-operate. Perrin gave me a lot of his time, of which he has so little. Although well past retirement age, he still advises Richemont and remains an influential personality in the luxury industry.

I chose these "Magnificent Six" for what they teach us and for the perspective they give. Their experience offers precious lessons for anybody aspiring to work in this industry and for those who are building its future. It was a genuine privilege for me to get to know their story. Now, here it is.

Alain-Dominique the conqueror

THERE ARE NO MORE LEADERS LIKE ALAIN-DOMINIQUE Perrin in the business of luxury. They disappeared mysteriously in the Internet age like dinosaurs millions of years ago. Where have they gone? What have they become? In charge today are schools of sharks, mostly men and a few women, all wearing grey suits with spreadsheets in their eyes, ready to sell their soul to meet their objectives and pocket their bonus. To match Perrin's vision, courage and panache seems just as difficult as remaining human amid the industry's predators with long teeth. All those who succeeded ADP walked in the shadow of his legend.

Perrin's story began in 1969 with a gold-plated oval Cartier cigarette lighter. Produced under license, it marked the first time a prestigious jeweler lent its name to a mass market product. The chic lighter proved an instant hit. Perrin sold hundreds of thousands of them. Buoyed by their success, he launched *Les Must* de Cartier. These "must have" items included sunglasses, perfumes, scarves,

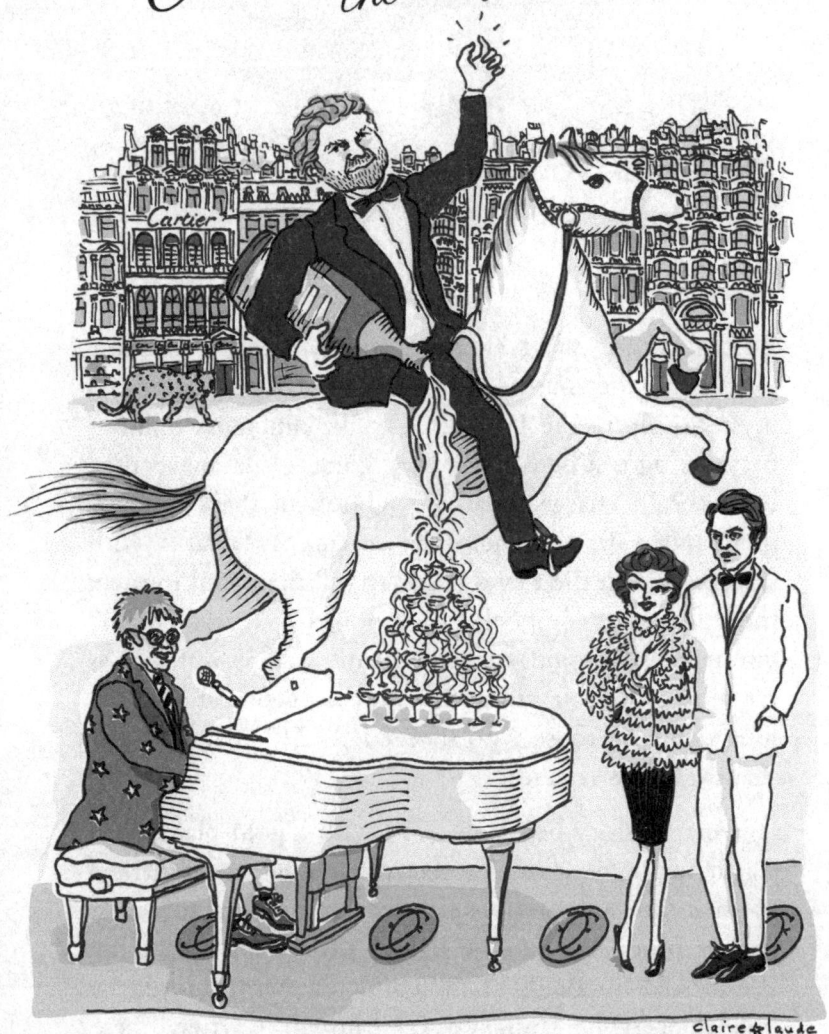

Alain-Dominique
the conqueror

claire★laude

watches and pens that embodied class and glamour at a fraction of the price of a traditional luxury accessory. From now on, Cartier would no longer be the preserve of American millionaires, royal families and maharajahs but a brand accessible to the fast-expanding middle classes. *Les Must* de Cartier, backed by 1970s and 1980s celebrities such as Adriano Celentano and Alain Delon, democratized luxury. With *Les Must*, Perrin reinvented luxury and the very notion of luxury itself. It was guilt-free luxury one could afford and display.

In the 1980s, rival pioneers would exploit this new form of accessible luxury to tap Japan's rising purchasing power. Henry Racamier and Yves Carcelle made a fortune at Louis Vuitton with Monogram bags and Jean-Louis Dumas filled Hermès' coffers selling silk ties, small leather handbags and scarves to the Japanese. In many respects, Perrin is of the same ilk as Giorgio Armani. The Italian luxury tycoon is roughly of the same generation, only eight years older. Like Perrin, Armani had an eye for beautiful products and built his empire with accessible luxury goods.

However, the concept of *Les Must* ruffled feathers among the conservatives that made up France's luxury trade group, the Comité Colbert. Cartier was duly booted out of the exclusive club in 1974, a year after *Les Must* was launched. But Perrin could not care less. "When Cartier was thrown out, Colbert was made up of the Chaumets, Boucherons and Van Cleef & Arpels, jewelry people who took themselves very seriously and did not understand this young man who was creating a revolution in luxury with his lighters," said Arnaud Bamberger, one of Perrin's acolytes and early disciples who led

Cartier in the UK for more than two decades. "I remember him saying 'if you don't want me anymore, I don't want you either.'" Perrin is a lone wolf. He likes to take firm positions.

Cartier's exile, which would last 40 years and end nearly a decade after Perrin left the brand's helm in 1999 to lead its parent Richemont, did not prevent him from turning the company into the world's No.1 branded jeweler. Today, Cartier generates in excess of 5.5 billion euros in sales every year, which is more than Tiffany or Bulgari.

Perrin is a man of disruption. What gets him out of bed in the morning is an audacious coup, an ambitious project that will shake things up. Perrin looks forward, not backwards. He never reaches his goal but overshoots it. His associates say his courage is viral and inspirational. Perrin is the kind of man who says: let's worry about whether there was a bridge once we have crossed the river, shall we?

A round-faced, bear-like character with hazelnut eyes, wavy hair and three-day stubble, Perrin carries the silhouette of a hedonist battling the extra pounds. He shows little patience for dimwits and does not tolerate any beating around the bush. His charm rests in his free spirit. At first, he might come across as brash and tempestuous, but if he likes someone, he will give that person the world.

In 1990, Perrin caused ripples by ditching Baselworld, the industry's biggest fair where watchmakers and jewelers present their new collections every year. Perrin found Basel too expensive. One could not eat or rest well there and look after clients properly. He took all of Richemont's brands, which at the time included Baume & Mercier, Cartier and Piaget, and set up a rival fair the following year in Geneva which he called the Salon International de la Haute Horlogerie, known as SIHH. With its plush cream-colored salons and all-day food and drink service, the atmosphere at SIHH is much more pleasant and intimate than Baselworld, where visitors can get lost in its never-ending labyrinths of gigantic, glitzy booths.

Following Perrin's departure, rival watchmakers and jewelers increasingly moaned about Basel's high fees and joined SIHH, where they said they were happier and had better access to relevant media and customers. Audemars Piguet, Richard Mille, Ulysse Nardin and Hermès are among the many brands that followed ADP. In July 2018, even the great Swatch Group, a Baselworld pillar with its Omega, Blancpain and Breguet brands, left the fair founded in 1917, putting its very future into question. Yet, when Perrin founded the SIHH in 1991, sceptics predicted it would last two years.

Antiques dealer

Perrin could sell sand to the Arabs, as the French say. When he was 22, he quit business school and left home. Back in the 1960s, there was no such thing as unemployment in France. On the contrary, companies scrambled to find workers. France invited laborers from its former North African and African colonies to do jobs Frenchmen did not want to do, such as cleaning the streets or driving garbage trucks. Perrin came across a newspaper ad looking for people to sell dowry essentials door-to-door. Not an easy job. One never knows when one's kids will get married, if they ever do. So why buy a dowry kit now?

ADP took up the challenge. The boxes contained linen, cutlery and other items for newlyweds. Reassured by his good manners, enthusiasm and energy, families let him into their homes, served him coffee or a glass of wine. While chewing the fat, Perrin cast an eye around for antiques. "This old chest of drawers takes a lot of space, don't you find? If you want, I could help you get rid of it," he would tell his credulous hosts. It turned out that Perrin had a flair for rare, fine objects. He bought old pieces of furniture, had them restored and sold them at a handsome profit. By the end of the summer, not only had he sold more dowry kits than everyone else in his team, but with all the money he had made from selling antiques, he bought himself a convertible Peugeot 403, Inspector Columbo's car. That was quite the status symbol back then for a man in his early 20s who had just flown the nest. Perrin proudly showed his new automobile to his father when he returned home. And later, he would eventually finish his business school studies.

The "*Les Must*" adventure

After having successfully developed his antiques business, it was time for Perrin to move on. In 1969, shortly after his father died, Perrin met French industrialist and former World War II resistance fighter Robert Hocq. The two bonded and Hocq asked him to help him develop a business around a new Cartier cigarette lighter that his company Silver Match had just started producing under license. Perrin agreed and surrounded himself with a team of young, dynamic salesmen. The lean gold-plated Cartier lighter would compete head-on with rivals such as Dunhill, which would later become a sister brand within the Richemont group, and S.T. Dupont, whose attempted merger with Silver Match collapsed.[1]

Sold at first in average tobacco shops, the Cartier lighter grew into a must-have item, triggering the idea of creating an entire line that would be called *Les Must*. "They had to be 'must-have' items that made you instantly cool, instantly 'in'," recalls Michel Guten, one of Perrin's early lieutenants and Richemont group veteran. At that time, Serge Gainsbourg's 1966 song *"Qui est in, qui est out"* was popular. Guten said the definite article *"Les"* was added to make the collection sound more French. One seminal discussion took place at the Parisian brasserie Au Pied de Cochon near the chaotic Les Halles market where, in the early 70s, one could buy anything from live chickens to a few hours of sex at any time of the day and night. Encouraged by the success of the lighter, Hocq, Perrin, Guten and others brainstormed over several bottles of wine about how to give middle class people more luxury at a reasonable price. "We understood the sea of possibilities that lay before us," said Guten.

---

[1] The descendants of Simon Tissot Dupont, who founded the company in 1872, would eventually sell their stakes to the U.S. company Gillette in 1971. Today, the Paris-listed company is controlled by businessman Dickson Poon who also owns London retailer Harvey Nichols.

After the lighter came the pen, the burgundy leather goods, the watch, the scarf, the sunglasses and the perfume. Perrin was in tune with his times. When launching a new product, he would always have more faith in his instincts than in marketing studies. ADP drew inspiration from the Cartier lighter's first ad published in 1969 that showed an oval golden lighter on a burgundy backdrop with a yellow flame. He was convinced that all *Les Must* products should share the same universe, shapes, codes as well as clearly recognizable features. Perrin confined his strategy for *Les Must* in a little "red book," in reference to the famous compilation of quotations by Chinese communist leader Mao Zedong. Oval would be the shape, first applied to the lighter and then to the pen, sunglasses and other products; and burgundy red would be the color. The double C-shape would make its way everywhere from the shop's door handles and carpets to sunglass branches.

Les Must products such as lighters and pens would also carry motifs from one of Cartier's best-selling jewelry items, the so-called *Trinity* ring of three interlocking bands made of three different types of gold. They were originally commissioned in 1922 by artist and film-maker Jean Cocteau for him and young writer Raymond Radiguet, the love of his life who died at the age of 20, only a few months after his acclaimed novel *Devil in the Flesh* was published. One ring was of pink gold, a symbol of love, the second of yellow gold, a symbol of friendship and the third in grey gold, representing fidelity. Cocteau wore it on his little finger. From then on, it became "the gay couple ring." Eventually, the story faded away and the rings resurfaced much later in 1982-1983 under a new name: *Trinity*.

Every *Must* product was numbered and had to be of excellent quality. It was slightly expensive but cost much less than traditional Cartier jewelry pieces. For example, in the 1980s, a Cartier lighter cost around 1,000 French francs, which in today's money, adjusted for inflation and purchasing power parity, represents around 240 euros—or 125 times more than the average BIC disposable lighter. Other *Must* items such as watches could cost 10,000 francs back then, or 1,500 euros.

Les Must collections generated excellent margins. With the fortune amassed from the Cartier licenses, Hocq had the means to actually acquire Cartier. He embarked on the ambitious project of reuniting all of Cartier's businesses, which had grown steadily apart over the company's glittering history. Long gone were the days when its founder, Louis-François Cartier, a jewelry apprentice who had inherited his atelier from his master in 1847, seduced Europe's well-heeled and royals with audacious pieces such as bracelet-watches and gem-encrusted cigarette cases. Cartier had also become popular with influential monarchs such as King Edward VII of Great Britain, King Alfonso XIII of Spain and Princess Eugénie, wife of Napoleon III. Edward VII called Cartier the "jeweler of kings, king of jewelers" and the brand became an official purveyor to the English royal family, which it remains to this day. Later, Cartier's regular customers included members of the American establishment such as the Rockefellers, the Fords, the Vanderbilts and the Morgans as well as royals from Spain, Belgium, Russia, Portugal and Albania.

By the early 20th century, Cartier had grown into one of the world's most prestigious jewelers. A shop was opened in London in 1902 and in New York in 1907. It was also recognized as a luxury watch specialist, using movements provided by Swiss watchmaker Jaeger, which a century later would become the sister brand Jaeger-LeCoultre within the Richemont group. The *maison* caught consumers' attention with unusual watch shapes such as the *Barrel* in 1906, the *Turtle* in 1912 and the *Tank* in 1917.

The grandsons of founder Louis-François Cartier—Pierre, Jacques and Louis—ran Cartier's jewelry businesses separately out of New York, London and Paris respectively. While they all called themselves Cartier, they were effectively three separate businesses. The lack of coherence in terms of designs and image eventually took its toll on the brand, as more and more people travelled and noticed differences. After the last of the three Cartier brothers died in 1964, their companies in Paris and New York were sold off to various investors while London stayed in the family a few more years. The businesses started drifting apart and losing appeal.

Hocq and Perrin's plan was to revive Cartier's innovative spirit and cachet and give it a contemporary twist, one that was fitting for the 1970s, an era of relative prosperity and ostentatious displays of wealth. Assisted by banker Joseph Kanoui, Hocq bought and reunited the various Cartier entities spread across the world and invited investors to share the risks. One of them was the South African billionaire Anton Rupert, who had built the Rothmans cigarette empire and had business interests ranging from wines and spirits to banking and mining.

Anton Rupert created the Peter Stuyvesant brand in the 1940s, packaging loose tobacco and snuff in his garage. He was credited with innovations such as king-size filter cigarettes, foil-wrapped packs and menthol filters. Anton was the father of Johann Rupert, Richemont's present controlling shareholder.

Rupert helped Hocq acquire Cartier New York and its subsidiaries in Latin America in the late 1970s, receiving in exchange the right to produce and sell cigarettes under the name Cartier. In 1979, Robert Hocq was killed by a car as he walked out of his office in Paris. Rupert bought out Robert's daughter Nathalie Hocq and progressively turned his minority holding into a majority stake in the early 1980s. Cartier became the main cash cow of Vendôme Luxury Group, the umbrella structure that would later acquire Dunhill, Chloé and Montblanc. The Richemont group was created in 1988 to help separate the Rupert family's South African activities from overseas operations and create a distinct entity for luxury activities. In the late 1990s, Vendôme was absorbed by Richemont group. Cartier still accounts today for more than half of Richemont's operating profit.

Belle Époque

All of those who worked with Perrin and witnessed the rise of Les Must remember it as the belle époque of their life. They were in their 20s and early 30s and lived as if there was no tomorrow. They had huge faith in Perrin and worked hard and played hard like he did. Perrin slept little and could toil until 3 a.m. at his office on Place Vendôme. He hired "mostly women, because they worked well." To motivate his troops, ADP drew inspiration from Antoine de Saint-Exupéry, author of *The Little Prince*, who wrote: "If you want to build a ship, don't unite your men and women to give them orders and explain to them each detail and where to find each thing. If you want to build a ship, make your men and women yearn for the sea."

"That was the *belle époque*," said Jean-Marc Jacot, a watch industry veteran who worked with Perrin on *Les Must* in the 1970s and led the high-end Swiss watch brand Parmigiani until 2015. "For me, Perrin is the only person who has really mattered in high-end watchma-king," he added. "He is the man who taught the Swiss everything they know about marketing a luxury watch. Remember, marketing is not natural for the Swiss, this is a country of engineers, of things well done. Chic and story-telling is not their forte. There were many people at Richemont ready to get down on their knees and give their life for him."

Les Must items had to be glamorous. For their quality and image to be faultless, everything had to be done in-house, from design to manufacturing and advertising. "Our model was anti-license," Perrin told me in his sunlit office on the top floor of the Cartier Foundation for Contemporary Art, a modern glass building in central Paris. "I am against licenses. It is an easy way to make money, but you lose control of your brand." The irony is that Cartier enjoyed a renaissance in the 1970s largely thanks to the success of the Cartier lighter produced under license. Perrin set up a solid supply chain. Cartier lighters were produced at a plant near Paris and watches were made by Switzerland's Ebel from 1972 to around 1988. Later, Cartier used the plants of Piaget and Baume & Mercier after Rupert bought controlling stakes in the watchmakers. When Perrin re-launched the Santos watch in the 1970s with a mechanical movement, he made a point of leaving the visible screws, first introduced by the jeweler on the watch case in 1904. Today, these screws are a key feature of the brand's watch and jewelry pieces. Many of its bracelets and necklaces carry the trademark dash inside a circle.

Les Must targeted the gift market and Perrin zeroed in on duty-free hot spots like Hong Kong and Hawaii. There was also Anchorage in Alaska, where planes linking Asia to America made a stopover of several hours and passengers had nothing else to do but shop. Perrin recalls Chanel sold lots of perfume there in the 1970s. Another popular destination turned into a major shopping hub was Guam. Japanese newlyweds flocked to Guam for their honeymoons. "We were lucky that the Japanese smoked a lot and loved Cartier lighters," said Perrin. They also snapped up sunglasses, bags and other *Must* items. Back then, gold imports to Japan were forbidden, forcing Cartier to make items in vermeil. Japan was Cartier's No.1 market, way ahead of the United States, where demand for luxury goods was more subdued. *Les Must* also sold well in the Caribbean islands and in Miami, Florida.

"Big Bang" Parties

If *Les Must* disrupted the luxury world, so did their accompanying "big bang" parties. By Perrin's own account, one of the most daring and dazzling events he organized was for the launch of the Santos watch in 1978 at Le Bourget Air and Space museum outside Paris. Perrin's plan was to hire half a dozen private jets from French plane maker Marcel Dassault and get them to pick up celebrities from all over Europe. They would disembark onto a red carpet leading to the museum amid crowds of journalists waiting to immortalize the moment with photos and films broadcast around the world. To win Dassault over, Perrin promised the event would generate fantastic publicity for his new Mystère 20 jets. "Ok, you're on!" said Dassault. "But you've got a nerve, hey!" added Dassault, squinting behind his round spectacles.

On a hot summer evening in 1978, Dassault's private jets took off for Milan, Madrid, Rome, Munich, Zurich and London to pick up the "beautiful people" on Perrin's list. He rounded up Ursula Andress, Marcello Mastroianni, Adriano Celentano, Alain Delon, Brigitte Bardot and Christina Onassis. Joining them was Horst Buchholz, who played in the western *The Magnificent Seven,* and the great toreador Luis Miguel Dominguín. Also invited were French singer and socialite Gerard Lenorman and Belgium's handsome car racer Jacky Ickx, several times winner of the 24 hours of Le Mans, Formula One races and the Paris-Dakar rally.

Everyone was filmed and photographed stepping out of the private jets and walking on the red carpet into the spacious museum. The Santos watch was unveiled in front of one of the original planes aviator Santos-Dumont flew himself. Champagne fountains flowed and spectacular laser shows wowed the black-tie audience. There was dancing until the morning and everyone walked out sporting the new watch. Later, Perrin hosted a similarly high-octane party in New York attended by Truman Capote and Andy Warhol. Then it moved to Rio de Janeiro, Buenos Aires, Tokyo and Hong Kong. "I launched the Santos watch nonstop for 18 months," said Perrin. "The impact of those parties was phenomenal. We got so much media coverage we could live without any advertising for six months. The watch sold incredibly well, much better than I expected. It was a planetary success," recalls Perrin with fervor, nearly 40 years later, smoking cigars in his Cartier Foundation office.

The Santos watch was named after Alberto Santos-Dumont, a pioneer aviator of Brazilian origin who flew all kinds of gravity-defying machines such as hot air balloons, early dirigibles and aeroplanes. In 1904, Santos-Dumont asked his friend Louis Cartier to make him a wristwatch that would enable him to keep both hands on the controls while timing flights, something he could not do with a pocket watch. The new Santos featured the same square-shaped case as the original, but it was in steel and gold, fitted with screws on the case and all over the bracelet.

In 1981, Perrin launched *Must* Cartier perfume for women and Santos *eau de toilette* for men with a lavish party in Versailles, attended by "trainloads" including the singer Dalida and actor Roger Moore. Guests were transported to the event in horse-drawn carriages. Both fragrance bottles featured traditional house codes such as the oval shape and burgundy red. The Santos bottle carried the trademark visible screws of the Santos watch.

Two years later, Perrin launched *Must* sunglasses. Elton John, who had built one of the largest eyewear collections in the world, had to be part of the event. Perrin had oval-shaped sunglasses specially made for Elton John, who performed at the sea resort of Port El-Kantaoui in Tunisia. A similarly grand event was held in Los Angeles attended by "le tout-Hollywood" (everyone who was anyone in Hollywood) including actors Jane Seymour, Zsa Zsa Gabor, Gene Kelly and James Stewart.

But the drawing power of *Les Must* came not only from countless celebrity endorsements. Every year, one or more versions of the pen, the lighter, the Santos, the Tank watch or other items were launched, creating that sense of momentum, newness and innovation that is crucial for a brand to remain desirable. Perrin made sure *Les Must* long remained associated with cool, rich and famous people who loved adventure and partying.

The ADP way

Arnaud Bamberger, a tall man with slicked-back hair, agreed to speak to me about Alain-Dominique Perrin over breakfast at the plush Prince de Galles hotel near the Champs Elysées in Paris. He introduced himself as one of the "few frogs" who enjoyed the privilege of having regular encounters with the Queen of England, her royal highness Elizabeth II. Cartier organized polo tournaments every year in Windsor Great Park, where celebrities hobnobbed with members of the royal family.

Created by Perrin in 1985, Cartier's International Polo Cup is now called Cartier Queen's cup. Perrin wanted Cartier to sponsor a sport that evoked elegance and strength, and decided polo was best suited for the UK. "It is important for the brand to continue to be associated with the royal family, as it was a century ago," Bamberger told me. Cartier also held polo races on the snow in the Alpine resort of Saint Moritz and on the back of elephants at Tiger Tops, in Nepal's Chitwan national park, with Beatles drummer Ringo Starr hitting polo balls with rattan mallets.

Sent by Perrin to London in 1992 "for a few years," Bamberger remained in charge of Cartier UK until 2015. For Christmas that year, his friends and colleagues received a card from him entitled "from chairman to doorman," with him dressed as doorman next to Cartier's historic front door on New Bond Street. Bamberger was succeeded by Laurent Feniou, an affable ex-Rothschild banker with a talent for public relations.

Before Cartier, Bamberger sold Lesieur sunflower oil. He had heard a lot about Perrin and longed to join Cartier's adventure. But how does one make the transition from oil to diamonds? Bamberger wrote a letter telling ADP how much he really wanted to work for him but had no idea what he could do. Three days later, he was screened by Perrin's headhunter. After passing muster, he met with Perrin, with whom he had a long chat and was hired on the spot to look after Cartier's exports.

Bamberger would later manage Cartier's retail operations in the United States. One balmy afternoon in the mid-1980s, Bamberger and Perrin were walking together on Rodeo Drive, Los Angeles' luxury strip. As they passed by a Ferrari showroom, Bamberger said he hoped to make around $100 million in sales that year. "You see this car?" asked Perrin, pointing to a Testarossa that at the time cost more than $200,000. "It is yours if you make sales of $150 million this year." At the end of the year, Bamberger came short of the target but Perrin, who never missed a joke, sent him a small crystal model of the Testarossa made by Daum.

Cartier's empire was built on Perrin's word, worth more than any contract or any six-figure cheque, his former associates say. "If you cannot keep your word, you have to buy it back from Perrin," Thierry Fritsch, a former Cartier executive and Chaumet boss, told me. Those who worked with Perrin say he was extremely demanding and yelled at them if they made mistakes. Fritsch, for example, said he was sacked seven times by Perrin. But when he decided in 1993 to leave to work for silverware maker Christofle, they parted ways on good terms.

Like a Japanese chef, Perrin always has several things on the fire at the same time. He lives with lists of things to do and people to call. He tries to remember people's birthdays and goes out of his way to help those in need, whether they work for him or not. In 1992, a Moroccan-born Cartier employee in Paris was hit by a handling trolley that fell on him and died instantly, leaving behind a wife and two children. Perrin found out the widow's in-laws stole his life insurance and took the children away from her, bringing them back to Morocco. He pulled a few strings, and within two weeks, the widow got French citizenship, which enabled her to get her children back and stay in France. In today's computerized and ultra-bureaucratized France, that could never have happened.

Later, Cartier's Paris store was burgled. Instead of fleeing, employees went through the back door and locked the thieves inside, transgressing established security rules. Perrin berated them loudly for risking their lives. "OK, you did not do what you were supposed to, but thanks to your foolishness, you saved me money, so here—take this," he said, handing each an envelope filled with cash. The move, also unthinkable today, would long remain engraved in their memories.

Perrin had as strong an eye for products as he did for talent. Anne Dellière, head of Richemont's marketing and strategic planning, is arguably one of Perrin's best recruits. Dellière, a tall, feline blonde with scrutinizing eyes, is the only woman to have survived for nearly 20 years in a senior position at testosterone-dominated Richemont. She is one of the group's most powerful women. In addition to overseeing media purchases, Dellière acts as a check-and-balance for chief executives. She questions whether their strategy is in line with each brand's heritage and image and whether it does not conflict with the strategy of other brands within the group. "ADP is about transmission," says Dellière about Perrin. "He genuinely wants to help get the best out of people." Dellière said he gave her the right to say what she thought, a privilege she uses sparingly.

It is strange that Dellière is not part of the group's senior executive committee, a body that remained mainly composed of men aged just under or over 50 for a long time. In 2016, Johann Rupert decided he had seen enough grey hair on his board and announced the departure of around a third of its members to make room for younger recruits and more women. And the board's renewal has continued since.

Rupert declined to talk to me about Perrin even though without him, Richemont would not have become what it is today. Rupert is not known for his fondness for journalists. His family is still the target of media attacks in South Africa, where it is seen as a symbol of "white monopoly capital." Perrin, who is eight years older than Johann Rupert, was involved with the group's businesses before his time, when his father Anton Rupert was still in charge.

ADP is a legend at Richemont and most of the group's more than 30,000 employees know his story. That does not seem to bother Rupert. Apart from a shared history, the two men have many things in common: a passion for rugby, gastronomy, good wine, and little tolerance for obsequious types and people who try to hide things from them. Both read a lot, which cannot be said of many overworked executives, whatever business they are in. They also have opinions about everything. Rupert's voice is much hoarser than Perrin's and in a group discussion, the two heavyweights invariably dominate the conversation.

Moving on

Cartier ended the *Les Must* adventure in 1997 on the brand's 150th anniversary. The line no longer reflected the zeitgeist. The word "*Must*" was progressively deleted from product names, stores and marketing campaigns as Rupert moved Cartier upmarket and focused on acquisitions. In 1999, having led Cartier for so many years, Perrin became chief executive of Richemont until 2003 and helped the group manage and integrate its investments in Van Cleef & Arpels, Jaeger-LeCoultre, IWC Schaffhausen and A. Lange & Söhne. Perrin remained a group executive until 2010 and a non-executive director until September 2016. Today, he still advises Richemont. For many years, he took part in meetings to discuss strategy, advertising and the group's pipeline of new products. He ensured collections were harmonious and in line with the brands' heritage. When Rupert was not present, Perrin took the decisions.

Dellière said Perrin could as easily describe the qualities of a V&A broach as the twisted leg of an antique chair. "He is really the eye of the group," she said. "Perrin will spot the small detail that will make this or that watch or jewelry product more beautiful." He would correct the length of a necklace, the position of a stone as the central piece or the shape and size of a panther's paw in a brooch. At Richemont, another man who has that talent and sensibility is Nicolas Bos, head of Van Cleef & Arpels.

Bos, who once had long hair, a gothic look and rings on every finger, is now in his 40s and looks like a Gallic version of Don Quixote. The Frenchman entered Richemont through the back door thanks to an internship at the Cartier Foundation in 1992. He then spent more than a decade at Van Cleef & Arpels, where he was creative and marketing director and head of North American operations before becoming chief executive of the jeweler in 2012. Bos has been a member of Richemont's management committee since 2014. In recent years, Van Cleef & Arpels has been Richemont's most successful brand, helping make up for weakness at Cartier. "There is no recipe in luxury, it is a conjunction of a story, a moment, a market and people," Bos told me. "You have to make the product relevant for the times and for a certain clientele. In jewelry, a big change can be catastrophic and a nice product is not enough, you need a good story behind it," he said.

Cartier Foundation for Contemporary Art

When François Mitterrand's socialists took power in 1981, Perrin sensed growing enmity towards luxury brands such as Cartier, Chanel and Hermès, particularly among left-wing intellectuals. Mitterrand's adviser, economist Jacques Attali, even evoked the possibility of nationalizing Cartier in an op-ed published in the daily *France-Soir*. Perrin took the threat seriously and sought a way of protecting Cartier. Art could be the brand's shield. By becoming associated with a place where artists could show their work, independent of public financing, Cartier would become an important patron of the arts and rise above any criticism. "I wanted Cartier to be respected by intellectuals," Perrin said. His initiative was backed by his long-time friend César, the French sculptor. Perrin admired César's audacity to call a crushed car art. "I loved his irreverence," Perrin said of the man with whom he celebrated Christmas until he died in 1998. Since then, Perrin is the executor of César's will.

The Cartier Foundation for Contemporary Art opened its doors in 1984 in Jouy-en-Josas, home to the famous HEC business school. It later moved to Boulevard Raspail in central Paris and architect Jean Nouvel, who would become a close friend of Perrin, was asked to design the project. "He wanted a modern building, a Parisian monument that would go well with Cartier's image," Nouvel told me in his vast Parisian office. "I presented him with the project of an all-glass building, on which clouds and trees would reflect. He paused for a few minutes and said: 'let's do it.' Alain is really someone who thinks fast and takes decisions quickly—unlike most people," Nouvel said. In front of the building stands a nearly two-century-old cedar tree planted in 1823 by French writer François-René de Chateaubriand, who used to live there. Nouvel has built many famous landmarks including Paris' Arab World Institute, the Louvre in Abu Dhabi as well as two Cartier factories in Switzerland and Richemont's headquarters in Geneva.

To this day, the Foundation's mission has remained the same: to showcase contemporary artists. Like Hermès' La Verrière art gallery in Brussels, it focuses on artists who are not yet major celebrities. The Cartier Foundation has never made a euro of profit, even if it sometimes sells a few catalogues and souvenirs. "Art is not destined to remain a domain for the rich of this planet. It must be accessible," Perrin told me.

One of the best-kept secrets of the Cartier Foundation is its spacious rooftop terrace next to Perrin's office, from where one can admire the Eiffel Tower, Sacré-Cœur Basilica and Montparnasse Tower. It is also home to a strange statue, a dwarf riding a fish by the Bordeaux artists' collective called Présence Panchounette. It guards the entrance of a large and luminous meeting room with Philippe Stark-designed transparent chairs. Another secret is that the Foundation houses many Richemont managers and staff, which explains the high level of security in the building.

When I first met Perrin a few years ago, I planned to write a story on what luxury leaders did outside the office. Some were into horse breeding, others into olive oil or cheese; Perrin was into wine. He had ploughed vast amounts of his Cartier-amassed wealth into cultivating and producing high-grade Cahors wine, of the fiery and full-bodied Malbec variety. Perrin bought château Lagrézette in the 1980s, a medieval castle complete with turrets and moldings. Its refurbishment lasted 12 years, during which he gave new life to its interiors, garden fountains and trimmed hedges. Château Lagrézette stocks Perrin's vast collection of antiques which include 16th and 17th century paintings, many of the Flemish and Dutch school, including artwork by Pieter Brueghel the younger. Perrin planted ninety hectares of vines around the castle. Some bottles got a grade of over 90 out of a 100 by wine authority Robert Parker. The business employs 40 and generates more than 5 million euros in annual revenue.

After three decades of patience and investment, Perrin's wine business finally started making profits in 2016. When investors moan about the fact that it can take eight to ten years to turn a fashion brand into a profitable business, they should compare that with wine. Fashion looks like a short-term project in comparison. Perrin has used his castle to play host to artists such as

Elton John, Tina Turner, Richard Gere and BB King. He also organized a meeting there between Tony Blair and Jean-Pierre Raffarin in 2002, the year the latter became France's prime minister.

Perrin used to play rugby and polo, ride horses, ski and sail. In his 70s, he enjoys hunting grouse and woodcock with friends in Scotland and England. He owns a house in La-Croix-Valmer near Saint-Tropez, where his wife likes to spend much of her time. He also has a chalet in Verbier and a house in Martigny, Switzerland. When you tell Perrin you would like to speak to his wife, he asks 'which one'? He married four times and is still on good terms with all of his former wives as he made sure they would never be in need. All of his children get along, friends say. In that way, Perrin resembles the larger-than-life writer and journalist Joseph Kessel, grandfather of all French reporters and author of the bestseller *The Lion*. Kessel continued to support many of his ex-girlfriends and ex-wives after they split. For that too, Perrin deserves his sobriquet Alain-Dominique *the conqueror*.

What about Cartier today?

After Perrin, Cartier was led by people who ploughed hundreds of millions of euros into turning the brand into a super high-end watchmaker that offered elaborate movements and complications. Under the leadership of Stanislas de Quercize, Cartier founded the Maison des Métiers d'Art in the Swiss watchmaking hub of La Chaux-de-Fond, home to Tag Heuer and Corum, where skilled artisans worked on enamels and wood marquetry.

While Chinese demand remained strong, Cartier found buyers for its ultra-fancy timepieces. But after Beijing launched its anti-corruption drive in 2012 and condemned ostentatious spending, expensive watches started gathering dust in boutiques. In 2016, Cartier was forced to buy back tens of millions of stock from cash-strapped retailers to help them stay afloat. The brand gave them credits for future purchases to "prevent rivals from force-feeding them," Johann Rupert explained in 2016. Jewelers and watchmakers can harbor relationships of power with distributors, coercing them into stocking expensive models that weigh on their budgets if they do not sell them quickly. Some of the repurchased stock was sold through internal company sales, while the remainder was recycled. At the time, Cartier was also keen to downsize its distribution network to preserve its aura of exclusivity.

Investing in high-end watches may have spruced up Cartier's image but it let down customers who were mainly interested in accessible jewelry and watches costing a few thousand euros. They were baffled by its 120,000 euro watches with elaborate complications for connoisseurs. Those who desired an uber-fancy watch generally opted for a Vacheron Constantin or a Patek Philippe, or a timepiece made by a small artisan—not a Cartier. The focus on high-end watchmaking confused Cartier's message. Jewelry and watch buyers were getting increasingly younger. Many successful Asian businesswomen bought jewelry for themselves. Women loved Cartier for its historic little red box and obvious status symbols that were the *Trinity, Juste un Clou* and *Love* collections with the visible screw. They were major cash cows for the brand. But Cartier's main entry-level jewelry collections remained largely unchanged for many years. The *Clash* collection, composed of tiny spikes and pyramid studs launched in 2019, helped renew Cartier's offering, together with the new *Drive* and *Clé* watches unveiled in previous years. However, their shapes were not particularly ground-breaking. Cyrille Vigneron, a Cartier veteran who left for a few years to lead LVMH in Japan, took the reins in 2016. Vigneron is well aware Cartier needs to work hard as competition is fierce and value for money has become a commanding principle for consumers.

Cartier has grown into a gigantic *maison*, "an ocean liner" to use ADP's language, with its more than 300 boutiques worldwide. The jeweler has organized dozens of exhibitions to showcase its heritage and history. Cartier also often commands the highest prices at auctions. In May 2015, Sotheby's sold one of the most expensive pieces of jewelry ever back then, a Cartier ruby for $30 million. But if Cartier is to remain strong in the 21st century, it will have to remain bold, take risks and never forget the spirit of adventure Perrin infused into the brand. Otherwise, customers will look for beauty and audacity elsewhere.

Jean-Louis the artist

JEAN-LOUIS DUMAS BUILT HERMÈS INTO THE WORLD'S most desirable luxury brand. The *Kelly* and the *Birkin* are not just handbags, they are the ultimate shopping trophy. Ladies from London to Shanghai all dream of owning one, not because of their price tags, which start at around 7,500 euros, the cost of a small car, but because they are nearly impossible to get. Since I started writing about Hermès in 2008, I have never met anybody who was able to buy a *Birkin* or a *Kelly* simply by going to a Hermès boutique. I have tried myself and never succeeded. You have to know someone or find a way of getting high up on waiting lists—even though the brand generally denies there are any—or be the first one to enter the shop and snap up the first available Kelly or Birkin bag, regardless of the color or the leather with which it was made. How many husbands and desperate boyfriends have gone through the nightmare of trying to buy one for their darlings? Going into the forest, killing a bear, bringing back its pelt and laying it by the

bed would be an easier task. "Let me tell you madam, if I received a pound for every person who asked me how they could buy a *Birkin* or a *Kelly* bag, I would not be speaking to you right now, I would be lying somewhere on a beach in Nassau," a personal shopping assistant at Selfridges in London once told me.

At a time when most items are made by machines or in sweat shops in far flung places, when it is nearly impossible to get a human over the phone when reaching out to a big company or organization, hand-made items such as the *Kelly* bag and the artisans who take more than 20 hours to sew them together in a comfortable atelier somewhere in France seem to be from a different era. Dumas had foreseen it: "The century of tomorrow will be a century of hands." The original French version comes with a pun: "*Le siècle de demain sera un siècle de main.*"

Soft power

Jean-Louis Dumas, who died in 2010, was a tall, slender man, with a half-bald head and wore a suit and a silk tie no matter what day of the week it was. He did not have a particularly striking physique. What caught one's attention first was his generous smile, which surprised and pre-empted his thoughts. His deep brown eyes sparkled with intelligence and audacity, downplaying the seriousness of his professor-like half-moon reading glasses. Dumas could delve into one's soul but he would not hide his in return to protect himself. On the contrary, he had the eyes of a child who constantly marveled at the world. His gaze expressed empathy and a quest for beauty. "What describes Jean-Louis the best are his eyes, he really communicated with them and with his drawings," said Christian Blanckaert, his friend, who ran Hermès' French and international operations for many years.

Dumas would rarely leave home without his little vertical red leather-bound sketchbook and his miniature metallic watercolor box, accompanied by a tiny phial of water. His illustrations were light in tone and their humor and spirit were similar in style to those by the popular French cartoonist Sempé. Dumas would send aquarelles to thank, congratulate, recount a moment or tell a story. He used them to make friends and allies. Those who built a relationship with Dumas guard his drawings like a treasure. But he was not the only descendent of Émile Hermès who knew how to draw. Many possess that talent. Not only are they born shareholders of one of France's most profitable companies—they start life with that gift. Jean-Louis' brother, Philippe, made a career out of it. He illustrated children's books and supplied Hermès with umpteen drawings that were printed on scarves, towels, plates and many other products. They were also used for invitations and in-house publications.

Dumas' artistic talent gave him tremendous soft power. He noticed things most people did not and saw beauty where it was hidden. Thanks to his drawings, he was able to express thoughts many struggled to put into words. Being able to draw, like being able to play music, allows one to convey a multitude of subtle moods and emotions. If Dumas had an idea about a product or a design for a boutique, he would draw it. His illustrations offered precise, detailed roadmaps his staff could understand and put into action. And not only did his drawings inspire troops, they gave Hermès a genuine artistic soul and personality.

Dumas built many bridges between the brand and the art world, which Hermès continues to exploit to this day. The company relies on a talent pool of dozens of artists, designers, calligraphy and scenography specialists who work on many different projects. Drawings, sketches, illustrations and art installations are used in all aspects of Hermès' communication. In 1973, Dumas launched a bi-annual review called *Le Monde d'Hermès*, which today has a circulation of 700,000 and is translated into 13 languages. It presents the latest collections as well as various original pieces of writing, photography and artistic work. Dumas would write the opening page of *Le Monde d'Hermès*, a task now aptly fulfilled by his son Pierre-Alexis Dumas, Hermès' artistic director who has grown into an eloquent personality himself.

Had Dumas not dedicated his life to Hermès, he could have become a professional musician or a photographer, his friends say. A passionate drummer, he played jazz in nightclubs in his twenties and travelled with a band to Eastern Europe and Scandinavia. Dumas always carried with him his Leica camera (a brand he loved so much, Hermès would eventually buy a stake in it). Dumas took photos of everything — places, people, animals, landscapes. His lens was his third eye and his photos served as notes and ideas he classified and kept to structure his thoughts.

Despite his busy life, Dumas found time to read books and share their content with staff and friends. Among Dumas' favorite authors were René Char, a friend of

George Braque and Albert Camus, who believed poetry could save the world. There was also philosopher Italo Calvino, and the seminal Greek classic *The Odyssey* by Homer. Dumas was always *au fait* with what was happening on the cultural scene. He would have read the bestseller everyone was talking about and seen the exhibition or film that was on people's minds. Dumas regularly commissioned texts from authors and Hermès still collaborates with many contemporary writers today.

Dumas despised routine and formal processes. He could have never worked for a big group such as L'Oréal or Procter & Gamble. At Hermès, he could interrupt a board meeting to talk about a wonderful book he had just read and would make everybody laugh with portraits he made of people while they talked. Such light, joyful behavior would not go down well with the technocrats in the driving seats of big corporations today. Dumas was notoriously late at meetings — sometimes by several hours — and owed much to his devout secretary Marie-Josée, who helped people remain patient and served them tea or coffee. Marie-Josée put a semblance of order in Jean-Louis Dumas' poetically disorganized life. Impeccably dressed, with her blond hair in a bun, she was a crucial member of Hermès' staff, known for being able to fulfil impossible missions such as finding plane tickets at the last minute. When Dumas left the office to go home on his bicycle on a Friday night or before holidays, his driver Bernard would bring piles of letters and notes to his house on which he wished to continue working.

At one time, there used to be a secret way into Dumas' office. You had to go to the lady who sold ties at the Faubourg Saint-Honoré boutique and tell her that you had a meeting with Dumas. She would open a door that led to the lift, which itself opened up in front of his office and Hermès' leafy roof-top terrace. Today, the penthouse garden is filled with white roses, magnolias and an apple tree that produces some thirty pots of jelly every year—a gift reserved for esteemed guests.

Hermès: the story

Jean-Louis Robert Frédéric Dumas was born on February 2nd, 1938, in Paris. He belonged to the fifth generation of descendants of Thierry Hermès, a French Huguenot Protestant who, in the first half of the 19th century, returned to France from Krefeld, Germany, to start a harness-making business. In 1867, Thierry Hermès won the prize for the best harnesses at Paris' second universal fair. Half a century later, with cars replacing carriages, his grandson Émile widened the company's activities to include leather goods such as travel bags, belts and saddles. Émile Hermès was one of the first to bring zippers to France, using them for clothes and bags. In 1922, he produced the company's first leather handbags, and 1937 saw the first Hermès silk scarves. After the war came the silk ties and the launch of the first scent, *Eau d'Hermès*. But it wasn't all easy. Hermès nearly went bankrupt after the 1929 depression and was saved by the goodwill of some suppliers. When the Germans occupied Paris in the 1940s, Hermès struggled to survive.

Robert Dumas developed a trapezoidal ladies' handbag called "tall bag with straps" in the 1930s. It had limited success until Grace Kelly bought the biggest model and a photo of her carrying it was published in Life magazine in 1956. The picture made it an "it" bag every elegant woman would want to have. In the mid-1960s, Catherine Deneuve's sister, the late actress Françoise Dorléac, reportedly spent her first major artist's fee on what was already back then called the *Kelly* bag.

A few decades later came the *Birkin* bag. It goes back to a chance encounter in 1984 between Dumas and British actress and singer Jane Birkin. The two were sitting next to one another on a Paris-London flight. Jane Birkin dropped her agenda on the floor, scattering the papers it held. "The day Hermès makes a bag with pockets, I will have that," she exclaimed, to which Dumas replied: "But I am Hermès." He promised her to make the bag of her dreams. Back in Paris, Dumas invited the actress to the Hermès workshop and the pair conceived what would become known as the *Birkin* bag.

Jean-Louis Dumas was the fourth of six children. He grew up in Paris near Place du Trocadero and spent his holidays in a small house in Normandy where he played with his cousins. "This is where he developed his sense of clan," said Menehould de Bazelaire, who was close to Dumas then and now looks after Hermès' museum and cultural heritage. Dumas studied law and political science at Paris' prestigious Institut des Sciences Politiques, known as SciencesPo. He joined a buyer training program at Bloomingdale's in New York in 1963, a year after marrying Rena Gregoriadès, an interior designer of Greek descent with whom he would live a love story for more than fifty years. Rena Dumas designed many Hermès stores and company buildings. Her husband said he was not "necessarily programmed to join Hermès" until his father Robert invited him in 1964. He was elected to the top job by the family after Robert passed away in 1978.

Robert Dumas had married Jacqueline Hermès, one of three daughters of Émile Hermès, a grandson of founder Thierry. As Émile and his wife Julie did not have any sons, the name Hermès was lost. Their grandchildren and offspring carry the family names of the men Émile's daughters married: Puech, Dumas and Guerrand. Only direct descendants of Julie and Émile Hermès can be members of Hermès' family-controlled parent company Émile Hermès SA.

Robert Dumas developed the brand's leather goods, ties and silk scarves business while his brother-in-law, Jean-René Guerrand, helped Hermès branch out into perfumes and launched *Eau d'Hermès* and *Calèche*. When Jean-Louis Dumas took the reins, Hermès was a dignified but somewhat fusty brand. Consumers from that time remember shop assistants in Paris as staid ladies wearing elegant blouses, pearls and thick spectacles. Jean-Louis gave Hermès a modern elegance that made the brand more relevant and desirable. He wanted to surprise customers and steer clear of clichés. Dumas preferred to take risks and try something new than re-edit or re-launch something old. "Hermès is not a creativity company, it is a renaissance enterprise," Dumas would tell journalists.[1] Today, there are tens of thousands of product references applied to shoes, jewelry, perfume, ready-to-wear, scarves, gloves, bags and tableware. And every six months, a significant proportion of them are changed.

[1] "Jean-Louis Dumas, Hermèsman," *Madame Figaro*, December 19, 2001.

If Thierry Hermès stood for craftsmanship and Émile Hermès for creativity, Jean-Louis introduced a third pillar: style. Dumas had a clear idea of what Hermès' allure should be and never veered from it. Stylistically, the company remained on the same course while he was in charge for nearly three decades, and arguably it still is. "I only found a fireplace that was well built by my predecessors, Émile Hermès and Robert Dumas. I put wood into it and blew on the embers," Dumas said in 2001.[1]

Many of the people Dumas hired remained in place for a very long time. In 1988, he invited Véronique Nichanian, who worked for Italian designer Nino Cerruti, to develop menswear and Hermès' men's universe in general. Nichanian, still in charge today, was hired five years after Karl Lagerfeld joined Chanel in 1983, putting her in the same longevity league as the Kaiser.

The first time Nichanian spoke with Dumas was over the phone. When he called, she thought one of her friends was playing a joke on her. "OK very funny, but really who are you?" she asked. Dumas laughed and answered: "No, no, it is really me, Jean-Louis Dumas. Please come and see me in my office, I would very much like to meet you." When Nichanian showed up, Dumas talked to her about everything but menswear—it was his way of getting to know people. She told him about the exhibitions she had seen and about her passion for Japan, a country he was very fond of himself. A week later, he invited her for lunch. Only he forgot to tell her that it would be in the company of all of Hermès' board members. A few days later, she received a one-page letter

[1] "Jean-Louis Dumas, le Lutin d'Hermès," *Série Limitée*, September 2001.

saying that she was invited to start working as Hermès' new menswear designer as soon as she could make herself available. Today, creative directors get expensive lawyers to negotiate thick contracts on their behalf. Every minor detail is laid out, from financial terms and holidays to non-compete clauses that prevent designers from working for other brands for several months should they part ways with the company.

In womenswear, Dumas renewed the creative leadership more regularly. In 1997, he shocked the industry by hiring iconoclast Martin Margiela to give the brand a new creative impetus. Margiela, the mysterious designer who never gave interviews or let himself be photographed, introduced new cuts and created simple, minimalist and comfortable looks for Hermès. When he left to develop his own brand in 2003, Dumas called Jean-Paul Gaultier to ask him for advice on who could replace him. Gaultier thought about it and called him back. "'I have found someone, but I don't know if you will be happy: it's me!'" he said. As they celebrated their partnership, Dumas wore Gaultier's traditional sailor's striped shirt and Gaultier a classic jacket and tie. Gaultier, another anti-conformist soul, provided Hermès with humorous yet ultra-elegant interpretations of its classics. He would play with the *maison*'s use of leather, including leather straps in his looks. He also invented a muff version of the *Kelly* bag.

Dumas introduced several new activities at Hermès including watchmaking, enamels, tableware, shoemaking and jewelry. In 1989, he bought Saint Louis, the oldest surviving crystal glassmaker in Europe, founded in the 16th century. Soon after that, Hermès acquired the silversmith Puiforcat. The two tableware companies today contribute more in terms of creativity and know-how than profit. Had they remained on their own, they would have gone bankrupt and vanished a long time ago, together with their unique craft and skills. Dumas enjoyed giving an aesthetic meaning to things. For him, a Saint Louis vase made with hand-blown crystal glass was not a simple object but the product of centuries of tradition brought to perfection.

The Hermès way

For Dumas, Hermès was not a brand but a signature. It was not a luxury goods maker but a provider of high-quality objects. The word marketing was banned. Hermès products were not expensive but costly, because they cost a lot to produce. Dumas saw himself not as a CEO but a "poet and a grocer" (*épicier et poète*), an expression today used by his nephew, the company's chief executive Axel Dumas. The word Hermès itself was to be pronounced in a specific way in the original French. One did not pronounce the H but made the liaison. Hence, "Chez Hermès," was to be pronounced "chez Zermès," and it is still the case today.

When announcing major news, Dumas would climb onto a stool. He excelled at moving people with simple words and spoke as well as he wrote. He regularly conveyed his faith in Hermès and in the work of its artisans and designers. Véronique Nichanian says Dumas never asked to see what she did before it was finished. "I trust you," he would tell her. Nichanian was amazed by how much freedom and responsibility she was given from day one. "Manage it as if it were your own small business," Dumas told her about menswear at Hermès. "Jean-Louis had a respect for creative people I have never seen elsewhere. At other brands, everyone is under huge pressure from the marketing and finance departments. At Hermès, we are given the time to do things well," she told me. While many fashion brands are now locked in a race to produce as many collections as possible every year, Hermès wisely never went down this road, Nichanian said.

Dumas' great-niece Pascale Mussard is one of the family's most creative minds and his spiritual daughter in more ways than one.[1] Like her great-uncle, her eyes seem to constantly marvel at the world, only hers are not brown but a rare light aquamarine. And Mussard has the allure of an artist. When I met her at her Petit h studio in Pantin, outside Paris, she was wearing an oversize mustard yellow dress, earrings composed of hand-blown Saint Louis crystal drops and a gigantic silver octagonal ring. Having led several Hermès departments including fabric purchases and communications, Mussard shared the artistic directorship with Dumas' son Pierre-Alexis for three years. But eventually Pierre-Alexis pushed her out, forcing Mussard to move on. That would prove to be for the best as it would force her to realize her dream. In 2010, the year Jean-Louis Dumas passed away, Mussard launched a start-up within Hermès called Petit h. Her company makes one-of-a-kind objects from unused

---

[1] Pascale Mussard is Jean-Louis Dumas' great-niece in the broad meaning of the term. The mother of Jean-Louis Dumas was the sister of the maternal grand-mother of Pascale Mussard.

Hermès supplies such as belt buckles, crystal glasses, crocodile skins, furs, and rolls and rolls of beautiful, unused silks and fabrics of all kinds. Her studio, near Hermès' main workshops, is an Aladdin's cave.

Petit h would become Hermès' laboratory of ideas. Its leather bracelets, miniature aeroplanes and boats are sold at Hermès' store on rue de Sèvres in Paris, and twice a year, for a few weeks, in various big cities around the world. Many objects created by Petit h have been adopted by what Mussard calls "Grand h," or "Big h"—or parent Hermès. "Petit h has allowed me to put in practice many things Jean-Louis taught me and one of them is being capable of re-inventing oneself and another, is to constantly think of ways to innovate," Mussard told me.

Discovering the world

A Paris-Match journalist once asked Dumas: "What do you think about when you get up in the morning? Dumas answered: "About life, about this phrase by an Indian poet: This morning a butterfly is preparing itself to cross the Bay of Bengal. Every day, we are like this butterfly. We just have to believe that the Bay of Bengal exists, otherwise we go around in circles."

When he was a young boy, Dumas dreamed of exploring the world, having read all Jules Verne's and Paul d'Ivois' mystery books. He famously broke his arm playing with the lift of Hermès' building. In 1959, at the age of 21, he made his first life-changing trip with two cousins, sponsored by Citroën. In a 2CV, the trio drove from Paris to Nepal and India via Afghanistan, "four years before the Beatniks got there," he said. The trip would mark the beginning of his love affair with India, where he would return regularly and make many friends.

But ultimately, Hermès would be his greatest adventure. Dumas thought of the company's staff as his extended family. And as such, they should discover the world at Hermès' expense. Dumas wanted his staff to share a collective experience of awakening to beauty. Every employee was invited to write down their dream trip. It could be swimming with rays, climbing Kilimanjaro or admiring Japan's blossoming cherry trees in the spring. They had to be exciting and realizable dreams. From October 2006 to March 2008, Hermès organized dozens of trips around the world. People gave their ideas and a lottery system was set up, overseen by a bailiff, who picked those who could go. Small teams were formed, drawn from all departments.

From Hermès' staff of about 6,000, 46 dream trips were selected. Christian Blanckaert, who headed Hermès' French operations, got to go horse riding in winter in Russia. He travelled with a group of nearly 20 people, among them French managers, Japanese store directors and a shop assistant from the United States. Galloping in deep, sparkling snow under a powerful winter sun with the golden cupolas of Orthodox churches shining in the distance "was probably one of the most beautiful and intense moments of my existence," Blanckaert told me.

Dumas knew that travelling helped one to know oneself better and widened horizons. He wanted his staff to travel together, so they could learn as much from each other as from their discoveries. Hermès organized trips to meet horsemen in Mongolia as well as tribes in Africa and India. A small group went to exchange know-how with silversmiths in a desert in India and brought crystal to melt on the spot. In 1995, Eric Popineau, atelier head at Puiforcat, showed how silver was hammered in France and in return, he discovered how it was done in India.

In the 1990s, Dumas offered a few people, including Véronique Nichanian, the opportunity to travel to Japan and learn a craft. She chose calligraphy. Claude Brouet, Hermès' women's ready-to-wear designer at the time, learned how to trim trees while others went for Japanese pastries. "It was a full week in complete immersion. First, I was in a school with kids, then I had a teacher for myself. What kind of man sends you like this, for free, with the sole purpose of enriching yourself? He knows that by enriching your world, he enriches your creativity and ideas and therefore the brand," Nichanian said. "How wise and intelligent it is from a human point of view."

Another measure Dumas implemented was staff exchanges. People spent a week in other departments to learn a new profession and find out about the company's other activities. Such initiatives brought cohesion among the rank-and-file and helped them adhere to the company's vision and ethos. "The better your staff understands the general direction of where the boat is going, the fewer instructions and orders you need to give them. They do things by themselves. And isn't it more exciting and motivating to take initiatives and try things out yourself than constantly having to get somebody's approval," Hermès' former CEO Patrick Thomas, who replaced Dumas, told me. In the same vein, for Jean-Louis Dumas, the best way to make a customer love Hermès was for the sales assistant to love Hermès himself or herself first. Only sincere and natural enthusiasm would make customers warm to the brand and open their wallets.

Dumas enjoyed citing the pioneering American carmaker Henry Ford: "A company that only makes money is very poor." For Dumas, "a company remains a unique terrain of social progress because it unites men and women around clear objectives [...] and because its success gives a sense of purpose to those who build it. [...] We try to be a *maison* that maintains itself when everything around it is in flux, but it will be the first one to move in the direction of our quest for beauty. [...] Our love of tradition will never undermine our ability to marvel."[1]

But if Dumas believed in leaving creativity completely free, he also thought it could benefit from having a little bit of structure. Every year, he introduced a theme around which Hermès designers, artists and illustrators would be asked to produce new interpretations of the brand's world. To celebrate the launch of each year's theme, Hermès still organizes no-expenses-spared events, traditionally held in unexpected places and attended by hundreds of journalists. I've traveled to many of them and was often impressed by their originality. A few notable moments come to mind. A Chinese woman dressed in a tuxedo playing Rachmaninov on a grand piano surrounded by carcasses in the meat section at Rungis, Europe's biggest food market, at 5 a.m. to celebrate the 2009 theme "a beautiful escape." For the 2014 theme "metamorphosis, a Hermès story," Sardinian polyphonies

[1] "Comment je vois les années 2000", Jean-Louis Dumas, *Figaro Économie*, January 1, 2000.

floated in the golden early evening light from inside Mont Saint-Michel's abbey church and over the surrounding sands exposed by the low tide. For its 2012 theme "the gift of time," lampion-decorated horse-driven carriages transported guests around the Jardin des Plantes in Paris as if in some kind of Tim Burton film.

Under Dumas, themes were more basic. In 1996, it was the year of music. Teachers were hired to give staff singing lessons in shops. Christian Blanckaert and Pascale Mussard took part in the final show at Buddha Bar in Paris. Blanckaert shed his jacket, tie and round spectacles to become a Hells' Angel, complete with a fringed black leather biker jacket and dark sunglasses. Mussard transformed herself into a sex kitten with a red wig and cut jean shorts. As they performed tunes by French composer Jean-Jacques Goldman, no-one recognized them. "I think the spirit at Hermès is to do things seriously but to never take yourself too seriously," Mussard told me.

In the year 2000, Blanckaert thought the advent of a new millennium should be celebrated. From a hospital bed where he was being treated for a minor health problem, Dumas approved Blanckaert's project to fly some 370 staff to celebrate Halloween in New York and hold a strategy briefing the next day. An entire plane was commissioned. This would be unthinkable today. If the plane crashed, no-one would be left to run Hermès. An entire hotel in New York was booked. However, once in downtown Manhattan, Hermès managers did not stay in their rooms. Like feral cats, they roamed all night. But everybody showed up for the 9 a.m. strategy meeting at Hermès' shop on Madison Avenue. The company's team-building events and staff odysseys continued well after the Sept.11 attacks in 2001. "I think any other *maisons* would have cancelled, but for Jean-Louis, these trips took on an even stronger meaning after the attacks," said Menehould de Bazelaire. Dumas was an eternal optimist. A Protestant like most in the family, he often quoted Martin Luther: "Even if I knew that tomorrow the world would end, I would still plant an apple tree."

Family business

Jean-Louis Dumas never missed an occasion to unite his troops. Long-serving employees were entitled to proper leaving parties. People would wear costumes inspired by the person departing and songs were composed to tell his or her story. For Blanckaert's departure, a group of Hermès executives donned his typical blue jacket, red tie and spectacles. When Dumas' secretary retired, top managers dressed up as Marie-Josée in a skirt, white blouse and white wig tied up in a bun. A professional make-up artist was hired. Songs were written for her and performed at a party in her honor.

Dumas' best and closest ally was his wife Rena. Of Greek descent, she had a natural, authentic beauty and elegance. Jean-Louis regularly said how lucky he was to be "such a wonderfully well-married man." Part of Rena's strength was counterbalancing her husband's energy and lightness. She was, however, an iron fist in a velvet glove, and a demanding person attached to her principles. Rena took an active part in Hermès' international expansion. Jean-Louis would find the locations and negotiate the rent, while Rena designed the boutiques. In major cities such as Tokyo, Brussels, New York and Seoul, the couple made sure the shops would have a room for art exhibitions, building ever more bridges between Hermès and contemporary artists.

Old money

Dumas had the means to live like a prince but he preferred simplicity. The house in Normandy where he spent weekends and holidays with his wife and children was modest, located near the sea and surrounded by woods and fields. In Paris, the couple lived in a comfortable duplex with a terrace that opened out onto the Esplanade des Invalides. At dinners at the Dumas', one rarely found CAC-40 bosses but rather creative types. If Jean-Louis and Rena formed a fusional couple and were busy building Hermès into a global brand, they struggled, like most modern parents, to find time for their children Pierre-Alexis and Sandrine. The relationship between descendants and the company their parents founded or worked for is never easy. On the one hand, they understand they are lucky to be born into a successful business, on the other, they cannot spend as much time with their parents as they would like. Many descendants choose not to pick up the baton, having developed a love-hate relationship with the company that stole their parents away from them. But Pierre-Alexis, Hermès' artistic director, took up his role with gusto. His sister, Sandrine, today works as an actress and a film-maker. She is not directly involved with Hermès but is a member of the company's controlling entity and has contributed to two theme-launch events "shall we dance?" in 2007 and "the gift of time" in 2012.

Hermès is the only luxury brand of this size that is more than a century old and still belongs to its founding family. Chanel, Louis Vuitton, Gucci and Dior are in other peoples' hands. Prada, Armani and Tod's are not in the same league in terms of longevity. Hermès smells of old money, a distinct fragrance. Those who thrive at Hermès are disarmingly humble, well-mannered with an innate sense of discretion. At Hermès theme launch parties, one always finds the company's two main bosses standing at the entrance, courteously greeting guests, irrespective of their importance or whether they know them or not. Today, such decorum is served by Pierre-Alexis and his cousin Axel Dumas, Hermès' chief executive since 2014. These ceremonial greetings, mostly forgotten today, speak volumes about the surviving family spirit and manners of the *maison*. "Hermès family members generally share the same mix of balance and rigor. People are courteous but never obsequious. Dignity is expressed with simple things," said Leila Menchari, one of Jean-Louis Dumas' closest friends who, for decades, created fantasy worlds for its Paris flagship's shop windows.

The Hermès clan was once close to several *haute bourgeoisie* families such as the descendants of the *couturière* Jeanne Lanvin, the jewelers Van Cleef & Arpels and the Taittingers of champagne fame. Pierre-Alexis Dumas married Sophie Bouilhet, a member of the Christofle silver manufacturing family, who gave him three children. Decades ago, there were many stories of Lanvin-Hermès marriages, of Lanvin guys picking up Hermès ladies working a few feet away. Former Lanvin designer Alber

Elbaz once told me that he asked Hermès if he could use the word Faubourg Saint-Honoré on one of its fabrics, even though it was registered as part of Hermès' trademark. Hermès Chief Executive Axel Dumas said yes "as Lanvin is our neighbor."

Staff at Hermès are suitably but not outrageously well paid and get a profit-sharing entitlement every year. Like at Chanel, employees tend to stay a long time in their jobs. Hermès cultivates a distinct tribal spirit in which newcomers may have a hard time finding their place. But if one is modest and talented enough, things go smoothly. There are two types of people at Hermès: family members and non-family members. Family members can, depending on circumstances, have much more sway over the company's affairs than non-family members, which is why they can sometimes get involved in more areas than external hires. No major strategic decisions will be taken without the approval of at least one descendent of Emile Hermès. Vetoes by family members are nearly impossible to override by external people.

Leila Menchari

One cannot understand Jean-Louis Dumas without talking to Tunisian-born Leila Menchari, the in-house artist and author of dozens of fairy-tale-inspired shop windows for the flagship at 24, rue du Faubourg Saint-Honoré. Menchari is a profound and multi-dimensional person. When I met her in 2015, she sat in her office like a queen, her nails impeccably done, her eyes heavily made-up, her hair perfectly arranged. It was not an office but a curiosity cabinet. The walls were covered in ostrich skin and elm wood. Pieces from her previous shop windows were displayed: a white organza skull, *Kelly* and *Birkin* bags in biscuit, plastic, tulle—anything but leather. In one corner stood the architect's table that the late Robert Dumas gave her. There were also many photos of her when she was younger, resembling a mix between actress Romy Schneider and a sphinx, standing by an eternally smiling Jean-Louis Dumas.

Menchari told me she still thought often of Dumas and his wife Rena. "They treated me like family and they are still family to me to this day," she said. She would spend Christmas Eve at their house, travel with the Dumas to Asia, India and Africa. She, in turn, would play host at her house at Hammamet in Tunisia, where Hermès' nose Jean-Claude Ellena would later find inspiration for the perfume *Un Jardin en Méditerranée*. As with all designers and artists at Hermès, Dumas gave her carte blanche. "I could really say what I wanted," she said. Every time a new shop window was presented, curtains were pulled down and champagne was popped. Menchari installed four different decors at the flagship each year, inspired by the theme chosen by Dumas.

Leila came to Paris at the age of 18 to study at the École nationale supérieure des beaux-arts. A friend of hers recommended that she show her drawings to Annie Baumel, a quintessential *Parisienne* in charge of shop windows and decorations for Hermès. When they first met, Baumel told Menchari: "I can tell that you're a dreamer. So, draw me your dreams." The young artist knew such an offer would not present itself twice. After seeing her work, Baumel told Robert Dumas: "Leila draws very well so I would like to keep her." And that was it. Menchari was hired in 1961. Over the years, her responsibilities grew and she eventually replaced Baumel.

One day in 1996, Jean-Louis Dumas asked Leila to come with him to Uganda to meet young boys and girls who had lost their families through war there. Contacted by a humanitarian organization, Dumas said: "I will not give them rice, but a future." He commissioned drawings from the children that would be used by Hermès for its shop windows and printed on towels, ashtrays, plates and scarves. The children would receive royalties. "They were naive drawings with a daring explosion of color," Menchari said. Many years later, she enjoyed meeting one of them who had become a computer programmer.

Even though she was over 80 and worked only occasionally for the company on specific decors to present new collections, Menchari kept an office at Hermès for a very long time. "Leila is a free electron. She lives outside of hierarchies and normal rules," explained Christian Blanckaert. He once suggested to her putting products in her shop windows that could sell better than the ones Menchari intended to display, to which she curtly replied: "Nobody tells me what I should put in my shop windows."

The workshops

At Hermès, the artisan is king. Without him or her, the brand has no *raison d'être*. Asked what a Hermès object was, Dumas would answer: "something that can be repaired." His view was that it had to be an object that improved with age. The leather or the fabric should become softer and the coat, shoes and bag even more comfortable. "I believe in products that are well made, in the intelligence of hands, in the constantly renewed powers of creativity. [...] We have to tackle the century with the will to accept a constant to-and-fro between cultural roots, know-how heritage and a smart use of the new technological means that are available to us. That way, we will sustain this 'fairy of quality' that provides a feeling of happiness which, over time, proves greater than the one imagined when the purchase was made."[1]

Originally, Hermès bags were made on the top two floors of 24, rue du Faubourg Saint-Honoré, and stocks were kept in the basement. The place was a beehive with employees on every floor making, packing, selling and designing objects of all kinds. With demand outstripping supply, Dumas commissioned a six-story workshop in Pantin, just outside Paris. Its inauguration in 1992 was "one of the biggest joys of my life," he said.[2] Designed by his Rena, it is an airy glass construction with a vast well of light in the center and square windows cut the size of a classic Hermès' scarf, or 90 cm by 90 cm. Capacity is limited to 250 staff to keep the workplace on a human scale, just like at every Hermès leather workshop in France. Artisans begin work at 7:30 a.m. and finish at around 4:30 p.m. A quiet atmosphere dominates, especially on the floors where the famous *Kelly* and *Birkin* handbags are made. Every artisan lives in his or her own bubble, piercing, polishing or sewing leather, with family

[1] "Comment je vois les années 2000," *Figaro Économie*, Jean-Louis Dumas, January 1, 2000.
[2] "Jean-Louis Dumas, Hermèsman," *Madame Figaro*, December 19, 2001.

photos pinned around his or her work station. Many of them have their ears plugged into music playing on a smartphone. I exchanged a few words with a muscular, mustachioed artisan who was hunched over pincers, meticulously sewing together leather hides with a thick needle. A pretty unusual sight: a bodybuilder earning a salary making dainty Hermès handbags.

The workshop had its own cafeteria, gym and kindergarten. Artisans worked there for 15 or 20 years and harbored no desire to leave. Some artisans travelled to give demonstrations at events around the world or beef up Hermès' repair shops. It takes years of training to perfectly execute every step required to make a Hermès handbag, from sewing with thread thickened with beeswax to finishing the edges. Many handbags require two, if not three days of work.

When Dumas left the company in 2006, Hermès organized a party at its Pantin workshop and artisans formed a guard of honor. Dumas, suffering from Parkinson's, cut a diminished figure by then. He beat a rhythm with his foot, partly due to his disease. "At least, it is useful for something," he joked publicly about his illness. Staff were torn between tears and laughter.

Advertising

Dumas thought customers were the brand's best advertisers. "Do not make anything vulgar, someone might buy it!" many remember him saying. But shortly after he became head of the brand, he thought it was time Hermès invested in ad campaigns. One of Hermès' first ads featured a young blonde in a jeans jacket with a Hermès scarf wrapped around her head. The idea was to surprise, transgress and show a different way of wearing the classic silk *carré*. Dumas wanted Hermès to be in tune with its times. To design the campaigns, he hired Françoise Aron, whom he had met at SciencesPo. She had just set up her advertising agency with Pacha Bensimon (who married photographer Gilles Bensimon). Their agency, now part of Publicis group, created ads for Hermès for four decades, an industry record considering how frequently brands change agencies. Bensimon and Aron, even when they were aged over 70, still took part in brainstorming sessions where Hermès' ad campaigns were born. They drew inspiration from the brand's annual themes, chosen a year and a half in advance, which "gives us time to cogitate," said Bensimon.

The guiding principle was to avoid banality. For example, when it was the year of Africa in 1997, they explored African women's gestures and postures. There was an ad with a woman carrying a child wrapped in a Hermès scarf on her back and a woman with a Hermès bag on her head. "We try to suggest and pass on messages as much as we can," Bensimon told me. When Dumas decided to do a campaign around Paris, he asked his team: "Right, now what does Paris evoke for you?" And people did their best to come up with something intelligent to say. At the end of the meeting, Dumas quizzed them to make sure they had listened and thought about what had been discussed. "There had to be a lot of spontaneity, freshness and inventiveness," said Bensimon. "Jean-Louis had about 10 ideas a second."

Hermès campaigns to this day never use celebrities or famous photographers, unlike most big luxury brands. "Hermès has many stories to tell so it does not need to have a star telling her own story," Bensimon explained. In the past decade, her agency experimented with photographers who never did advertising or fashion photography but mainly ethnographic or wildlife pictures. Thanks to them, Hermès expressed a different point of view. Recent hires included photographers such as Hans Silvester, known for its portraits of African tribes and Eric Valli, the Himalaya specialist who has also done work for Louis Vuitton.

In her souvenir box, Bensimon came across a cartoon in which Dumas painted senior Hermès board members' reactions to her ads, all caricatured, including him with his balding head and half-moon glasses. "He made fun of everybody," Bensimon remembers. "You could not find this in any company today." Back in the 1980s and 1990s, one could laugh during meetings and make jokes. Today, people are mindful of what they say and of what others will think. Self-censorship rules. Many topics such as religion, homosexuality and race have become taboo. In 1986, Hermès launched an ad for perfume *Bel Ami* that featured a pencil drawing of a woman lying naked on a bed that said: "He wears perfume, she abandons herself." "It was an audacious ad which today would be unthinkable," Bensimon told me. In recent years, the brand's ads have remained centered around nature and the wilderness.

Running the business

Money and profits should not be an end in themselves, but Dumas kept a close eye on sales. He knew profitability was important even if making spreadsheets was not a passion. One day, a senior luxury executive asked him at a party about Hermès' results. "See for yourself!" Dumas said, pulling out a handkerchief from his pocket on which the results had been handwritten.

Dumas did not mind throwing money out of the window "as long as it was from the garden into the house and not the other way around," recalled Blanckaert. When Dumas became chief executive in 1978, Hermès had around 120 points of sale, employed 650 people and made revenue of around $50 million. Today, it runs over 300 boutiques, generates annual sales in excess of 6.5 billion euros and employs more than 15,000, of which nearly half are artisans. In its silks business alone around Lyon, it relies on more than 800 staff.

Another major plank of Dumas' strategy was that each store should be inspired by local cultures and differ from the others to surprise the travelling customer. That was in contrast to many big brands such as Louis Vuitton and Prada whose stores used the same cookie-cutter formats for years. Each Hermès store director picked the products he or she would stock. Twice a year, more than 900 store representatives come to Paris for an event called "Podium," at which they choose merchandise. They are obliged to pick from each of the brand's 16 *métiers*, or departments, meaning that they need to select not just scarves and handbags but also furniture, tableware, jewelry and watches. As a result, each store has a unique product offering. Hermès customers can be sure the item they bought in one city will likely not be found in another.

To secure access to the best suppliers and raw materials, Dumas led an ambitious vertical integration, continued to this day by his nephew, the consensual Hermès veteran Guillaume de Seynes. He has many hats as he is in charge of manufacturing, equity investments and also heads Hermès watches and shoe brand John Lobb. De Seynes oversaw investments in Vaucher Manufacture, one of Switzerland's most prestigious high-end providers of watch movements. Hermès also invested in numerous watch parts suppliers as well as tanneries all over France, silk manufacturers and crocodile farms in Australia and alligator farms in Louisiana.

In 1993, Jean-Louis Dumas took the company public. The move facilitated share transactions between family members and provided them with an up-to-date market price without having to hire lawyers. Even though Hermès is listed on the Paris bourse, it has always behaved like a private company, paying little attention to analysts' criticisms or share price swoons. It waited until 2014 to invest in a user-friendly website that carried press releases and financial statements. The company's free float is small, which has contributed to making its valuation the highest in the European luxury goods galaxy measured in terms of price to earnings per share or PE ratio. In 1993, Hermès shares were worth around five euros. In 2010, the price stood at 100 and by 2019, it was more than 600 euros. Even Hermès shares have become luxury items.

When Patrick Thomas joined Hermès in 1989, his mission was to simplify the company's decision-making process and clarify the lines of command. "Before, there was no chart of hierarchies. Somebody would say I will look after this and she or he did. There was no document supporting or backing people's jobs," he recalled. Decentralizing decision-making was an arduous task because Dumas used to vet every decision. Even if people's responsibilities became more clearly defined over time, Dumas remained involved in many areas of the business until he left in 2006. "Jean-Louis was the director of everything. It is only when he became ill that everyone's functions became clearer," recalled Stephane Wargnier, who ran Hermès' communications department under Dumas and now does the same job at French brand Petit Bateau.

After Patrick Thomas retired in 2014, he kept an office at Hermès and continued to look after the company's Chinese luxury venture Shang Xia, his pet project launched in 2010. The brand sells 4,000-euro hand-woven Mongolian cashmere felt jackets and bamboo covered white porcelain tea sets for 2,500 euros in Paris, Shanghai and Beijing.

After Jean-Louis

Hermès remains desirable as a brand but the company has grown into a much bigger organization than it probably ever intended to be. New bosses are in place. Different layers of authority and responsibility have emerged. Decisions take much longer than they did 10 years ago. At Hermès' public relations department, people need to ask permission to send a press release.

What Dumas, Carcelle and Perrin have in common is that when they were in charge, their respective businesses were much smaller. As the undisputed leaders, they could take decisions quickly. Complex issues could be resolved in a matter of days. Today, power at Hermès, Louis Vuitton and Cartier is much more divided between various factions within the company and the devil of corporatism is everywhere. People at the three companies regularly complain behind closed doors about how many e-mails and meetings are required for things to start moving. And the trend is likely to get worse before it gets better.

When Dumas' nephew Axel Dumas became Hermès' chief executive, it marked the return of the family to the helm. Intelligent and a fast thinker, Axel knows how to be courteous and charming, but he is a much more reserved figure than his uncle or his candid predecessor Patrick Thomas. Axel Dumas says he is a caretaker, just like Patek Philippe's famous ads. In an interview he said: "I am just the tenant for the next generation."[1] This philosophy contrasts with the spirit of many executives at high-end brands whose priority seems to be boosting sales and profits, even if that might harm the brand's image in the long run.

Once Axel took full control, he set up a new executive leadership. He may not have all of his uncle's artistic talents, but he does insert the occasional poetic lines in financial statements. For example, one Hermès trading update stated: "In 2016, Hermès will celebrate 'nature at full gallop.' Through horses, its first ever customer, Hermès

[1] "Inside Hermès: luxury's secret empire," *Forbes*, Susan Adams, September 8, 2014.

has developed a genuine and profound bond with nature, built on inspiration, admiration and respect. Nature inspires us by its vitality and the dazzling beauty of all the precious creations it offers, for which we will be eternally grateful."

Axel always had supporters within the company, but his legitimacy received a boost when he buried the hatchet with Bernard Arnault in 2014. The battle between LVMH and Hermès was the most acrimonious in recent history, reminiscent of the ruthless fight for Gucci between Arnault and Pinault more than 10 years earlier.

A few months after Jean-Louis Dumas passed away in 2010, Arnault shocked the luxury world by revealing that he had surreptitiously built up a 17 percent stake in Hermès thanks to equity derivatives that allowed him to avoid disclosure. The French stock market watchdog AMF later revealed in its investigation that it had been built up over many years. Once the public relations bomb exploded, LVMH relentlessly continued to increase its holding to over 23 percent. The noose got tighter. Hermès retaliated by launching legal action against LVMH on allegations of insider trading and stock price manipulation. Hermès family members accused one another of treason and of having jeopardized the company's independence by selling shares to Arnault.

At Hermès' annual results presentation, I heard Patrick Thomas say: "To seduce a beautiful woman, one does not start by taking her from behind!" LVMH fought back with proceedings against Hermès for libel. The battle intensified in 2013 after the AMF fined LVMH some 8 million euros for failing to properly disclose the stake-building. When the conflict with LVMH started, Hermès family members regrouped to strengthen the company's defense. Descendants of Emile Hermès placed their stakes in a holding called H51 that bound them for two decades and represented 50.5 percent of equity, making a takeover virtually impossible.

Under the 2014 deal between Arnault and Dumas, LVMH agreed to redistribute the bulk of its Hermès stake to the group's shareholders, ending four years of legal battles dubbed the "handbag war." The truce marked the first time Arnault—whose LVMH group had gobbled up more than 70 brands in the past four decades, including sizeable ones such as Roman jeweler Bulgari—abandoned the pursuit of a prized target. In 2017, Groupe Arnault, Bernard Arnault's family holding, used its 8.5 percent stake in Hermès to finance LVMH's purchase of Christian Dior, which was the group's parent until then. Few people understood the complex financial transaction to acquire Dior, of which LVMH was a past master, but Hermès family members understood what it meant for them. Arnault was really letting go, even if officially he had kept saying that he did not want control.

A key figure who helped broker the deal between LVMH and Hermès was Thierry Breton, a top member of France's Protestant establishment, ex-finance minister and former boss of telecoms operator France Telecom. He now heads the Paris-listed IT services group Atos. Diplomatic and tenacious, Thierry Breton helped LVMH and Hermès conclude a truce. At LVMH, his name is rarely mentioned. Yet, Thierry Breton chairs the committee of wise men who will oversee Arnault's succession when he passes away.

Hermès bosses sleep too well, luxury insiders say. Its handbags, scarves and perfumes continue to enjoy strong demand despite financial and geopolitical crises. Hermès did not see LVMH coming and the company's managers are under less pressure than their counterparts at groups such as LVMH, Richemont and Kering. The chief executive of one of the world's biggest luxury shoe brands once told me in confidence that he fought tooth and nail to get the best rental terms on a prestigious address for a new shop in China while his counterpart at Hermès got a spot next door on much worse terms but that did not seem to bother him.

For a long time, Hermès remained old-fashioned in many ways, which was partly what made the company and the brand so endearing. It had preserved a certain creative freedom and family aura that made it special and different. But something happened in early 2018 that made me think Hermès had changed. Pascale Mussard was forced out of Petit h, the start-up she created in 2010 after Dumas passed away. Petit h was a commercial success. But management at Hermès had decided the time had come for Mussard to leave. The company had imposed on her conditions that made it impossible for her to stay, sources with first-hand knowledge of the situation told me on condition of anonymity. It turned out she never had the opportunity of discussing her exit from Petit h with various senior Hermès executives. It just happened. And the company took weeks to officially admit she had left. The statement Hermès issued and sent me is nowhere to be found on Hermès' corporate website.[1] Pascale Mussard would not reply to my requests for comment.

[1] "Senior Hermès family member Pascale Mussard exits Petit h," *Fashion Network*, Astrid Wendlandt, March 1, 2018.

What happened to the human face Hermès once so actively promoted and people sincerely believed in? What happened to the lunches Hermès managers organized to flesh things out? Officially, Hermès says there is no problem. Mussard wished to leave the brand. In Hermès' defense, since she was over 60, perhaps the company thought it was time for Mussard to retire. Her departure could signal new cracks in the unity between Hermès' family members that was instilled by Jean-Louis Dumas and cemented by LVMH's attack. A family behind a company remains a family. Its members are not saints but normal people who can get into fights. A family is like a volcano; it can erupt any day.

Yves the geostrategist

Yves Carcelle built Louis Vuitton into the world's No.1 luxury brand. He conquered the world with it and planted LV flags in every upcoming and hip corner of the planet. For him, the world was a giant Risk board game and he was one of its most talented players. Carcelle knew when to move, forge alliances and go on the offensive. Under his leadership, Louis Vuitton's empire expanded, country by country, city by city, until eventually, its gigantic size and omnipresence became a threat to its perceived exclusive luxury brand status.

Overflowing with energy, Yves Carcelle was a self-made man who reached to the stars, powered by his love of people and a passion for beauty and perfection. His integrity, rigor and empathy made him one of the best, if perhaps the best manager LVMH has ever had. Why? Because people really enjoyed working for him. Carcelle encouraged staff to outperform and aim for excellence — leitmotiv of LVMH's 156,000 employees today. If Bernard Arnault's group had only one face, aside from

his own, it was Yves Carcelle's. The man embodied the group's values. His grandeur, panache and vision inspired colleagues and, in turn, customers.

Carcelle had a helmet salt-and-pepper coiffure, a permanent grin and mischievous eyes. He was your typical Latin man who talked with his hands, loved women and made no secret of it. He was ready to live as many adventures as life had to offer. Like Alain-Dominique Perrin, the man oozed freedom. Yet paradoxically, *carcer*, the Latin root of his family name, means prison.

Karl Lagerfeld once told me of Carcelle: "Yves was happy when he was on the road." An indefatigable traveler, Carcelle spent most of his time abroad. The airplane was his office. It was where he could best focus. No phone calls, no text messages. Nobody knocked on his door. He could devise his plans for the world while flying high above it.

Carcelle led Louis Vuitton for more than 20 years until 2012. Together with Bernard Arnault, he turned a small 19th-century luggage maker into a global brand that today provides jobs for 20,000 as well as for hundreds more suppliers, artists, consultants, photographers and other luxury mercenaries. During his tenure, Carcelle more than tripled Louis Vuitton's network of shops to over 400 and multiplied by more than 10 its annual turnover. By 2019, it was estimated to have reached over 12 billion euros or 13.5 billion dollars. The brand famous for its Monogram bags still contributes more than half of LVMH's operating profits, according to analysts, as does Cartier for Richemont.

Yves Carcelle deserves a special place in the pantheon of luxury leaders because he was one of the few who was able to remain human, available and generous in spite of the company's formidable growth. Carcelle knew how to speak to every employee and could cite the first and last names of all Louis Vuitton store directors and country managers, which meant memorizing hundreds of names. I heard many stories of managers surprised Carcelle remembered where they had gone on holiday and other details of their private lives. These were small tokens of attention that meant the world. In fact, it would be fair to say that Carcelle paid more attention to his staff than to his own family. In return, employees worked long hours, including weekends, and were steadfastly loyal to him.

But this loyalty would be Carcelle's undoing. Bernard Arnault grew frustrated over the years that Louis Vuitton employees would listen more to the brand's boss than to its owner. Officially, Arnault disputes that. But several former managers told me that Arnault could not always do what he wanted with Louis Vuitton because Carcelle stood in the way. He would politely listen to what his boss had to say but afterwards, he would turn around and do what he thought was best for the brand. At times, that meant disregarding Arnault's input. By about 2010, when the industry enjoyed a short rebound after the financial crisis of 2007-2008, Arnault possibly sensed the luxury business had entered a new cycle. The consumer had changed and Louis Vuitton had become ubiquitous and over-exposed. The brand needed a new roadmap and creative reboot to save its exclusive aura but Carcelle remained an obstacle. He had to go.

Considering Louis Vuitton's stellar performance and results several years after Carcelle left in 2012, Arnault was probably right. He may not be the most charismatic and warmest of luxury leaders but he has a sixth sense when it comes to business and strategy. Carcelle's story offers a precious lesson for anyone working or aspiring to work in the luxury business. Here is a man who gave his life to a brand, who did not see his children grow up and went through two painful divorces. And all this for what? He was brutally sacked and discovered afterwards that he was suffering from a rare and incurable form of cancer that wiped him out in less than a year. "Perhaps Yves' greatest mistake was that he was not able to pass on the baton and eventually, he died from it," a person who worked many years with him told me.

The world is my oyster

The first time I met Yves Carcelle was in 2008 at a conference on India organized by Comité Colbert, France's luxury trade group. India looked like an impregnable fortress. Legislation was hostile to foreign investment and red tape was fierce. Most big cities were devoid of luxury strips. Brands could only enter by opening a small shop in a five-star hotel or in the country's two or three relatively upmarket malls. But Carcelle believed in that market. "One should not give up on India," he told me right after the conference. "India will open up one day—for sure." As he was about to elaborate, he said: "Come with me in my car, we will continue to talk there." As we were whisked away in his Renault sedan, to attend Comité Colbert's lunch at the plush Bristol Hotel in Paris, I thought to myself: "Wow, finally a luxury chief executive who is not afraid of a journalist." Carcelle was almost always informative in our chats, either on or off the record, and our mutual trust and respect grew over time.

Carcelle's era is synonymous with the golden years of the luxury industry's globalization, which started in the late 1970s and continued in earnest until around 2014. For most of the past four decades, the recipe remained simple: open flagships in the right places, wow the press with lavish, star-studded parties and lift prices every year. Luxury goods needed new twists and turns of course, but customers were much less demanding than they have become today, particularly in Asia, the industry's main engine of growth. When Carcelle passed away in 2014, Paolo de Cesare, Printemps' longstanding boss, said it marked the end of an era. Frantic land-grabbing was over. The CEO of the French department store said: "There was luxury before Carcelle and after Carcelle." After Carcelle passed away, most mega-brands, including Louis Vuitton, Prada and Gucci, closed or moved shops and downsized in certain areas to preserve their exclusive image.

Yves Carcelle had a flair for the next luxury market and acted as a trailblazer in terms of hot spots for boutiques. Wherever he opened a shop in an emerging market such as China, others such as Prada and Chanel invariably followed. He was the luxury industry's geostrategist. Carcelle was often first in a country, in a city and in a neighborhood, taking the plunge and usually being proven right. Had he been alive today, he would have been light years ahead in scoping out promising markets in places such as Iran, Egypt, Pakistan, Nigeria and South Africa. A boutique is not just a place where people buy things. It is crucial for brand awareness and communication. And location is paramount.

The diplomat

Had he not gone into luxury, Carcelle could have made a career in diplomacy. A professional charmer with clear ideas about what he wanted and where he was going, he knew how to tune into people and make them feel understood, no matter what their social or cultural background was. He made them believe that he was genuinely interested in them—a rare talent in a world in which most men and women listen mainly to themselves. "When you spoke with Yves, he made you feel as though you were the most important person in the world," said one former associate. Many people I spoke to about Carcelle could not be quoted. They did not want to get into trouble with the powerful luxury brand and LVMH. On planet Luxury, executives love to badmouth each other in private, but most people I met seemed to like and respect Carcelle. They described him as a breath of fresh air in a high-strung industry. "When you mention Yves, I think of open, brilliant, professional and visionary," Patrick Chalhoub, CEO of Chalhoub group, LVMH's main distribution partner in the Middle East, told me.

At Comité Colbert, Carcelle played an important role, notably in international affairs. "Yves brought an exceptional energy to the Comité Colbert," said its Chief Executive Élisabeth Ponsolle des Portes. "He had a great notion of common interests and generosity and instilled a formidable spirit of solidarity between members."

Carcelle's curiosity about other cultures knew no bounds. He kept himself well-informed and read *Le Courrier International*, a weekly compilation of foreign press coverage of world affairs. Nothing excited him more than finding out about a region's dynamics, politics and customs. He enjoyed thinking about how the *maison* could engage with consumers in new markets and make them open their hearts—and eventually their wallets.

Striking the right chord with local authorities and media was a complex and delicate affair, particularly in the early 1990s when luxury was barely present in many parts of the world. At that time, in half of Europe, in large parts of Asia and in Latin American communist strongholds such as Cuba or Colombia, luxury goods such as Louis Vuitton bags were regarded as superfluous items flogged by capitalist exploiters of the working class. Carcelle joined Louis Vuitton in 1990, right after the fall of the Berlin Wall and just before the Soviet Union's implosion. At that time, China was starting to open up and embrace capitalism, but the communist party retained control over the economy and every aspect of society. Younger generations welcomed luxury goods but their parents and grandparents harbored a more negative attitude. Carcelle's job was not only about getting luxury-suspicious nations to embrace to Louis Vuitton. It was also about elevating the whole industry's profile and reputation. He worked hard to convince local governments and foreign buyers that luxury goods were not expensive, shameful symbols of Western decadence but the incarnation of refinement and the product of centuries of craftsmanship.

Carcelle, together with Alain-Dominique Perrin, Jean-Louis Dumas and others of their generation such as Chanel's Bruno Pavlovsky and Dior's Sidney Toledano, played the role of ambassadors of French culture and taste. Through their respective brands, the Japanese, Chinese, South Koreans and Russians discovered France. When Carcelle passed away in 2014, France's Culture Minister Fleur Pellerin called him "a visionary … one of the great ambassadors of French elegance and *savoir-faire.*"

Like most great luxury leaders, Carcelle did not have any aristocratic or luxury background. These men were on a mission to democratize luxury and spread its gospel around the world. Rising upper middle-class consumers could afford Louis Vuitton's small leather goods for $200-$300 and $600 canvas bags just like they could afford Cartier lighters costing the equivalent of 150 euros or sunglasses worth 200 euros.

From sponges to handbags

Yves Carcelle was born in Paris on May 18, 1948. He was the only child of Lucie and Paul Carcelle, a civil servant who worked for the French Senate and afterwards the Monnaie de Paris, the capital's money printing institution and museum. The job gave the family a flat near the banks of the Seine in the Latin Quarter. Later, Carcelle would joke that he could see his childhood bedroom from the opposite side of the Seine, from his 5th floor

Louis Vuitton office on rue du Pont-Neuf on the Right Bank.

After graduating with top grades from Paris' highbrow Louis Le Grand high school at the age of 16, he completed his military service at Salon-de-Provence aviation base in the south of France, where he met his first wife Françoise. Aged only 18, he entered the École Polytechnique, known as "X", the alma mater of umpteen CAC-40 bosses, government officials and award-winning researchers. Afterwards, since his ambitions were in commerce, he also got an MBA from Insead, one of France's top business schools.

Armed with such prestigious degrees, Carcelle could have applied to big groups such as L'Oréal, Renault, Elf Aquitaine or Alcatel. Instead, he started as a door-to-door sales representative for sponges and other cleaning products at consumer goods group Spontex.[1] The job helped him hone his negotiation and people skills and come up with ingenious selling techniques. For example, he would ask a flirtatious girlfriend to enquire in drugstores whether they stocked products he sold but were not displayed. Half an hour later, Carcelle would enter, proudly presenting the items his attractive lady friend had looked for. His method proved infallible. "You have to be a good salesman if nothing else," Carcelle would later say about the skills required to make it in luxury. "And you have to know how to deal with people."[2]

---

[1] Alain-Dominique Perrin also started his professional life as a door-to-door representative, only he sold dowries.
[2] "Yves Carcelle, businessman who turned French fashion house Louis Vuitton into one of the world's leading luxury brands," *The Independent*, Chris Maume, September 1, 2014.

After sponges, Carcelle joined Absorba, a children's clothing brand based in France's textile hub of Troyes, where he moved with his family. He was promoted from head of projects to marketing boss and shortly afterwards, in 1985, he landed his first CEO job at linen brand Descamps, owned by France's leading thread producer DMC. At Descamps, Carcelle worked with Jean-Marc Loubier, who would later migrate with him to Louis Vuitton. "Already at that time (when at Descamps), Yves was a man of action, a self-starter who figured things out quickly and made do with what there was," said Loubier.[1]

Carcelle's impressive turnaround of Decamps caught the attention of Bernard Arnault, a young entrepreneur who had just acquired Boussac Saint-Frères with the help of French bank loans backed by the French government. The textile group owned, among other things, Christian Dior and the Bon Marché department store in Paris. "I noticed a tremendously passionate man with a very agile mind," Concetta Lanciaux said about her first impressions of Carcelle. Lanciaux, who would become LVMH's head of HR, worked for Boussac Saint-Frères after a stint at Intel in the United States. She was into importing modern American management techniques to France. "Yves was very human, you felt like you could immediately connect with him." Lanciaux remained one of

---

[1] After Louis Vuitton, Loubier would run Celine and later set up a luxury group called First Heritage Brands which owns Belgian leather good maker Delvaux, shoe brand Robert Clergerie and storied French fashion brand Sonia Rykiel, which went into judicial liquidation in 2019, putting 130 people out of a job. First Heritage Brands is backed by Hong-Kong billionaires Victor and William Fung, associated with the logistics and retail conglomerate Fung Group.

Arnault's closest advisers for 23 years. But at some point, she too had to leave LVMH. In 1989, Arnault hired Carcelle to look after Christian Lacroix but he stayed there only a few months. After Carcelle moved on to oversee the group's strategy in 1990, Arnault gave him the keys to the Louis Vuitton *maison*—for better or for worse.

Racamier's heritage

For the record, it was not Yves Carcelle who drove Louis Vuitton's first major international push but Henry Racamier, a tall, shrewd businessman with a long nose, square spectacles and slicked-back hair. Racamier introduced Louis Vuitton to the Japanese and cemented its reputation in France. He also used Louis Vuitton to acquire Moët Hennessy, building the foundations of what would become the LVMH group.

Racamier took the reins of Louis Vuitton just as he was going into retirement in 1977, having sold his steel business to Germany's Thyssen. Louis Vuitton back then was a healthy, medium-sized business in which his wife, Odile Vuitton, great-granddaughter of founder Louis Vuitton, was a shareholder together with other members of her family. The leather goods maker employed less than 100 people and generated the equivalent of around 10 million euros in annual sales. It had a manufacturing plant in the Paris suburb of Asnières and two stores, including one on Avenue Marceau[1] in Paris where Japanese

---

[1] The place is now occupied by a Radisson Blu Hotel.

tourists queued to snap up Monogram travel bags. Louis Vuitton was smaller than Hermès in terms of sales back then—today its turnover is around twice that of Hermès. In the late 1970s, the No.1 luxury brand was Gucci, which is now still bigger than Hermès in terms of revenue.

In the 1980s, Japan's economy was booming, new giants such as Sony and Toyota were emerging and the Japanese consumer's buying power was on the rise. Travelling to Paris and buying a Louis Vuitton bag was the ultimate status symbol for middle- and upper-class Japanese.

Racamier understood Louis Vuitton would be much more profitable if it had its own shops than if it continued handing over fat margins to third-party retailers. Over the decade he was in charge, Racamier opened more than 100 shops and developed the brand's presence in Japan and in the United States. By 1989, Louis Vuitton had created 2,000 jobs and generated sales of around 700 million euros, or more than 60 times what it made before Racamier's arrival.

Racamier also elevated the brand's public profile thanks to major sports and social events. He got Louis Vuitton to sponsor vintage car contests at Bagatelles Gardens outside Paris and in 1983, the brand became the main sponsor of the America's Cup yacht race. Founded in 1851, the America's Cup is the oldest trophy in international sport, predating the modern Olympic Games by 45 years. The Louis Vuitton Cup was the challenger selection series for the America's Cup. As of 2013, just after Carcelle had left Louis Vuitton, the race was branded America's Cup World Series and Louis Vuitton sponsored all the races. But Arnault and Michael Burke, who were never big fans of the sailing race, let it go to Prada in 2018 and the Italian luxury brand became its main sponsor.

Racamier floated Louis Vuitton in 1984 on the Paris bourse. Two years later, he bought champagne maker Veuve Clicquot, which also owned Givenchy perfume. For him, the deal was a way of diversifying operations. The following year, Racamier expanded further in wines and spirits by orchestrating a merger between Louis Vuitton and Moët Hennessy, the owner of Moët & Chandon champagne and Hennessy cognac. After the October stock market crash of 1987, shares in the newly combined group tumbled, clearing the way for Bernard Arnault to pick up stocks on the cheap and build a strong position within LVMH. After a bitter two-year battle with Racamier and other old guard figures such as Alain Chevalier at Moët Hennessy and André Sacau at Louis Vuitton, Arnault took full control of LVMH in 1990.

Building blocks

One of the first things Carcelle did when he became chief executive was clean up Louis Vuitton's distribution network in the United States, where the brand had around 200 points of sale. Carcelle cut them to 130 and turned wholesale accounts into leased concessions, which gave the brand more control over image, merchandising and staff. Along with Arnault, Carcelle was one of the first to understand that the luxury battle started with boutiques. When you owned your own stores, you could better manage not only communications but also your own stocks and margins.

Carcelle and Arnault ruled that Louis Vuitton would never do discounts. It was short-term pain for long-term gain. This policy would protect Louis Vuitton's image from being hit by discounts slapped by U.S. department stores on products that stayed too long on shelves. To this day, Louis Vuitton, together with Hermès, Dior and Chanel, are among the only major luxury brands that never do discounts. They organize private sales for staff and media but those remain discreet. This also explains why these brands are still around today.

Arnault also decided that Louis Vuitton's handbags had to be made in France even though, in the 1990s, many industry peers were starting to have things produced more cheaply abroad. Louis Vuitton secured its supply chain just like its rivals Hermès and Chanel did, snapping up suppliers and tanneries to safeguard quality and production facilities. In France and Italy today, there are barely any independent tanneries or leather goods manufacturers left. They all belong to the big luxury groups. That makes life difficult for small leather goods brands and shoe-makers who struggle to get access to the best hides and artisans.

Carcelle set up a centralized merchandising system that allowed Paris to know in real time exactly what was being sold and where, and to align production accordingly. When a product became popular at one shop, internal systems triggered automatic renewal orders. Carcelle's successor Michael Burke would later reverse that strategy, introducing a scarcity policy instead—like the one followed by Hermès for decades, letting demand outstrip supply,— to help move Louis Vuitton more upmarket.

Conquering the world

"My engine is passion. For 20 years, I have woken up every morning thinking of new commercial territories and new products," Carcelle once said in an interview.[1] One of the first regions he focused on was Asia. He thought one good way of getting people to know the brand was to travel through the country and grab their attention by sponsoring a major event. In 1998, Carcelle organized a five-day rally in China that started in Dalian, on the Yellow Sea near the North Korean border, and ran west more than 1,200 kilometers right up to Tiananmen Square in Beijing. To the delight of millions of bystanders, more than 100 rare vintage cars such as millionaires' Ferraris and maharajahs' Rolls-Royces and Bentleys roared through China's countryside and remote villages. All of them were emblazoned with *Louis Vuitton China Run* stickers. The Chinese government put more than 10,000 policemen at the company's disposal to handle security. "Chinese people were cheering. We were hosted by every city's mayor and representatives. It was incredible," said Anne-Catherine Grimal, who took part in the rally. Now she looks after Moët Hennessy's communications after a stint at Le Bon Marché and a long career at Louis Vuitton.

[1] "Yves Carcelle," *Objectif Languedoc Rousillon*, Idelette Fritsch, May 2013.

In early 1990s Asia, there were no luxury malls, neighborhoods or streets. Like in India a decade ago, the only entryways were high-class hotels. Louis Vuitton and Cartier opened their first shops in China at the Palace Hotel in Beijing in 1992. At the time, the Chinese military controlled the retail sector. To enter the communist country, capitalists had to negotiate with men in uniform. Recruitment was no easy task as locals knew nothing about the industry, nor about brands' history and how to share it with customers. The two brands hired staff from hotels as they were the only ones who knew something about service and had any exposure to luxury. Carcelle later opened Louis Vuitton boutiques at the Peninsula Hotel in Hong Kong and at Hiltons in Singapore and Kuala Lumpur. In Japan, Carcelle could rely on the retail network built by Racamier. He had opened the first Louis Vuitton stores in Tokyo and Osaka in 1978 and the first free-standing store in the capital's Ginza district in 1981.

"If you think about it, contemporary luxury is really a creature of Asian consumption," argued Jean-Marc Loubier, who worked for a decade with Carcelle at Louis Vuitton until 2000. "It was built on the rise of Asian powers." First, it was Japan, then China and South Korea. During those years, the industry was also powered by the explosion of air travel and global tourist shopping. The region's upswing showed in the luxury sector's results. Back in the 1990s, for example, more than 60 percent of Louis Vuitton's business was with Japan.

For Carcelle, opening shops was an obsession. Not only did he choose locations wisely, he vetted every detail, from design to staff. In 2002, he inaugurated the brand's biggest ever flagship in Omotesando, Tokyo's luxury strip. The facade of the nine-story flagship resembled a pile of trunks of various sizes, complete with an event hall, a VIP lounge, a penthouse and offices. Carcelle chose the design of Japanese architect Jun Aoki with the approval of Kyojiro Hata, the man who made Louis Vuitton the biggest success story in luxury in Asia. A diplomat, Carcelle made sure Hata did not feel side-tracked but part of the Omotesando flagship project.

Under Carcelle, Louis Vuitton embarked on a major push in other emerging markets such as South America and Eastern Europe. Louis Vuitton was one of the first luxury brands to open a boutique in Moscow's pedestrian Stoleshnikov Lane in December 2002. Today, it is one of the Russian capital's most popular luxury shopping streets.

Carcelle broke new ground in Paris as well. In 1995, he set up a Louis Vuitton shop in the heart of Paris' Left Bank, opposite the Saint-Germain-des-Prés church and next to literary haunts Les Deux Magots and Café de Flore. At the time, the neighborhood was known for its record shops, bookstores and jazz clubs. Years later, more brands would follow, including Ralph Lauren and even the jeweler Chaumet. Where there is now an Armani shop at the corner of rue de Rennes, there used to be the famous Drugstore café, where people met for drinks and bought books and magazines until two o'clock in the morning. Shop windows that were once brimming with books and records are now full of clothed stiff mannequins. Sadly, fashion today sells better than books.

Image makers

Jean-Marc Loubier, who oversaw communications at Louis Vuitton, wished to give the brand a literary aura to strengthen its spirit of travel. The company started publishing city guides, travelogues and sketch books. It backed a literary collection called "Travel with" ("*Voyager avec*") and published works by writers such as Virginia Woolf, Ernst Jünger and Blaise Cendrars. Louis Vuitton's publishing activities continue to this day, led by editor Julien Guerrier. But in spite of their quality, his books make less noise than Nicolas Ghesquière's outlandish fashion shows.

To mark the centenary of the LV Monogram in 1996, Louis Vuitton asked an eclectic group of high-profile designers to conceive items that would be produced in small quantities. The collaborations would be unveiled during Paris' haute couture shows in January. "The idea was to showcase different cultural views," said Loubier. Designers Vivienne Westwood, Azzedine Alaïa, Helmut Lang, Manolo Blahnik, Sybilla, Isaac Mizrahi and Romeo Gigli created all kinds of bags and products. The best-seller was Alaïa's invention, the Alma bag (the half-circle shaped tote) half-covered in leopard prints.

Louis Vuitton's main story was about travelling with class. People wanted to be seen carrying LV-embossed bags and suitcases. One creative soul who captured well that spirit of travel was photographer Jean Larivière, whose work gave a romantic streak to Louis Vuitton. Larivière produced breathtaking shots of landscapes in remotes places such as Tibet and the Sahara. Some of his best shots included gold LV letters magically appearing on boulders with majestic mountains in the background. Another was a gigantic LV composed of small rocks laid in the sand in the desert, with a caravan of camels passing in the distance.

Star photographer Annie Leibovitz produced one of Louis Vuitton's most memorable campaigns. One photo showed former Soviet leader Mikhail Gorbachev, looking anxious in a car passing by the Berlin Wall with a Monogram bag next to him stuffed with Western magazines. There was also James Bond actor Sean Connery sitting on a pier in the Bahamas with the caption: "There are journeys that turn into legends." In another one, Bono and his wife Ali Hewson carried Louis Vuitton bags as they stepped off a tiny propeller plane in Uganda's Savannah. The caption read: "Every journey began in Africa."[1] The campaigns presented travel as a process of self-discovery while strengthening Louis Vuitton's image as the ultimate symbol of power and elites. The successful project, overseen by Antoine Arnault, helped Bernard Arnault's son make his mark within the group. Antoine Arnault worked for many years with Yves Carcelle. Today he runs LVMH's Berluti shoe brand and is head of the group's communication and image.

[1] In 2018, Louis Vuitton revisited a similar sensibility and spirit of travel theme with a campaign featuring actress Emma Stone filmed and photographed in the Californian desert.

Branching out into fashion

Louis Vuitton's 1996 collaboration with designers for the centenary of the Monogram was such a success that it inspired Arnault to invest in a ready-to-wear line for the brand. His HR supremo Concetta Lanciaux travelled to New York to ferret out the ideal designer. She interviewed several journalists and came back with the names of two designers on the rise: Marc Jacobs and Michael Kors. Arnault and Carcelle went for Jacobs, who they thought fitted better with Louis Vuitton. They tapped Kors in 1997 to develop ready-to-wear for the group's Celine brand, a chapter in the designer's life few remember. Kors left Celine in 2003 to develop on his own label with LVMH's financial backing. The Michael Kors brand would grow into a huge company, listed on the New York Stock Exchange, rivalling Ralph Lauren and Coach.

Jacobs embodied the "grunge" fashion movement of the 1990s. He described it as "a bit trash, a bit funk and a bit chic." At the age of 24, he was the youngest designer to receive the New Fashion Talent award from the Council of Fashion Designers of America and would later get several other CFDA prizes. Carcelle was not particularly passionate about fashion but surrounded himself with people who were. He clicked with Jacobs and gave him carte blanche.

Jacobs' first fashion collection presented at Paris Fashion Week in March 1998 was minimalist, sober and slightly subdued, with two-tone felts in grey, pale and dark colors, accessorized with mules. No handbags. The designer wanted to establish Louis Vuitton as a bona fide fashion label and get people to focus on the clothes. It was also a way of getting them excited about what would come next. "The idea at the beginning was to build the brand's image. I think that there was no real target in terms of profitability," said Agnès Barret, who led Louis Vuitton's ready-to-wear at that time and now runs her own head-hunting firm in Paris called Agent Secret. But if ready-to-wear would never represent a very significant source of revenue for Louis Vuitton, it powered the brand's diversification into accessories such as shoes, which became a huge business, as well as belts and sunglasses.

In 2007, Bernard Arnault estimated that since Jacob joined the brand 10 years earlier, sales had doubled every five years. The designer's budgets would grow accordingly, and his shows would have more and more impact. Many people remember the jaw-dropping black LV steam train pulling up into the Louvre courtyard for the brand's 2012 show. Models gracefully disembarked in dark draped suits with oversized hats and buttoned shoes, escorted by clerks carrying their Vuitton bags. Jacobs also sent supermodel Kate Moss down the runway clad in a black bodysuit, strutting down the aisle with her skinny legs and theatrically smoking a cigarette. For another show, the model jumped off a full-size merry-go-round set up for the occasion. Other mesmerizing moments included Jacobs' collection inspired by artist Richard Prince's naughty nurses portraits, with looks composed of dip-dye vinyl corset dresses covered with sheer white organza blouses.

In a documentary film on Louis Vuitton and Marc Jacobs, French journalist Loïc Prigent shows the designer wearing geeky yellow spectacles, feeding on protein bars and goji juice and talking about his inferiority complex vis-à-vis artists.[1] "I have always felt intimidated by the art world," Jacobs said in the film. "The art world is up here," he explained, raising his hand aloft, "while fashion is down here." In the film, Jacobs also roams through galleries buying art pieces for his own private collection. After Richard Prince, Jacobs collaborated with many other artists including Takashi Murakami, known for his multi-color smileys and monsters, the psychedelic polka dot master Yayoi Kusuma and graffiti artist Stephen Sprouse. Murakami's spring/summer 2003 collection with multi-colored LV bags was one of the best-selling ever. "I believe in the clash of cultures, in inspiration, in fecundity," Carcelle said. "One should never judge designers based on the image we want to give them. There is with Marc a profoundness that is often hidden by a humorous discourse. But it is somebody whose creative inspiration is genuinely profound."

The film also highlights one of Louis Vuitton's most grandiose parties just outside Tokyo. Under a giant cupola built for the event, the capital's elite and whoever counted in fashion danced wildly and downed more than 1,000 magnums of champagne. "What one needs to do to sell one's brand!" Carcelle tells Prigent with an ironic smile at the party. "You see the things you have to do to conquer markets!"

[1] *Marc Jacobs & Louis Vuitton*, Loïc Prigent, Arte Vidéo, 2007.

Always everywhere

Yves Carcelle was the first one to push the heavy glass doors of the head office on rue du Pont Neuf at 6 a.m. every day to catch calls with Asia. He was also the last one to leave, after having spoken to America. Luckily, he could function with four hours of sleep. Carcelle loved to make jokes and was generally light-humored, but he could also be quite strict and severe. Meetings had to begin on time. If one was scheduled for 8 a.m., it was not to start at 8:05 a.m. Staff had to come prepared, otherwise they got flak. A few employees would make the mistake of thinking that they could party with him until the wee hours and not show up the following morning at a 7 a.m. meeting. One regional head of communications failed to wake up on time and sure enough, Carcelle decided that his future was no longer with the brand. He never told him directly. That was left to HR. "But the problem was that everyone felt like they were part of his first circle and when they understood they were not, they were disappointed," said one of his former regional managers.

Carcelle knew that parties were essential for team-building. "Most people look at each other differently once they have had a few drinks together outside of work. And truth is, you are less likely to have an argument with someone with whom you partied and had fun than someone you barely know," one of his former staff told me. Carcelle organized all-day seminars on strategy once a year in every region and ended them with theme parties. People reminisce with watering eyes about the fêtes Carcelle organized on New York rooftops, at

Stockholm's Nobel prize landmarks and on Hawaiian beaches with flowery leis around their necks.

But Carcelle was not particularly good at hiring people. When he interviewed candidates, he did most of the talking. It was a way for him to verify that the person's sensibility was close to his. "Yves was a terrible recruiter. He had a penchant for people with extraverted personalities like his, so he had a natural empathy for those people," said one of his former lieutenants.

When Carcelle arrived in a city where there was one or several LV shops, he was so eager to find out how things were at the boutiques that he would not stop at his hotel to drop off his things first. If there were many customers inside when he arrived, he would wait outside. "Yves had genuine respect for his staff, which is how he built his reputation," said one person who worked for him for many years in eastern Europe. Right after the earthquake and tsunami that caused the Fukushima nuclear disaster in 2011, Carcelle rushed to Japan to check up on his teams.

One person who knew Carcelle well was Catherine Vautrin. She was head of products at Descamps back in the mid 1980s when Carcelle was CEO and she later followed him to Louis Vuitton where she looked after the brand's ready-to-wear department. "Yves was very direct and told people what he expected of them," Vautrin told me. "Yves was both accessible and efficient. He was also sufficiently strong and confident to let us take the initiative and make mistakes." Carcelle also taught her never to burn bridges and keep good relations with everybody. "He is the kind of guy who would sack you and you would still want to tell him thank you," she added. Carcelle helped her land her first CEO job at sister LVMH brand Emilio Pucci in 2000.

Perhaps one of Carcelle's biggest weaknesses was that he could not draw the line between professional and private life. His second wife Rebecca gave him two children, but he would not see them much more than the first three he had with his previous wife Françoise. François Delage, head of Louis Vuitton Asia Pacific under Carcelle, said many lieutenants like him struggled to find the right work-life balance. "When I was boss in Asia, my social and professional life were totally intertwined," Delage said. After seven years with Louis Vuitton, I had two kids but I was divorced. If I could do it again, I would pay more attention to my private and family life." Delage later became CEO of diamond specialist De Beers Jewellers, the jewelry distribution company co-owned by LVMH until 2017. Looking back on the years he spent with Carcelle and the kind of manager he was, Delage concluded: "Yves was always present everywhere."

Dark days

Carcelle protected his staff and shouldered alone the pressure Bernard Arnault piled on him. Arnault was a constant source of misery for Carcelle but he was also the one who made him shine and excel. During his last years at Louis Vuitton, Carcelle had full-body massages after his weekly Monday meetings with Arnault to evacuate stress. Even though they respected one another, the two men competed against one another. They worked together for more than twenty years yet Arnault and Carcelle continued to call each other "Monsieur."

Carcelle and Arnault had a lot in common. They were entrepreneurs for whom rigor was a religion and both had graduated from Polytechnique. But in terms of personalities, it was Ying and Yang. Carcelle was an ebullient extrovert, while Arnault is distant and closed-up. Carcelle spoke with enthusiasm, Arnault's voice is low and monotonous. Carcelle was down-to-earth. Arnault is a ghost-like figure with an emotionless stare.

Carcelle suffered from the fact that "BA" never invited him to his house for drinks and harbored much warmer relationships with other senior LVMH executives such as Sidney Toledano, who ran Dior for more than two decades. Members of Arnault's first circle included lawyer Pierre Godé, his confident and architect of his corporate raids, who died of cancer in 2018, and Nicolas Bazire, a French establishment figure in charge of mergers and acquisitions and of the family holding Groupe Arnault. There was also Antonio Belloni, the deputy who helped with acquisitions in Italy such as Bulgari, and Michael Burke whose relationship with Arnault goes back to the 1980s, when two two friends made ill-fated real estate deals in Florida and Arnault returned to France to buy Dior owner Boussac Saint-Frères. Burke has held many jobs at LVMH including Fendi CEO, deputy CEO of Christian Dior Couture and head of Louis Vuitton in the United States.

"For more than 20 years, Arnault tried to impose his will at Louis Vuitton but Carcelle resisted," said one of his former regional directors. "And people were incredibly loyal to Yves, which disturbed Arnault even more."

Arnault knew that sooner or later, Carcelle would have to go. Had Carcelle taken on board much more what his boss had told him, perhaps he would have remained longer at Louis Vuitton and at LVMH. Arnault does not like it when people do not deliver the results they promised. He goads his staff by putting them in competition against one another. "Every manager is like a horse in the starting block every morning," one former senior LVMH executive told me. "They run against each other. But it is true that there are a lot of good horses in that stable." And this race to perform helped LVMH rise to become the world's biggest luxury group and is the reason why so many people want to work for it.

Carcelle's former classmates were unanimous in saying the man had a slight problem with authority, which Arnault must have felt. When he was at Polytechnique, he was behind some of the most subversive plans to escape his superiors' orders and missions. This could explain why it was so psychologically difficult for Carcelle to cave in to Arnault's demands. Carcelle was his own boss and could accept no other.

Arnault tried several times to sidestep Carcelle. In 2000, Arnault appointed him head of LVMH's fashion group, the umbrella unit for fashion brands that included Loewe, Kenzo, Donna Karan, Emilio Pucci and Celine. Arnault put Gianluca Brozzetti in charge of Louis Vuitton. Later, he who would run jeweler Buccellati. Around one year later, he would name another Italian, Marcello Bottoli, as the new head of Louis Vuitton. The two Italians struggled to impose themselves. Louis Vuitton staff continued to consider Carcelle their ultimate leader and he could not refrain from meddling in the brand's affairs, making life impossible for his successors. Throwing in the towel, Arnault put Carcelle back behind the steering wheel in 2002 with a remit to drive Louis Vuitton's expansion in emerging markets.

In 2010, Arnault probably sensed the luxury industry had changed. Competition had become fiercer, particularly from accessible luxury brands such as Furla, Michael Kors and Longchamp. There was also quite a bit of "anti-logo" in the air. Emerging markets' customers had become sophisticated and educated about luxury brands much faster than expected. They had developed an appetite for exclusive, one-of-a-kind items. The $700 Monogram Louis Vuitton canvas bag had lost its appeal. Most fortunate secretaries had one and could purchase it everywhere. It was difficult to believe that 30 years earlier, the majority of customers in emerging markets did not even know that such brands and products existed.

Louis Vuitton had to regain its former glory. It needed a new artistic direction and more original and expensive designs. It also needed to put major brakes on its global expansion to enhance its perceived exclusivity. But Carcelle would not listen. He continued to open boutiques in far-flung places, including in Mongolia's capital Ulan Bator in 2009. Louis Vuitton opened a shop next to the Government Palace. It was one of the first luxury brands to enter the former Soviet country, along with Ermenegildo Zegna. "Carcelle would tell Arnault look at this beautiful castle I have built—but Arnault would focus on the cracks that were starting to appear," a former associate said. Carcelle's mindset seemed to remain stuck on global conquest. He did not want to understand that the times had changed, that small was beautiful and that there was growing demand for discreet, minimalist, rare and expensive items.

Chantal Gaemperle, LVMH's head of HR, found a replacement for Carcelle. Jordi Constans was a Spaniard who headed Danone's fresh dairy products division. The man had more experience with a cow's milk than its hides and was more of a marketing than a retail expert. That suited Arnault just fine as he did not want someone who could challenge his ideas, particularly in retail. "Jordi arrived saying there were too many products. So, this had to come from 'BA,' you could tell that this did not come from him," said one former Louis Vuitton country manager.

Arnault did not warn Carcelle that he was going to be replaced. The geostrategist only found out when LVMH put out an official statement announcing Constans' arrival in September 2011.[1] The news sent a bullet to his heart. Carcelle was a broken man. At his last Louis Vuitton fashion show, he told me: "Please don't ask me any questions now, just let me enjoy my last show."

Unfortunately, Arnault bet on the wrong man as the group soon announced that Constans was ill. To end uncertainty over who would succeed Constans, Arnault picked long-serving Michael Burke, who had just taken on the top job at Bulgari. Arnault knew Burke would

---

[1] "Throughout 2012, Mr Constans will familiarize himself with the LVMH Group, specifically Louis Vuitton, and will succeed Yves Carcelle at the end of this process," the group statement said. In it, Arnault added: "I am delighted that Jordi Constans is joining the group. Initially, he will have the privilege of working with Yves Carcelle, who has led Louis Vuitton with remarkable success since 1990."

not baulk at his demands and would duly execute his strategy.

Carcelle had a rare and incurable form of kidney cancer that had been active since 2007 but was only discovered in 2013. It would bring him down in just over a year. His father had died of a similar disease. Before exiting Louis Vuitton, Carcelle suffered several blows. The taxman carried out a thorough investigation of his personal wealth in 2010, which in France can be like enduring KGB torture for months. It led to a heavy fine that weakened him financially and psychologically. The following year, his wife Rebecca filed for divorce.

In the last months of his life, Carcelle continued to travel, holidaying with his children on the Seychelles Islands, and looked after his Sarus wine business, an estate named after a Chinese bird that symbolizes longevity. Among his passions, there was sailing and there was wine. "Wine is for man the just representation of the value of time," the Sarus wine brand quotes him as saying on its website. The estate grows Syrah and Cabernet Sauvignon vines on the clay and limestone-rich soil of the Hérault region in the south of France. The estate is also home to several art installations, including one called Driftwood that dominates the landscape of rolling hills.

Louis Vuitton after Carcelle

"Yves loved Louis Vuitton more than anything," wrote Antoine Arnault in a booklet put together in homage to Yves Carcelle after he passed away at the age of 66. "He was Louis Vuitton. He was so proud of this beautiful house he helped grow with my father, so that it became the No.1 of luxury," Antoine Arnault said. "How many times have I not seen him roam about the corridors and kiss staff as if they were warm tasty buns [...] and he would call them all by their first names! [...] One evening, we were together in Asia, and I asked him how he managed to be in such good shape despite the jetlag: 'I will rest when I am dead,' Carcelle answered. Nobody, including you Yves, expected it would happen so quickly."

Between 2011 and 2013, Arnault changed Louis Vuitton's entire creative and management leadership. After replacing Carcelle with Constans and Constans with Burke a little over a year later, Arnault appointed his daughter Delphine as Burke's No.2 in 2013. Delphine Arnault had worked with Sidney Toledano as Dior Couture deputy chief executive for five years.

Like most of Arnault's captains, Burke and Carcelle competed against one another. Carcelle did not have the same close, long-running relationship Burke had with Arnault. Unlike Carcelle, Burke does not want to be loved by his staff. Love for him is at home, not in the office. A straight-talking pragmatic manager, Burke focuses on results, on things that can be measured. He is also more concerned about Louis Vuitton's financial performance than Yves Carcelle was during his last years.

When Burke took the job in 2012, Louis Vuitton's corporate culture changed dramatically. The spirit went from being one of a big family united around a leader and a project to one of performance at all costs and survival of the fittest, like at many other LVMH brands, several former members of staff said. "I think all of those who were lucky enough to work with Yves Carcelle feel as if they had all been his children. They treasure what he has taught them," said Agnès Barret, who oversaw the brand's burgeoning ready-to-wear business in the late 1990s. Staff were bruised by his abrupt departure. "Everybody was in shock when they found out Carcelle was leaving. I even saw people crying in corridors," said one former associate. Some staff suffered in silence to keep their jobs while dozens of others, especially those who were regarded as too close or loyal to him, were sacked or fled to rival brands before getting the boot.

Between 2013 and 2016, dozens of Louis Vuitton staff in Paris and other cities in Europe went on sick leave, citing stress and depression. Many did not return. At the time, LVMH flaks played down the trend. They told me that it was not an issue for the brand and there were fewer departures at Louis Vuitton than at other brands. In 2015, a senior Hermès executive told me that he received dozens of emails from Louis Vuitton employees looking for a new job. Some LV staff joined rival luxury groups such as Kering and Richemont or independent brands such as Moncler and Valentino.

Others migrated to Fendi, back then led by Pietro Beccari, one of Carcelle's spiritual heirs. Beccari did not wish to talk to me about Carcelle for this book, arguing that it was not "something that he was used to doing." After bringing Fendi above the psychologically significant one-billion-euro sales mark, Beccari longed for a new challenge and was even considering leaving the group if Arnault did not give him something else interesting to do, several sources close to the group told me. So Arnault offered him the leadership of Christian Dior Couture and Sidney Toledano took the helm of LVMH's fashion division, overseeing the growth of smaller brands. Carcelle held that same position when he briefly left Louis Vuitton's executive seat in the early 2000s.

Carcelle had a tendency to forget the brand did not belong to him. He was merely its temporary caretaker. Louis Vuitton existed before him and would thrive after him. But that did not stop Carcelle from giving his life to the *maison*. His story speaks volumes about the drawing power of luxury and the sacrifices people are ready to make to be part of the dream. The tale of Carcelle's rise and brutal fall is one of the most poignant in the luxury goods galaxy. He might no longer be with us, but the memory of his star still twinkles.

Good leadership

A READY RECIPE FOR SUCCESS IN LUXURY DOES NOT exist. It is a subtle combination of various factors: a good story, in tune with its time, told by an exceptional designer and executed skillfully by a leader. But what is a good leader? Can somebody name one in charge of a company or a country? Many seem so disappointed by the current state of affairs and disenchanted by the world in general that they have lost faith in the very idea of leadership itself. Perhaps good leadership is a myth.

When thinking about leaders the caliber of Alexander the Great and Napoléon, leadership seems to be about a certain divinization of man. It conjures up images of nimbus, of cheering crowds, of inspired men and women who dismiss their daily worries to focus on something bigger than themselves. The notion of great leadership is the injection of something almost shamanic into an institutionalized and rationalized world.

For the Russian writer Alexander Solzhenitsyn, one of the greatest tragedies of humankind is that the qualities and talents required to be a great leader — courage, determination and the ability to federate men and women around a project that gives meaning to their lives — are incompatible with the turpitudes required to get to power, which involve backstabbing, lying and manipulation.

Considering how many mediocre people lead companies and countries around the world, one can only note a major deficit of good leaders. Yet there are so many huge problems to tackle, starting with saving the planet. For José Neves of Farfetch, a great leader is someone who is able to convince others that they can realize their own dream by taking part in his. For Hermès' late Jean-Louis Dumas, good leadership is like playing a game of Mikado. One needs to find ways of making changes without letting the whole structure collapse, a tactic that befits a long-established brand such as Hermès. In the business world, a good leader is not necessarily an entrepreneur and vice-versa. An entrepreneur is someone who has a vision, spots an opportunity and turns it into a viable project, while a good leader is someone who inspires and stimulates his teams. Some rare individuals can be both.

Brands disappear or fall by the wayside because there was no more market for their products or because they were poorly managed, generally by people who let their egos drive their actions instead of a long-term vision. The luxury world is full of brands that were harmed by bad leadership and never recovered from it. Some of them have been reduced to licenses or empty shells while others disappeared altogether. For example, perhaps the brand Christian Lacroix never made a profit because the designer's beautiful outfits looked more like costumes than clothes and were often not very easy to wear, while Emanuel Ungaro never found the right creative and management duo after its founder sold the business to Ferragamo in 1996.

The specificity of this sector is that good leadership is about a partnership between two people, the CEO and the artistic director. It relies on someone with business nous and a talented designer and storyteller. The right brain and left brain need to get along. If the designer is great but disagrees with the chief executive on strategy, this is bad news for the brand. If the chief executive does not understand where the creative director is going, odds are that consumers won't either. A good CEO must have a relatively good aesthetic sensibility. He or she needs to make sure that the designer's work is in harmony with the brand's heritage and values.

"Pressure at big fashion brands has become very strong because revenues are huge and stakes are high," argues Ralph Toledano. "Fashion companies need to redouble efforts to put back some humanness into their businesses, otherwise technocrats and processes will dominate creative teams. If your managers do not know how to remain human in spite of the pressure, you quickly get burnouts."

Some people like José Neves argue that one does not necessarily need an MBA from a prestigious university to be a good leader. He cites the example of Holli Rogers, whom he hired during her sabbatical from Net-a-Porter where she was fashion director, to be CEO of Browns, Farfetch's multi-brand fashion boutique. "Holli once asked me if she was a good CEO," he recalled. "She said:

'I am completely unprepared, I do not have an MBA, I have never studied management, I do not know how to read a profit and loss account or a balance sheet.' I told her that she was the perfect CEO for Browns. You know why? Because people love working for her. Every time I speak to her employees, they say, 'Holli is amazing, we love Holli, thank God she is the CEO of Browns.' So, forget the balance sheet and power points, there are other people who can do that for you. But what other people cannot do is inspire your staff the way you do. A good leader can be a woman, a man, old, young, very academic or a university dropout. None of this really matters." In 2019, on top her job as CEO of Browns, Holli Rogers became Farfetch's Chief Brand Officer and joined the company's executive board.

One thing people tend to forget is that one works first and foremost for a person, not a company or a brand. The company and brand name come after. This point may sound trite or obvious but listening to the grievances of so many underappreciated and overworked luxury employees, it might put things into perspective. If a leader inspires you, if you admire him or her, if he or she looks after you in every sense of the term, understands your strengths and harnesses them, you will give your job everything you've got and it will bring you in return that sense of fulfilment you were always longing for.

But if your boss is a tyrant with no passion or ambition other than becoming rich — and there are plenty of opportunities for that in luxury — then work will become tedious and your survival instinct will tell you to go explore options elsewhere. "It's all about people" is a refrain everyone knows well but that is regularly forgotten.

If a manager cannot make staff dream, how is he or she supposed to make customers dream? Luxury is, after all, about cultivating dreams. And if a manager is not sensitive to beauty and cannot be moved by it, chances are that he or she will not make it in the luxury business. A luxury CEO who does not read books, never visits art exhibitions and is generally disconnected from the cultural life in his or her home country and in major target markets, is likely to do more damage than good to a brand. Philistine CEOs in the luxury business do not leave a positive legacy.

Like in most big organizations, staff at major luxury brands have become anonymous. Most do their own thing in their own corner, sending e-mails and avoiding contact. Internally, the company is divided into baronies, each led by a firm hand. Rare are the times when people from different departments interact. For example, social media managers tend not to talk much with shop assistants and product designers. "Due to the sheer size of many luxury brands, it is difficult to find people who have a 360° view, unless they have set up their own fashion business," says Sidney Toledano, ex-CEO of Christian Dior Couture and now head of LVMH's Fashion Group, which includes brands such as Celine and Givenchy. "People in luxury too often have tunnel vision. They operate in silos. They are hard-working, intelligent but the probability that they have lived strong experiences is becoming smaller because responsibilities are more spread out now than they were in the past. Looking ahead, the luxury goods industry will need to find answers to this."

The value of access

Adding to the growing lack of human contact, most people do not have much proximity to the CEO or the brand's designer, even though they are the best placed to tell them about strategy, identity, values and projects. Staff tend to deal with intermediaries or lieutenants, mostly via emails or phone calls rather than in person. Actually, most senior bosses do not get that much more access to the company's chief executive and designer than their rank-and-file. The company's chiefs only interact with a *garde rapprochée*, or inner circle. Some luxury leaders harbor some kind of cult of personality, thinking that if they become too accessible, their staff will not fear and respect them as much. In Russia, since even before the Romanovs, those with power were those who had "access to the body" of the president or the tsar. In Russian, it is called "*dostup k telu*" (доступ к телу). The more arduous and complicated is that "access to the body," the more power it confers. Gregory Rasputin, the legendary confident, adviser and healer of Russia's last empress Alexandra Fyodorovna Romanova, embodied the power conferred by unbridled access to the executive chambers. Before he was thrown, still warm, into the glacial waters of the Neva river after being poisoned, shot and beaten, Rasputin at times wielded more authority in Saint Petersburg than Tsar Nicholas II himself.

Power isolates leaders and makes them retrench. Luxury leaders are no exception. Regular access to the CEO or designer remains the privilege of a handful of men and women, who fight tooth and nail to preserve it. A case in point is Bernard Arnault, whom some people at LVMH impishly call "God." Only around 25 LVMH senior managers have regular access to Arnault. Arguably the man whom many at LVMH also call "BA" is more of an entrepreneur than a leader. He skillfully spots opportunities and talents. He is a fast thinker but not the one who harangues troops (though he has made efforts recently) or finds magic words that make people dream. His captains have much more contact with staff.

However, for most people, Arnault is the undisputed king of the luxury business. His staff consider him their boss. They defend him and venerate him for his intelligence and flair, even if most people rarely see him and some never.

When the luxury industry embarked on its global expansion many years ago, people applying for jobs would get at least one meeting with the big boss. Today, most new recruits never see Arnault, Pinault or Rupert. Officially, most companies will tell you that they believe personal exchanges are important. They organize lots of meetings and all-day strategy briefings that end with fancy dinners to get colleagues to interact. But on a day-to-day basis, the lack of human exchange feeds anxiety and a sense of loneliness and anonymity among employees. It is telling that some luxury brands are thinking of hiring a "Chief Happiness Officer," a job first born at Google. The CHO's mission is to stimulate troops and look after their well-being. Some companies have figured out it was important for productivity. Actually, every CEO should be a CHO. Investors should be wary of brands that have a CHO as it may signal that staff are unhappy. Perfume brand Guerlain, which belongs to LVMH, set up a "happiness committee" in December 2017. However, that did not prevent some employees from having burnouts and from being put on sick leave by their doctor.

Watch industry veteran Jean-Claude Biver was entrusted by Bernard Arnault in 2015 to lead LVMH's watch division and revive the fortunes of Tag Heuer, its biggest brand. For the 66-year-old executive, this new mission was a welcome challenge. The first thing he did was organize a series of breakfasts throughout the year with small groups of employees in offices around the world. He wished to get to know them but more importantly, he wanted them to get to know him better and understand where he wanted to take the brand. His method worked. Tag Heuer, helped by its repositioning and new connected models, has been enjoying one of the highest sales growth rates in recent years against the backdrop of a depressed watch industry.

Biver already had a strong track record. In the 1980s, he resuscitated Blancpain (part of Swatch Group) and did the same for Hublot in the late 1990s and 2000s before selling it to LVMH. "A good leader for me, is someone who is not afraid of surrounding himself or herself with staff who are more competent in their field than him or her, who knows how to take responsibility for a team's failures, who can forgive their mistakes and will also share with them successes," Biver told me. "It is also someone who knows how to transmit knowledge, experience, visions, errors and doubts."

In 2016, Biver gave a lecture on Switzerland's watch-making industry to the annual meeting of the International Journalists Ski Club (Ski Club International des Journalistes or SCIJ) in the Alpine resort of Champéry, of which I am a member. He told about 200 SCIJ members how the industry was built by Protestants living in exile in the Swiss mountains. The following day, Biver joined in the fun and slalomed effortlessly through heavy crusted powder snow, something only excellent skiers can do. Over a cup of mulled wine at sunset, he told me: "In everything you do, you have to be first, unique and different. First, unique and different." He was a living example of that.

What is more precious than a job?

Employees today are tired of the system. The social contract that once ruled is no more. In the 1990s and 2000s, it was normal to work until late in the evening and during weekends, or cancel planned holidays if something big happened. It was socially accepted. In exchange, at the end of the year, one could expect a good appraisal, a pay rise or—at the very least—continued employment in the new year. Today, there is no such guarantee. Everyone is on an ejection seat. And many among the younger generations do not want bonuses or pay rises. They prefer time off to travel and do other things than work. They want to post photos of their experiences on Facebook and Instagram and get lots of "likes." They will not let themselves get harassed by stressed out bosses sending them emails out of hours. Twenty years ago, one could do that. Not anymore.

The good leaders of tomorrow will be those who can make people feel their contribution is valued, that the company has strong values they adhere to and that they are working on a project that matters to them. It will be those who know how to reward hard-working employees and express gratitude in a sincere and intelligent way. It will also be those who are able to retain and foster the talents without which, they know too well that they are nothing. On that subject, General Charles de Gaulle had a point: "To be a truly great man, one needs to know how to remain small."

Some economists predict that jobs, particularly in mature and developed countries in Europe and North America, will become scarcer as companies outsource to machines and low-cost countries to continue making more profits. This will lead to a further rise in social inequality and tensions between the haves and the have-nots. A weighty and unlikely speaker on this theme is Johann Rupert, one of South Africa's richest men. During his speech at the FT Luxury Summit in Monaco in 2015, the South African billionaire mentioned a book he had just read called *Robots Will Steal Your Job, But That Is OK*, written by a 20-something Italian named Federico Pistono. Rupert encouraged everyone to read it.[1]

In one of his TED talks, Pistono makes a depressing point: "Most people spend all their daytime at jobs they

---

[1] *Robots Will Steal Your Job, But That is OK, How to survive the economic collapse and be happy*, CreateSpace, 2012.

hate, only to make money and buy things they do not need and to impress people they do not even like." He also reminds us that we live in an economic system based on constant growth, yet the earth's resources are finite. Pistono calls for people to figure out a more sustainable alternative system. But if many companies have taken initiatives to become greener and more sustainable, much of it is lip service since our economy remains based on the exploitation of limited resources and maximization of profits, and people still need to earn money to survive.

Rupert said Pistono's book made him think about tomorrow's world. "What keeps me awake at night is how society will cope with structural unemployment, envy, hatred and class warfare," he told his audience in Monaco, Europe's wealthiest city per capita. "People with money will not want to show it. If your child's best friend's parents are unemployed, you're not going to want to wear anything showy." Rupert is right. Wealth inequality shows no sign of abating. The top one percent of global wealth holders now own the equivalent of 50.1 percent of all household wealth, up from 45.5 percent at the beginning of the millennium, according to Credit Suisse Research Institute's 2017 Global Wealth Report.

Whether we work in luxury, automobiles, pharmaceuticals or engineering, we are all at the mercy of our managers' ambitions and fears. Everyone has tales of random, unfair annual appraisals and there is nothing they can do about it. There is no appeal, no escape door. Nobody is held to account. To feel better, they tell themselves they should be happy to have a job—if they still have one. The corporate world is the last autocracy.

The luxury industry as a whole, including groups such as LVMH, Chanel, Prada, Richemont and Kering as well as independent brands such as Ferragamo and Moncler, has created millions of jobs around the world in the past few decades. Yet most people, including politicians, do not realize that. If you ask a random person in the street who employs more people, Google or LVMH, most likely the person will answer Google. Yet in 2019, LVMH employed more than 156,000 people while Google had nearly 100,000 staff. The market value of Alphabet, Google's parent, in 2019 was more than four times that of LVMH. However, major employers such as L'Oréal (which had 86,000 staff in 2018) and LVMH are not rewarded for helping keep lots of people off the streets and on a payroll. Parents get social benefits and tax rebates for raising children. Why couldn't we incentivize companies to employ large numbers and make managers feel good about it instead of constantly finding ways of getting rid of staff? Social inequalities and strife will only get worse if profits continue to be so much more important than jobs.

More Gypsies please

Most industry leaders say their mission, aside from making their shareholders rich, is to promote talent and creativity. But luxury HR bosses seem to be lacking such creativity. They keep hiring the same profiles over and over again. After having worked for various luxury groups, people become exchangeable pawns in the global game. They all have the same types of degrees, the same mindset, the same style and even spend their holidays in the same resorts. The same thing happens in many other industries.

Alain-Dominique Perrin has been bemoaning the lack of diversity among Richemont's higher echelons. "I have told Richemont HR people many times that they always hire the same kind of people with the same background and experience. Instead, we should hire a non-negotiable proportion of 'Gypsies,' of people who have ideas and are self-starters. It is more important to hire people with ideas than people with diplomas. You need those too but not only," he explained to me. "Luxury technocrats need to surround themselves with troublemakers, with disruptive people who will give them a different point of view regarding strategy, products, shops and many other things. It is these people who will help managers make the right decisions."

Many luxury businesses have become gigantic, generating billions in revenues, with subsidiaries and shops in every part of the world. "If luxury brands do not change the way they hire people, then these huge steamboats will become trains on rails—boring and predictable, the opposite of what a real luxury brand should be," Perrin argued.

When people start applying formulas in this industry, it is usually the beginning of the end. "You have to find the right balance in an organization between those who are very creative and think out of the box and those who bring structure. Otherwise you go nowhere," argues Marie-Aude Stocker, Director of People, Development and Prospective at Van Cleef & Arpels, Richemont's best-performing jewelry brand. Stocker has worked more than 20 years at Richemont, including 14 years at Cartier. "At Van Cleef & Arpels, we say that we look for '*pierres de caractère*' (stones with character), which means we don't only look for skills but also for personalities." One of the challenges of tomorrow, she says, will be helping experienced managers stay up to date in their field and keep the gap as narrow as possible between those who were born with the Internet, so-called "digital natives,"and those who learnt only later in their lives how to embrace the digital world.

The reality behind the dream

An anecdote went around Paris in 2016 about Delphine and Bernard Arnault that shows "BA" has a good sense of humor, even if he does not show it very often. As Arnault and his daughter were reviewing Nicolas Ghesquiere's latest collection, Delphine, who had recruited the French designer, told her father: "Yes, I know it is very niche." In French, *niche* denotes both a small brand and a doghouse. Arnault shot back: "Well, one should be careful that the *niche* does not become so small that the dog can no longer get into it." Ghesquière had joined Louis Vuitton in 2013 after beautifully resuscitating Balenciaga, building on its founder's constant search for new looks and fabrics.

Many young people idealize the world of fashion. They think that it is a magical world populated by beautiful, graceful and talented people. When they start working in the milieu, they get a cold shower. They realize pretty quickly that it is a fierce jungle, in which only the strongest survive. Creative people tend to be hyper-sensitive souls who are not equipped emotionally to cope with backstabbing and ruthlessness at work. They take everything to heart and are not very good at shielding themselves.

I once met a young lady who worked for Nicolas Ghesquière for over a year but did not wish to give her name for fear of being blacklisted. So, I will call her Juliette. While she worked at Louis Vuitton, Juliette had no life — which "comes with the job" most people in fashion will tell you. She started early and finished late every evening. Colleagues gave her strange looks if she left at 6:30 p.m. to go see a play or a movie. "It is fine to stay until 11 p.m. if you are having a creative moment but most of the time, I just felt imprisoned in some kind of strange masquerade," Juliette told me.

Even though we had been in contact through a mutual friend while Juliette was working at Louis Vuitton, I only got to speak to her once she had left the *maison*. It was as though she had been part of a sect. Nobody — including our common friend and her family — had had much regular contact with her until she left Louis Vuitton. But most fashion houses (not only at LVMH) are rather hermetic in spirit. And the industry's culture of secrecy at all costs does not help. One realizes that one was living cut off from the world only after pushing the exit door, by choice or by force.

At Louis Vuitton's design studio under Ghesquière, a lot of designers came from abroad. Few knew Paris and they would never discover the City of Light, putting their heart and soul into their work. Some came from Prada and Celine, where they had held more senior positions.

Juliette, who graduated from a prestigious European fashion school, was surprised to see that many designers like her worked on three-month renewable contracts. "I had the impression, every time, of signing the same kind of contract people at supermarkets got. It was debasing," she said. The short-term contract gave her no compensation for extra time. It was a flat fee and she often had to endure weeks in a row without weekends off. Junior designers like her were paid a few hundred euros more a month than the minimum wage. That was the case at most fashion studios and many young recruits accepted those terms. But not Juliette. After six months, she asked for an explanation for the low pay and precariousness of her contract from the human resources department and was served a well-honed speech: "It is an opportunity for you to work for another collection and this contract is the only solution we could find to keep you on board." Never was she told that she was valued or what her superiors thought of her work. Some at the studio stayed several years on such short-term contracts. French labor laws make it costly and difficult to lay off an employee if things do not work out, which is why so many big luxury brands use such contracts. The practice of handing out three-, six-months- or one-year contracts is widespread, not only in the luxury goods industry. Every public and private organization or company uses them. The French government constantly tries to find ways of preventing companies from relying too heavily on short-term contracts but to little avail.

When pressure and stress got out of control, some designers broke down in tears and colleagues rarely offered support. "If you cannot cope, you can leave—there are about ten people waiting outside the door who want your job," Juliette remembers hearing. Designers had little access to Ghesquière. He made rare appearances at the studio and when he did, he locked himself up. The only person who was able to speak to him directly was Natacha Ramsay-Levi, a designer who joined Louis Vuitton with him from Balenciaga. She was the main link between the designer and his team. "Natacha was the one who had meetings with us and who told us what the new collection would be about and what Nicolas wanted." Juliette said. "We were told that having designers around him prevented him from concentrating, so he did not want to see us," she added. The room where Ghesquière reviewed looks was called the "Vatican." It was all-white, with a white carpet and mirrors everywhere. Nobody had access except him and Ramsay-Levi, who eventually left Louis Vuitton to become Chloé's artistic director in 2017. There are many tales of designers who cut themselves off from the world to create. "Already at Balenciaga, Nicolas isolated himself a lot," said one of his former associates at Balenciaga who, like Juliette, did not want to be identified. However, not every designer lives in an ivory tower.

Under Marc Jacobs, the atmosphere at Louis Vuitton's design studio was different. People who worked with him said he was approachable, spent time with everyone and sometimes had lunch and dinner with staff. The ambiance at Louis Vuitton's menswear design studio under Kim Jones was also more collegial, several industry sources told me.[1] But to be fair, Jones was under less pressure, since menswear was a smaller business than womenswear and budgets were accordingly smaller.

[1] In 2018, Kim Jones left Louis Vuitton to design Dior's menswear.

Life at Louis Vuitton was no easier than at many other major fashion houses such as Givenchy under Riccardo Tisci. Staff there were constantly exhausted. The Italian designer drove his teams mad, demanding changes at the last minute before the runway show, according to several headhunting sources who did not wish to be named. Givenchy, along with Louis Vuitton, were among the big fashion *maisons* that had their fair share of burnouts. Givenchy went through at least four CEOs during the twelve years Tisci designed for the brand.[1] The Italian designer left Givenchy in 2017. The following year, he joined Burberry, triggering yet another round of musical chairs. In 2018 and 2019, fashion headhunters in Paris and London said several members of the designer's creative studio wished to leave but it was not easy for them to make the move. Salaries at the British brand were the highest in London's fashion ecosystem, which itself was much smaller than in Paris or Milan. "I have to deal with a fair amount of 'Burberry refugees'," said one London-based head-hunter. "But the problem is that they do not know where to go next."

Burberry declined to comment while Louis Vuitton said at the time that turnover at the brand was normal. The French brand explained that it was natural for a brand of this size to have many people come and go. However, bosses at big fashion labels are starting to realize that high turnover incurs significant costs and affects

---

[1] There was Marco Gobbetti, today CEO of Burberry, then Fabrizio Malverdi, who moved on to run Brioni, Susan Whiteley who did not last a year and Sebastian Suhl, who is now at Valentino. Then came Philippe Fortunato, who joined from Louis Vuitton, and who was still in charge of Givenchy in 2019.

corporate well-being, which risks stifling creativity, a brand's lifeblood.

At Ghesquière's studio, Juliette said every designer had to come up with new ideas and produce as many alternatives as possible, among which, only one would be chosen, if at all. For example, she would have to produce 10 variations of the same pocket on a jacket just to be sure that every option had been reviewed. "In the end, I think Nicolas only used 10 percent of what people showed him," Juliette said.

She thought the creative process used up a lot of fabric and created unfathomable amounts of waste. "The fabrics budget for one year is huge, it could probably dress hundreds," she said. LVMH has adopted a sustainable development policy that aims to minimize the use of natural resources. And since Juliette's time, LVMH has made some efforts to reduce waste. But isn't fashion about trial and error? One has not yet figured out a way of creating collections without prototypes that end up in the bin. Also, isn't the very idea of luxury not linked to waste? As the fashion industry is coming under scrutiny and criticism is mounting over its damage to the environment, such practices could change sooner than we think.

Juliette's experience at Louis Vuitton's design studio brings a healthy dose of reality into the dream. Yet, after all that she has been through, she would go back if she could, she said. Looking back, she feels lucky to have had her baptism of fire at such a prestigious brand. Nothing will discourage her. She knows the ropes now. And working for Louis Vuitton does open a few doors.

José the revolutionary

José Neves is the leader of tomorrow, the Steve Jobs of fashion. His vision is based on technology and new business models, as it was for Apple's legendary founder. Neves believes software can really improve lives. It just needs good intentions. A self-educated geek, he considers computer programming a form of art like design, sculpture or painting. He grew up with that skill and it is part of his life.

In technology, as in fashion, anything that works today will be obsolete in a few years. One step ahead. That is where Neves knows he needs to be. He constantly thinks about how to remain relevant. He strives to foresee which technology will shake up the fashion business. His vision has proved right until now. If the winds continue to blow in the right direction, he should keep his course and track record.

Born in 1974 in the Portuguese shoe-making hub of Porto and grandson of a shoe manufacturer, Neves seemed more destined to work in that field than become a poster

José
the revolutionary

child for the online fashion revolution. After countering several flops in fashion retail, in 2008, he created Farfetch, the world's first luxury Internet marketplace. Ten years later, it would become Europe's best answer to Amazon in the field of fashion and luxury and float on the New York Stock Exchange with a valuation of more than $6 billion.

Neves' pitch was as follows: Fashion is a $250 billion global industry with customers all over the world. Yet, there is no marketplace various retailers can go to and sell their products like on Amazon and Alibaba. "But Amazon and Alibaba don't get the fashion industry and the fashion industry does not get them either. So, someone will create a platform for the global luxury and fashion industry, and we believe it is us," says Neves, who speaks English with a distinct Portuguese accent.

Farfetch gnaws at the heels of behemoths such as Amazon, which in September 2018 became the second company after Apple to reach a stock market value of $1 trillion, handling around half of all e-commerce in the United States.

Having learned to code from the age of eight, José spent more time as a young boy solving problems and writing software programs than interacting with other kids and getting into trouble. Playing with computers was easier and just as interesting. Little did he know that what made him look autistic and asocial would give him the skills to build a multi-billion Internet giant. Neves works as easily with zany fashion types as with results-driven software engineers. He speaks both their languages.

Farfetch's approach triggered a revolution by coercing fashion brands and boutiques to cooperate, particularly on sensitive issues such as price. They had to ditch their traditional self-interested, zero-sum ways of operating. The logic behind Farfetch was that when boutiques combined their stock on the Internet, they offered more choice to customers than if they stayed on their own, hence shoppers had a better chance of finding what they were looking for and of pulling out their credit card. Farfetch made the pie grow bigger, Neves argued. Therefore, there was more for everyone to share.

Neves boasts the look of a defiant rebel with his Che Guevara-style beard and dark hair. His brown eyes sparkle with passion when he talks about his projects and his long forehead invites one to guess what he is plotting next. A tall, slender man, he has gleaming white teeth and seems relatively fit for someone who spends so many hours in meeting rooms and airplanes. The man has racked up thousands and thousands of miles crisscrossing the planet to get fashion stores and brands to join Farfetch. His passport regularly runs out of pages for visas and immigration stamps.

Farfetch grew out of José's fascination with concept stores which he sees as "curators of fashion." Start-up brands depend on these independent distributors since at first, they do not have the means to open their own store. By putting these boutiques' stock online, Farfetch gives budding brands the visibility they crave. On Farfetch, a Shanghai businesswoman can order a handmade leather clutch from small Parisian brand laContrie just as easily as a lady in Milan can order a dress from the Russian designer Vika Gazinskaya without leaving the comfort of their living room.

Neves chose the name Farfetch to express the idea of something coming from afar. What started as a small club of trendy shops has grown into a huge company with many major labels such as Fendi and Yves Saint Laurent selling directly on its website. Later, it grew even bigger thanks to alliances with important distributors such as JD.com in Asia and Chalhoub Group in the Middle East. By 2019, Farfetch had partnered with 1,100 stores and brands that were selling directly on the site and carried in total more than 3,000 brands. In the space of a decade, Farfetch has linked up stores and designers with consumers in nearly every single country in the world. By 2019, it had 1.8 million active users and operated in many countries such as China, Russia and Brazil where there was no strong local player.

The Internet has shaken every major pillar of the global economy but perhaps its biggest impact has been on retail, where there have been seismic waves of layoffs. The retail sector is North America's biggest employer with more than 15 million workers.[1] Malls, department stores and boutiques have been closing down as they lost ground to competition from the Internet and failed to adapt to consumers' fast-changing habits and tastes. Farfetch became for boutique owners a welcome raft in the tumultuous ocean of online fashion.

---

[1] *Re-engineering retail*, Doug Stephens, Figure 1 Publishing, 2017, p. 200.

Working together

Neves has accomplished something unheard of in the fashion business: making rival brands, designers and boutiques work together. It's war out there. Power games and petty battles are routine. Brands poach designers and staff from each other regularly. Retailers try hard to exact bigger margins from brands and better terms such as low-risk return policies. Some shops think so highly of themselves they think they can get away with not paying young brands for their stock for months. Some actually never pay anything. It seems that the more prestigious the shop, the less inclined it is to give any money to young designers for their work. The famous Milan shop 10 Corso Como founded by fashion star Carla Sozzani, sister of the late Vogue Italia editor-in-chief Franca Sozzani, has a reputation for not paying small brands for the stock it sells on their behalf. Contacted about specific complaints from some brands, the boutique never replied to my requests for comment.

Some megabrands force retailers to buy more merchandise than they think they will be able to sell. And if they refuse, these brands threaten to stop working with them altogether. If some retailers have too much stock, they resort to discounts, which sets them on a collision course with brands as sales harm their image. Fashion and luxury brands have no qualms opening a flagship right next to a multi-brand boutique that has been promoting their wares for years. They hardly say 'thank you' for having built a market for them. That also contributes to creating bad blood between brands and boutiques.

This permanent arm-wrestling could help explain why so many managers have oversized egos. To survive, fashion executives and retailers tell themselves they are so much better than their peers. Without that attitude, they believe people will walk all over them. Taken together, they make up a pretty paranoid bunch, convinced they should remain as secretive as possible, since everyone wants to steal their brilliant ideas. It took a strong-willed, smooth operator like José Neves to make the industry understand it needed to change its mindset. The success of Farfetch provided proof that competitors grew stronger if they combined forces. But for the isolationists in power for decades, Farfetch's cooperative spirit heralded a significant paradigm shift.

Neves believes that fashion "is an ecosystem in which the animals do not know that they need the other animals. You need the flies, you need the fish, the worms and bacteria. All these relationships are symbiotic. Same for fashion. Boutiques need the brands, the brands need the boutiques and the customer needs the boutiques and the brands, but if you ask them individually, they say 'I do not care…' It is our core business to make sure brands, customers and boutiques are aligned. It is the way the platform works. We force people to work together. They do not have a choice," he explains.

Andrea Molteni belongs to the third generation of Moltenis who run Tessabit's boutiques in the swanky resort of Como at the foot of the Italian Alps. "Fashion is perhaps the one industry in which people, who are supposed to be partners, actually compete against each other," he said. "So, José's ideas really go against the spirit of that industry… At first, retailers' response to José was:

why do I need you? I am already the best in the world," he recalled.

Natalie Massenet, who in 2000 was one of the first to create a successful online high-end fashion retailer called Net-a-porter (NAP today is controlled by Richemont), describes Farfetch as "an example of the 'collaborative economy,' when businesses historically seen as competitors work together to offer the best possible customer experience and support the world's luxury fashion brands. Farfetch aggregates the most beautiful fashion curated by the world's best boutiques and designer stores with the widest selection of styles into one easy-to-shop API (application programming interface)-enabled platform. It is a simple idea that is staggeringly difficult to execute that Farfetch has cracked. It's no coincidence that all the most successful companies, Facebook, Amazon and Apple are also API-enabled platforms."[1]

Revealing of his collaborative way of doing business, Neves hired Massenet after she left Net-a-porter in 2015 even though her company had competed against Farfetch for the same fashion buyer for years. However, Farfetch's business model could not be more different. NAP buys stock from brands and ships it to consumers around the globe from its warehouses, whereas Farfetch itself never owns any stock. That belongs to the stores and brands that sell it on the Internet platform. Neves has had a few bad experiences with unsold stock on his hands and learnt his lesson. Farfetch makes most of its revenue by receiving a cut of the value of the transaction, which by

---

[1] Massenet wrote these lines on her Instagram account when she joined Farfetch in Jan. 2017 as non-executive co-chairman. Massenet was chairman of the British Fashion Council from 2013 to 2017.

mid-2019 stood at a little over 31 percent on average. Massenet believed that offering customers more choice and service was the way forward. Moreover, she said: "We need to connect the inventory in all of the world's stores to the consumer more efficiently, and in doing so, we support full-price sales, and serve the brands and multi-brand retailers by powering their stores. When the opportunity came up to team up with José, I did not hesitate one bit. In supporting Farfetch, I can continue the evolution of my quest to better serve the fashion consumer that I started in 1999."

It is not easy every day for Neves to be fashion's Mr. Nice Guy. He constantly needs to defuse tensions between brands and boutiques and between boutiques, brands and customers. Much of the tension centers on the sensitive issue of price. Once a brand sells a garment to a retailer, be it a department store or an online boutique, it cannot control at which price it is sold to the final customer. It has become the property of the retailer. Yet brands have no qualms about putting pressure on retailers to adhere to certain price lists for each country and region. They call it a "recommended price" but retailers are asked to implement them to keep good relations with the brand. "We often stand in the middle" amid brands, boutiques and customers, explains Neves. "We do not set the prices ourselves. We help brands and boutiques navigate this whole conundrum." Hence, there can be differences in price for the same product across regions, which can upset customers. For example, a boutique in central London will have a price in pounds that is usually higher than the price in euros charged by a boutique in Milan, partly because retail costs in London tend to be higher.

Farfetch's algorithms select the merchant seller that is closest geographically to the client and offers the best service measured by how fast the product is sent and how efficiently returns and problems are dealt with. "The way to be consumer-centric in luxury is not the Amazon way — to drive retailers to the lowest price possible," says Neves. "That does not work in luxury. Farfetch is a mediator, a consensus-builder. We always talk about a 'win-win' mindset. We want to be brand-friendly and boutique-friendly, but it is a delicate balance." Some brands regularly ask Neves if Farfetch will keep boutiques onboard since so many brands sell directly on the site. He keeps repeating that boutiques form an essential part of Farfetch's identity. They act as curators and their point of view is core to Farfetch's value-adding proposition. The same applies when a boutique asks him not to take on a certain brand because of a concern or grievance it has. Neves stands his ground and answers that the more brands there are on Farfetch, the wider the choice customers have and the more buoyant will be demand.

Internet refuseniks

Some luxury and fashion brand managers still pretend the Internet never existed. They are simply not excited about it and probably never will be. Neves points to a generational issue and an emotional rejection of all things digital. "When something does not excite you, you rationalize it and find excuses not to do it," he says. "Take exercise, for example. If you do not want to do exercise, you will find all sorts of excuses not to do it, like this friend who died of a heart attack while running, etc."

Luxury and fashion brands could ignore customers' tastes and spending habits in the 1990s and the early 2000s. Customers travelled much less than they do today. They could not tell that every boutique looked the same and sold more or less the same products, only costing as much as 60 percent more in Asia than they did in Paris. The Internet forced luxury brands to be transparent and harmonize prices across regions. To borrow a well-known expression, the Internet made the luxury world "flatter."[1] Experts predict that if under 10 percent of luxury goods purchases are made on the Internet now, that figure should climb to 25 percent by 2025. In business terms, that's as good as tomorrow.

"A few years ago, you could afford to forget the customer as long as you controlled a few things," Neves recalled. "First you controlled the press. If you were friends with Condé Nast and Hearst, then they would say nice things about you and you would give them advertising, so in effect you controlled the media. Then, you controlled the distribution with your beautiful shop on Fifth Avenue or New Bond Street, and then you controlled the product creation process. So, you could forget about the customer. They had two or three magazines to read, one or two streets to shop and the industry got lazy and complacent."

Neves believes the old way of building a fashion business, which is still used today, will be dead soon. The

---

[1] I am referring of Thomas Friedman's *The World is Flat*, the bestseller on globalization in the early 21st century.

old system had a certain sequence to it. A designer produced a collection, presented it at fashion week, opened the showroom to retailers, delivered it six months later, editors came in, PR companies distributed samples all around the world, photo shoots got done, people went to department stores and bought the products they saw in magazines. That system no longer works. Hardly anyone now buys something they saw in a magazine. Most people spend more time on social media than flipping through publications. Condé Nast and Hearst are fully aware they need to reinvent themselves.

The Internet makes every luxury item easy to locate and purchase. The argument that a luxury object should remain scarce to preserve its perceived exclusivity is flawed, Neves argues. If a brand is not on the Internet, it is not controlling its story and in effect, it is letting other people tell its story. The brand's products will end up being sold on the Internet, whether it likes it or not. Consumers or sites controlled by Amazon or Alibaba will take care of that.

Yet the fashion sector still counts a significant number of Internet refuseniks. The most high-profile is Chanel. In November 2017, Chanel's fashion boss Bruno Pavlovsky told a crowd at the Vogue Fashion Festival in Paris that "if you give everything to everyone immediately, then you lose exclusivity."The brand still "considers that consumers' visit to our shop is very important" as is its selling ceremony, he said. However, Chanel has been looking for ways to provide more personalized services. In February 2018, it struck a deal with Farfetch to adopt its "augmented retail" technology, which will be explained later in this chapter. However, Chanel made it clear it would not sell its wares on Farfetch. That would be going too far. Chanel invested in Farfetch as part of the deal, a smart move considering Farfetch was about to float a few months later.

Meditating leader

Neves always dresses the same: a white shirt, a designer black suit and black leather shoes, without socks, from Swear, the brand he founded in the 1990s. But under his predictable appearance, lie multiple personalities. The first José one meets is the charming, mild-mannered entrepreneur, surprisingly humble for someone who has toiled in fashion for so long. Then there is José, the warrior, the nothing-can-stop him character, the terrier who will never let go, the man who can handle huge pressure and sign several deals in a month worth hundreds of millions of dollars. And finally, there is José, the wise, the calm force, the gentleman who thinks before he speaks, the José who pauses before taking a major decision.

A communist at the age of 18, Neves later became a Buddhist and still considers himself close to that faith. He is not into praying at temples but practices meditation regularly, either during yoga sessions or when he jogs alongside houseboats on Regents' Canal in London, near his house in Shoreditch. Meditating helps him manage the pressure that comes with running a fast-growing Internet start-up. "Since the brain never shuts down, meditation is more about being aware of all the stuff your mind is coming up with, not about emptying your mind," Neves explained. "Being aware of the transitory nature of your thoughts and emotions, you cannot help feeling frustrated, angry or impatient. It is part of being human. You just have to tell yourself that these feelings will not last," explains Neves.

His Achilles heel is constantly worrying about things. He tends to worry about whether his family, staff, friends, partners and customers are happy, even though he knows that one cannot do anything about the happiness of others as it depends on them, not on him. "But I have a natural tendency to make sure everyone is happy," he said. "I know that this is my default mode."

Fashion people love a good party, but Neves is not into mingling with strangers. He will avoid group gatherings if he can afford it. "When I go out, I go out and I can party until 3 a.m. but it is more the exception than the rule," he said. "For me, going from fashion show to fashion show and from soirée to soirée is my idea of hell." By his own admission, Neves is a relatively closed and taciturn person. He is conscious of the fact that he does not display much *joie de vivre*, which is why he feels socially awkward sometimes. Melancholy is a recurring state of mind. Maybe it's because he spent much of his childhood alone and did not have many friends to play with.

Geek turns entrepreneur

When he was eight years old, José received a computer for Christmas. It didn't come with any video games, so he started coding and solving problems with it. Interacting with a computer became José's preferred form of entertainment. As he applied himself to it, he became a talented programmer. At 13, José created a software program that could predict football match results and he sold it to a local newspaper. A little later, he helped his mother Augusta write her doctoral thesis on how children could learn mathematics thanks to computer programming.

Neves has lived alone since the age of 13. He chose to stay in Porto under the supervision of his grandparents when his parents moved to Lisbon. "I became conscious quite early on, that you have to sort out your own shit and that no-one is going to do it for you," Neves said. "You can kick the furniture, shout and blame other people but in the end, you need to look at yourself. Instead of pointing the finger at someone, you need to look at your own resources." From that time on, José's survival instinct grew, as did his self-reliance and resource-fulness.

José studied economics at the University of Porto. Bent on becoming an entrepreneur, he believed it was more important to know how to read a balance sheet and run a profit and loss account than grow into an even bigger whiz kid. After two years at university, when he was 20, he got itchy feet. He set up his first company which created software programs for dental clinics. José partnered with Cipriano Sousa, a young computer programmer he met through his mother. Sousa would eventually take part in every one of José's adventures. Today, he is Farfetch's Chief Technology Officer and runs teams of hundreds of computer programmers and IT specialists from Portugal to China. Like Bill Gates and

Steve Jobs, Neves quit school and never finished his five-year economics degree, having completed only four.

But the business of dental clinics was perhaps not the most exciting for the young entrepreneur. Back in the 1990s, textile and shoe production was booming in Portugal as European fashion companies were looking for ways to lower costs. Neves' father decided to ride the wave and set up his own shoe factory at the age of 45, turning his back on the pharmaceuticals industry in which he had toiled most of his life. "It was a complete disaster," recalls his son. "My father knew nothing about shoes. He was ripped off by suppliers, robbed by employees, abused by customers." José's father's venture in shoemaking lasted around five years. "It was a traumatic experience," concluded José. But it got his son into fashion.

Working with his father, José met designers and brands from all over Europe. Father and son attended trade shows in Las Vegas, Milan and Düsseldorf. At the age of 22, José discovered the world and met interesting, well-dressed fashion people. "People looked great. The parties were fantastic," he remembered. He also understood that he did not want to be just a shoe manufacturer but climb up the value chain. José and Cipriano decided to produce enterprise resource planning (ERP) software for the shoe industry in Portugal. It seemed a good idea since there were hundreds of bustling shoe factories. But if software development was his thing, Neves had always wanted to explore more deeply the fashion business and get his hands dirtier. In 1996, he founded a shoe brand he called Swear. Originally, Swear was about futurist, wacky platform shoes, influenced by Japanese *mangas* and electric pop.

José set up a Swear boutique in Covent Garden and built an online site, which in the mid-1990s was no mean feat. Amazon and eBay had just opened shop and online banking was embryonic. It's hard to believe that 20 years ago, banks did not know what José talked about when he asked for a merchant's account online. When someone bought a pair of Swear shoes online, one person in the Swear shop had to enter the credit card details manually to process the purchase. "I remember seeing the potential of the Internet the day we launched," recalled Neves. "We started getting orders from Japan, from Australia, which we processed from the shop. To me, it was quite clear the potential of having your creative vision accessible 24/7 by the whole world was going to change fashion forever."

As Swear gained momentum, the young Portuguese entrepreneur decided to move even further up the value chain and dabble in e-commerce. He set up an online shop called thing-is.com that sold mainly small, little-known European brands like Britain's Budicca. Three years later, in 2000, the Internet bubble burst. Newspapers were full of stories about fallen dot.com stars such as fashion retailer boo.com that had gone bust. They spooked those who had massively invested in the sector and Neves' investors pulled the plug fairly quickly. José recalled being told: "If these guys with 200 million pounds (at boo.com) could not make it, it is not going to be you, this 25-year-old guy from Portugal, who was going to cut it." Neves was left with piles of unsold stock, the kiss of death in retail. To turn clothes into cash, he opened a boutique on Conduit Street, in the hip part of Mayfair, which he called bStore. Within a year and a half, bStore had an e-commerce version up and running. It later moved to Savile Row, the high-end menswear shopping street. The episode helped Neves understand that owning stock was a real gambit. And it fed his thinking about what would one day become Farfetch. The website, which gets a commission from every sale, leaves headaches about stock overhangs to boutiques and brands.

Building Farfetch

At first, fashion executives and boutiques did not understand Neves. They saw him as a nice Portuguese shoemaker with a weird, ambitious project and would not give him the time of day. Determination is perhaps the one quality an entrepreneur needs to get his start-up off the ground. If Neves had taken no for an answer, Farfetch would have remained a nice idea scribbled on paper. One always hears people say dreams are impossible. Luckily, Neves never listened to them.

For a long time, luxury giant LVMH was intrigued by Farfetch. Neves would meet with senior group figures who could see the potential, but they were not quite ready to join his platform. It took years of patience to convince store managers and stiff-upper lipped fashion bosses to endorse Farfetch. One of the first stores to partner with Farfetch was Paris' Maria Luisa, the multi-brand boutique set up by late Maria Luisa Poumaillou, a revered fashion talent spotter and one of the first retailers to support young designers such as Martin Margiela and Helmut Lang in the late 1980s and 1990s. But glory is not always synonymous with commercial success. In its near 30 years' existence, Maria Luisa hardly ever made a profit. After every season, it was left with unsold clothes, shoes and accessories that dug into its finances. Maria Luisa was known for her fine taste but also for buying things ordinary people could find difficult to wear and therefore buy. (That is why the most profitable model is to be mainly a shop window like colette was).[1] Maria Luisa survived thanks to her husband Daniel Poumaillou, who, from time to time, mopped up losses by selling antiques and paintings.[2]

"When José came to see us, we were thinking ourselves about what we could do to get our designers better known and open new retail channels for them," said Daniel Poumaillou. "So, when José appeared, it was exactly what we were looking for. […] And the man was so human, so nice, we felt like we spoke the same language." Boutiques send to Portugal one of each item they wish to sell on the site so that Farfetch staff can take photos and upload them on its website. Around five days later, products are returned with a Farfetch tag that tracks their movements.

---

[1] Colette, which closed in Paris at the end of 2017, had a different business model than Maria Luisa. It did not buy stock. It simply promoted designers and brands and sold only a few items. Brands displayed there obtained great visibility, which boosted their sales elsewhere.

[2] The Maria Luisa name in France was sold to Printemps in 2016 after Maria Luisa lost her battle with cancer and passed away. She had moved the Maria Luisa shop to Printemps' Paris flagship in 2009 after closing rue du Mont-Thabor, off the St Honoré fashion strip and a stone's throw from colette. Today, her husband Daniel Poumaillou runs the Maria Luisa international franchise in China and Qatar, where shops have been opened in recent years.

Maria Luisa's stock appeared on Farfetch as early as 2008 but the partnership did not last long, partly because of Maria Luisa's recurring losses. Farfetch launched with a little under 20 trendy retailers, which included l'Éclaireur and the high-end shoe specialist Biondini in Paris, Feathers in London and the Danish designer and talent spotter Henrik Vibskov. A year later, the number of stores selling on the site climbed to 100. Between 2010 and 2012, José met many fashion chief executives. They were interested in his ideas but "were hesitant about the project as José was way ahead of his time," recalls Susanne Tide-Frater, a veteran retail consultant who revamped prestigious stores such as Harrods and Selfridges. She now advises Farfetch on strategy.

But there were a few early backers like Frederick Lukoff, chief executive of Stella McCartney,[1] who thought his idea was brilliant. Neves remembers coming back from his meeting with Lukoff in 2010, thinking to himself: "Finally, there are some CEOs who are getting it." Other early fans were Rick Owens, Fendi and Valentino, who back in 2015 were among the first brands to join the Farfetch platform directly. Fashion entrepreneur Anne Chapelle, who has invested in brands Ann Demeulemeester and Haider Ackermann, immediately understood José's vision. "Oh my god! Can I invest?" she told Neves. She declined to comment for this book.

In the early days, Farfetch's first employees shared offices in London with Neves' shoe company Swear and Grey Matter, his shoe manufacturing software provider. Swear lent money to Farfetch to pay for salaries and

---

[1] In 2019, Lukoff left Stella McCartney to become CEO of the Dutch brand Scotch & Soda.

operating costs. There were moments when Neves did not know if he would find 30,000 euros to pay staff on time. But as he owned all three companies, it did not matter. It only did when the first investors showed up. They were told they needed to first repay debts to Swear and his software company before they could invest in Farfetch. At the time, Swear employed 60 people and made 5 million euros in annual revenue. If Farfetch did not work, Neves' other businesses would have gone under.

"I could see myself at the time: I was 33, with no CV, no diploma, three bankrupt companies," Neves said laughing. "It would not have been a pretty sight. It was a poker gamble. Win all or lose all. I put all the chips on the table. You think you have a good hand, you think your idea is great, but it may well be that somebody else has a better idea than you," he added. His software company, which employed six people, was absorbed by the newly created structure called Farfetch.

Farfetch's first major investor was Frederic Court, a private equity pro from France who set up his own fund in London in 2015 called Felix Capital after having led investments in businesses such as France's Dailymotion, an online video platform now part of Vivendi media group. With the success of fashion retailers Asos and Net-a-porter in the UK and discount models such as Yoox in Italy and Vente-Privée in France, Court was convinced Europe had more entrepreneurial adventures to offer, particularly in digital, fashion and lifestyle. "My intuition was that there were more things to do in that space," he said. "I have always been fascinated by market-places, the transformation of retail and the challenge of managing stock in the Internet space." Back in 2008 and

2009, he followed Farfetch from afar, reading its newsletter. "At the beginning, I was not sure I understood what José was doing, whether Farfetch was an online fashion magazine or an e-commerce website," Court recalled.

Then, in 2010, he finally met José. He thought he had taken risks and was able to make the business grow with few resources. "This was exactly the type of thing I wanted to invest in. It was disruptive and had the potential to create something unique," Court said.[1] He foresaw that once all the best boutiques in the world had joined Farfetch, they were not going to tie up with another partner.

José the deal-maker

In 2013, Neves convinced Condé Nast, the publishing house behind *Vogue*, *GQ*, and *Vanity Fair*, to invest $20 million in Farfetch. The deal raised its profile and gave it access to precious content and contacts. Condé Nast gained exposure to the booming online fashion sector and its investment would prove to be a wise one. Two years later, Condé Nast decided to get involved in e-commerce on its own and launched, after repeated delays, the website Style.com in 2016. However, selling clothes online is a different business than publishing magazines. By late spring 2017, the site was hemorrhaging cash and the project clearly was a

---

[1] Court made the initial investment in Farfetch in 2011 when he was still with private equity firm Advent International.

commercial flop. Style.com had started in the UK, the most overcrowded fashion e-commerce market in Europe, with Net-a-porter, Matchesfashion and department stores that were very active online. People from Style.com's editorial department did not talk with the e-commerce and IT teams and vice-versa, which led to problems with the implementation of strategy. In June 2017, Neves came to the rescue. Farfetch bought the name and website Style.com for $12 million in future Farfetch shares and hired a few members of staff. The deal enabled Condé Nast to get rid of its e-commerce problem. However, it was presented as an alliance that would give Farfetch more editorial content. In return, Condé Nast would send its readers shopping on Farfetch.

The following week — we are still in June 2017 — Neves secured Farfetch's future in China, the world's fastest growing luxury market, by clinching a deal with JD.com, the country's second-largest e-commerce company. JD.com injected $397 million into Neves' company and gave Farfetch access to its logistics network, its high-end service and its social media partnership with WeChat, the popular chat application in China.

Since Farfetched launched in China in 2015, the Asian market had always represented "the next big opportunity," Neves said, "in the luxury, e-commerce space generally." The Chinese luxury customer, who barely existed 20 years ago, today represents around 50 percent of revenues for some big luxury brands, claiming the dominant position held by the Japanese in the 1980s and 1990s. The global importance of the Chinese consumer has only begun if one considers the sheer size of the economy, its demographics and the fact that less than 10 percent of Chinese have a passport.[1]

Neves saw there were very few local players in China. There are mainly three big companies—Alibaba, JD.com and Tencent—and the search engine Baidu. Together, they run the Internet in China. "So, for us, it was very clear that we needed to form an alliance and JD.com as it was by far, hands down, the partner we wanted to work with, so we went straight to them," Neves said. Later in 2019, Farfetch acquired JD.com's Top Life website and merged it with its Farfetch China operations. Farfetch also strengthened its business in China by acquiring CuriosityChina, a leading integrated marketing and social commerce company.

Lion's share

When I asked Neves in 2018 about the profitability of his company, he replied: "It is not a priority for now." It was as sensitive a topic for him as it had been for Natalie Massenet, who had also held back on Net-a-porter's profitability for years to focus on market share. Both knew that not being profitable made strategic sense. Investing in the future of a company was more important than squeezing cash out of it. "Investors actually demand that the company invests within reason (not like boo.com) and we keep it under control," Neves said. "Fundamentally, our business is profitable. You are acquiring a customer for 10 and you

[1] *The Bling Dynasty, why the reign of Chinese luxury shoppers has only just begun*, Erwan Rambourg, Wiley, 2014.

know that statistically that customer is going to return 30
or 40, so three or four times what you invest today. So,
you would be a madman if you did not invest as much as
you could, if you did not acquire as many customers as
you could before others did. It is as simple as that. And it
is perfectly under control, perfectly part of the business
plan. We measure it every month. If I was profitable, I
would be fired by my investors."[1] Asked when would
Farfetch be profitable, Neves said it could be immediately—just like Amazon chose to become profitable when
it decided it was time to be. Neves said the most profitable part of Farfetch was its core business, the cut it gets
from every sale, particularly from European boutiques
selling to the rest of the world. "Over the next ten years,
the luxury industry is expected to grow to an estimated
$500 billion, and online sales will potentially grow to
represent an incremental $100 billion opportunity," Neves
said. "Farfetch is uniquely positioned to capture the lion's
share of this opportunity."

Farfetch visit

The entrance to Farfetch's office in London, near Old
Street in east London—the British capital's "Silicon
roundabout"—was hidden by scaffolding and tarpaulins
when I visited it the first time in 2017. The place was
under construction just like the company itself. A recep-
tionist with raven black hair who looked like someone

[1] José Neves was speaking before Farfetch's New York flotation.
Now, as a publicly listed company, profitability has become more of
a focus point.

out of *Star Trek* sat behind a huge marble desk with
Farfetch engraved on it. Plasma screens showed Farfetch
ad campaigns and films about José Neves. Then opened
up a vast lofty space decorated with Swedish walnut
tables, steel tubes, grey concrete walls and round glass
ceiling lights. As if on a mission, twenty-something
women in jeans and sandals, laptops under their arms,
dashed into a meeting room called via Condotti. All of
the company's meeting rooms were named after famous
luxury strips such as that one in Rome. There were no
offices, just open spaces. Most people did not look older
than 30.

Near the kitchen, prizes for Farfetch such as the
Sunday Times Tech Track 100 Best Emerging brand award
and the Ernst & Young Entrepreneur of the year, were
on display. Such awards usually gather dust in a chief
executive's office, but they were here for all to see. Breakfast was free in the kitchen corner, with everything
healthy one could desire from yoghurt to muesli and all
kinds of milk. Large windows gave onto a terrace whose
bar tables and stools, bean bags, hammocks and sitting
benches seemed ideal for drinks on a Friday night,
London weather permitting. Farfetch staffers met there
on Friday evenings to give each other feedback and
publicly thank one another. Instead of going to the traditional British pub, where people drunk and gossiped
about work after hours, socializing happened under
Farfetch's roof.

Focus on values

In April 1974, two months before José Neves was born, Portugal was rocked by the "Carnation revolution," when army rebels seized power after an almost bloodless coup that ended more than forty years of dictatorship. Neves' mother Maria Augusta jumped atop a tank to celebrate the new era and live the moment. Carnations, in full bloom at the time, were put into the noses of rifles and pinned on army uniforms. "I think my risk-taking comes from my mother," says Neves. "As I was born in the middle of the revolution in Portugal, perhaps I am a revolution child." Neves likes the idea of revolution. In fact, "be revolutionary" is one of Farfetch's six values. However, revolution for him is more about disruption than destruction, collaboration more than war. For Neves, values are essential. They form the bedrock of corporate culture.

When one starts a business, everyone is ultra-driven. Staff work long hours and share meals. They are constantly in contact with the founder. Things work relatively smoothly until a company gets to around 100 to 150 people. Afterwards, it gets complicated. "One of my big mistakes was not realizing that the culture and the values were being lost as we grew, and they were becoming completely unclear, even for us—the senior management," recalled Neves. A catastrophic hire made him realize how important corporate culture was.

A person Neves chose for a very senior executive job—who cannot be identified here—looked smart, acted smart and had an impressive CV after working for a big luxury company. The individual asked all the right questions during the interview and provided all the right answers but actually did not fit with the company. The person behaved in a hierarchical and patronizing manner while Farfetch's staff were approachable. The individual in question could not understand how José could chat five minutes with a junior member of staff on his first day at work. And minor things started adding up. "So, we realized that it was really time for us to make clear our values and express them," Neves said. He created working groups to come up with words that expressed what Farfetch was about.

"Before, my old style of interview was very functional, asking people about their skill set, why they were right for the job, etc. Now I ask questions such as: one of our values is 'be human.' So, what does that mean for you?" says Neves. If the person cannot give him an authentic situation during which he or she lived the importance of that value, then there is a risk that person is just paying lip service to the idea and deep down, does not share the company's values.

Staff came up with six core ideas: be revolutionary, be human, be brilliant, think global, amaze customers and *todos juntos*. That last idea means "all together" in Portuguese, Neves' native language. "Since half the company was Portuguese, it was only right that one of its values should be expressed in Portuguese. It was also a way of celebrating the diversity of the teams," Neves explained.

Cipriano Sousa, Farfetch's CTO, whose relationship with Neves dates back to their dental clinics period in Portugal in the early 1990s, says motivating staff is his number one priority. When he speaks to Neves, they do not talk about technology but about how the pair can fuel enthusiasm. They tell their employees that they are building the world's No.1 platform for online fashion and luxury with technology nobody has developed yet. They say Farfetch is in the top league with other global online players such as Amazon.com and Booking.com in terms of number of visitors, transactions and geographical reach.

"We employ hundreds of engineers, so it is easy for them to lose focus. It is super important for us to remind them what they are here for, and what they want to accomplish," explains Sousa. The company regularly holds workshops to explain Farfetch's strategy and make sure staff understand where it is going. "I do not have a boss but a friend who supports me and gives me room to develop my own strategy and take decisions," says Sousa. "Each team has their own mission. We do not impose any specific goal, we want them to come up with their own goals and objectives. We just tell them: we have this problem, tell us how we can solve it."

Despite the star status he reached in his field, Neves is still basically the same person they've always known, his friends and associates say. He keeps people on their toes but gives staff a second chance if they make mistakes. The main thing that has changed with the years is that he takes a little bit more time to make major strategic decisions as the stakes are bigger. Neves continues to hate disloyalty and lack of passion. He also has little time for bullies and arrogance. However, he loves people who are different, who have their own point of view and are not afraid of expressing it. "I find it really inspiring when I talk to people who are very successful and yet are able to remain simple and do not put themselves on a higher level," Neves says.

"José has very strong views and is good at bringing people to share that view, rather than dictating how things should be done," says Tom Stafford, a partner at DST Global, the private equity firm founded by Yuri Milner, Russia's most influential technology investor, who backed Internet success stories such as Airbnb, JD.com, Alibaba and Facebook. Other investors in Farfetch include IDG, Temasek, Eurazeo, Global, Index Ventures, Vitruvian, Condé Nast International and Chanel.

Store of the future

One question Neves constantly asks himself is how to remain revolutionary and a positive force in the luxury and fashion industry. The answer cannot just be a website. One still needs to pay attention to the old bricks-and-mortar shop since it is where 90 percent of transactions take place. So, Neves looked for ways to connect physical shops with the digital world. Many retailers already allow people to order online and pick up their purchase in a store, or order in a shop and have the goods delivered at a given address. Offering customers such options bears the unappealing name of omni-channel, which one could easily confuse with a remote control for television.

"I have noticed that, if say for example, you have 20 minutes to spend in a shop, a lot of that time will be used by the shop assistant to look for stock, check inventory, call another store to see if they have your size, ask your name to see if you are in the system. And because you are a foreigner, they cannot spell your name correctly, you almost need to write it on a piece of paper. Those 20 minutes should be used to tell the story of the brand," Neves said. "Time is the ultimate luxury, you can mine for diamonds, you can mine for gold, but you cannot create time. It is fundamentally rare... So, if you are a luxury company, you need to devote time to your customer so that you can tell them your story. And this is what we are trying to build but it is not easy."

Farfetch, which is in a race with Amazon in the field of online retail technology, has designed an operating system, or API, to which other start-ups or technology providers can connect themselves. Neves' plan is to build another community on top of the one he created through Farfetch, this one centered on services in stores and online. After bringing together cool boutiques and brands, Farfetch's "Store of the Future" project is about uniting start-ups specialized in retail. In 2018, Neves set up the Farfetch Dream Assembly, a startup accelerator program. The project was unveiled two weeks after LVMH announced its own Maison des Start-ups located at Station F, a gigantic start-up campus in the 13th arrondissement of Paris, where the group invited luxury-dedicated start-ups to develop their business.

In the world of start-ups, what happens Neves explained, is that a group of entrepreneurs raises 2 million euros in funding for a big idea. Then, it will go to a major brand that will say, "let me think about it." And six months later, the brand will still be thinking about it, and by then, the money will have run out. "This happens all the time, every single day," says Neves. His plan is to build an ecosystem in which start-ups can help stores connect to the digital world. "We are only going to get to the final dream if we are open and stay open and bring everyone with us," he said.

Neves estimated that there were more than 200 retail tech start-ups selling applications ranging from digital mirrors to mobile in-store payments. "Our idea is to go to the brands and say this is the future. It is crazy that you do not know the customer who comes into your store and you are not treating them in a personalized way. Instead, you are spending time on things that can be robotic, automatic. This makes no sense. We want to go to the start-up community and tell them we already have the retailers and brands."

"Let all the fashion and IT companies of the world unite!" said Susanne Tide-Frater, Farfetch's advisor on strategy, who also looks after the "Store of the Future" project. "The technology Farfetch is developing is like a language that everyone in fashion can speak. It is the Esperanto of fashion IT." For her, Amazon is the biggest threat to the high-end fashion world. "Look at what they did to the book industry, what they have done to prices and margins. Margins in fashion have already been so squeezed, they cannot be any more," she said.

The "augmented retail" technology could take a few years to be rolled out. It has been trialed at Browns East in Shoreditch, a former printing plant in east London turned into a Browns outlet in October 2017. When customers enter Browns East, they are greeted on their phone. The app keeps track of the things they browse and touch thanks to RFID chips fitted in each item's tags. At any time, customers can pull up their wish-list on their phone. They can also disappear into a private

changing room (which needs to be booked ahead) featuring walls lined with soft pink fluffy carpet and circle-
shaped wooden doors. In the middle, stands an imposing
digital mirror that is more than two meters high. When
the customer enters, his or her name appears on the
digital mirror's screen. It says: "Hi there (name of the
shopper)," "Welcome to Browns East. There's all kinds
of things coming your way." By touching the screen, the
wish-list appears in the upper right-hand corner of the
digital mirror. Each item can be called up and examined
more closely by enlarging the photo. The digital mirror
also acts like a personal assistant that gives information
on the availability of sizes and items available at other
shops on the Farfetch platform. A customer can also order
a product from the warehouse and get it delivered within
60 minutes.

Neves' entrepreneurship spirit is infectious. Even his
wife, the Brazilian-Portuguese marketing specialist Daniela
Cecilio, succumbed to the bug after a few years working
at Farfetch.[1] Daniela created a fashion search mobile
application called ASAP 54. Her ambition was to create
for fashion what Shazam did for music. She raised around
$1 million from angel investors such as Eventures and
Novel TMT as well as from Fréderic Court and Carmen
Busquets, one of the early backers of Net-a-porter.
Busquets has also invested in Farfetch as well as in many
other important players in the sector such as Moda
Operandi. Once the deal was closed, another $2 million
came from Asian investors. "Our first meeting together

---

[1] Daniela helped set up and run Farfetch's back-office functions
such as styling, photography and VIP customer service. She also
helped Farfetch enter Brazil.

with Daniela and José was magic," Carmen Busquets told me sitting on a sofa decorated with antlers in her Parisian apartment near Avenue Montaigne, filled with contemporary art. "I became closer to Daniela than to him, as she was the entrepreneur I wanted to invest in. But I knew José was a great leader and I always spoke very highly of him even if I wasn't an early investor in his company," she said.

As Daniela struggled to monetize her application, in 2016, she transformed it into a shopping concierge service. People could send a photo of an item they wanted to buy, and a personal concierge would purchase the product and ship it to them. The service was something Neves wanted for Farfetch and he used Daniela's start-up to test it. The project was a success. The VIP concierge service called "Fashion Concierge" had an average value of $2,000 per purchase and more than 80 percent of its clients were return customers. Daniela's company was acquired by Farfetch in November 2017 for $2 million in Farfetch shares and its concierge service was integrated into the website's VIP proposition. If a customer wants something not available on Farfetch, now it can get a personal shopper to buy it and send it.

But if in-store technology is an important plank of his plans for the future, Neves wants Farfetch to remain at the cutting-edge online as well. In 2015, he set up Farfetch Black & White, a unit that sells e-commerce technology and services to fashion and luxury brands. They can purchase part or all of its solutions, from the day-to-day running of their website to customer service, online payment and marketing. Black & White competes with rivals such as Yoox, which used to power and manage the website of all Kering brands except Gucci. As of 2019, brands using Black & White included AMI Paris, Thom Browne, JW Anderson and Emilio Pucci. The services provider enables Farfetch to build relations with brands that go beyond the sale of their products on the platform.

Despite all this activity, Neves never abandoned the Swear shoe brand he created in 1996. Before he founded Farfetch, he passed the executive reins to Ben Demiri, a Kosovan molecular biologist turned fashion manager based in the UK. Swear London was relaunched in 2017 as a customization brand selling chic and cool leather sneakers made in Portugal. Customers can pick a style and put their initials and the shoes are shipped within 48 hours. They can also create a completely new shoe and receive it within a week or two.

Demiri and Neves quickly understood the fantastic opportunity customization represented for the industry. In 2014, they founded Platforme,[1] a customization specialist that would later work for brands such as Nicholas Kirkwood and Karl Lagerfeld. "We felt that there was real fatigue in the market around value for money," said Demiri. In his view, customization got rid of many problems plaguing the sector, the main one being off-price sales. People were only ready to pay for things that were customized and premium. Otherwise, no-one was ready to pay full price for anything. Customization also killed ubiquity, i.e. the same product everywhere from Shanghai to London. A made-to-order item was by definition

---

[1] Platforme would become the holding company for Swear London and for Six London, a shoe manufacturer working under license for small brands.

unique. Customized products also meant no waste and unsold stock. "Customization creates a more personal relationship between the brand and the customer. There is also a real engagement with manufacturers. They get paid more since it involves more craftsmanship and for them, it adds human value to the product," Demiri explained. In recent years, Dior, Louis Vuitton and Fendi have been stepping up investment in customization to preserve the perception of exclusivity—as well as margins.

Tomorrow's challenges

All e-commerce marketplaces try to solve the same problem: channel retailers' stock to as many consumers as possible. Farfetch is not without rivals and its business model is not without weaknesses in the long term. Over the years, it is possible that some fashion brands will become more confident about e-commerce and want to leave Farfetch to focus on developing their own websites. That way brands could return to their initial instinct of working on their own (and against others) and joyfully abandon the spirit of co-operation imposed by Farfetch. As sales generated by their own website grow bigger, they will be increasingly tempted to put pressure on Farfetch to lower its commission fees.

But Neves answers that there is room in the market for both models: selling on one's own website and on Farfetch. And once a brand leaves Farfetch, it loses access to millions of customers from around the world and to the multi-brand environment that stimulates demand.

Farfetch faces mounting competition from Internet powerhouses Facebook and Instagram, which are getting better at selling fashion. And there is of course Amazon, which has made no secret of its ambitions in the sector, even though LVMH has said that there was "no way" it would ever do business with the marketplace.[1] But that has not prevented Amazon from entering the fashion and luxury market and from sponsoring Fashion Weeks and prizes in countries like Japan. Like Farfetch, Amazon seeks to promote young designers thanks to these events. Farfetch has invested in artificial intelligence — as has Amazon — to offer more personalized services and suggest products to customers based on their past preferences and purchases. The battle between Amazon and Farfetch has only just begun.

In 2019, Farfetch moved to differentiate itself and answer consumers' concerns about the environment by launching a new concept called "Second Life." It allows customers to trade in their designer handbag (to be sold as a second-hand item) for credit to be spent on future purchases on Farfetch.

Retailers and brands know they need to step up investments in in-store experiences and in media content online to grab and retain customers' attention. In March 2019, Farfetch upped the ante by introducing "Farfetch Communities," daily posts and stories from "tastemakers" such as boutique owners, actress Chloë Sévigny and other

[1] "We believe the business of Amazon does not fit with LVMH full stop and it does not fit with our brands," LVMH Chief Financial Officer Jean-Jacques Guiony told investors at a quarterly sales conference call. "LVMH says no way will do business with Amazon," *Reuters*, Astrid Wendlandt, October 16, 2016.

well-known and lesser-known personalities. The initiative gave the website a more authentic voice and helped it stand out. It also helped define and express more clearly what Farfetch stood for as a brand, a problem the company took several years to tackle seriously. Farfetch has had branding issues perhaps because the tone of its editorial content changed several times over the years, which somewhat blurred its identity.

Had Porter, Net-a-porter's magazine, expanded rather than downsized and built a much bigger presence on the Internet, it would have been a strong competitor in terms of editorial content. Porter publishes interviews and real stories with a focus on inspiring women, an editorial line established by its founder Natalie Massenet, herself a former fashion journalist. Massenet was one of the first to make fashion shopping online a form of entertainment. The Net-a-porter website features videos and reports about celebrities and the fashion world on top of carefully curated looks one can purchase and get delivered right to one's front door. Rival Matchesfashion has also started paying more attention to editorial content. It publishes podcast series and video interviews with all kinds of creative personalities from designers to musicians, some of them recorded at its Mayfair townhouse in London. Meanwhile, online fashion retailer LuisaVia-Roma staged an extravaganza fashion show in Florence in June 2019 curated by star fashion editor Carine Roitfeld to celebrate its 90th birthday. Images and films of the event that ended with a Lenny Kravitz concert and a party attended by designers such as Virgil Abloh, who designs Louis Vuitton's menswear, fed social media and the LuisaViaRoma website with strong editorial content for weeks.

As online fashion retailers and brands increasingly behave like media companies, Farfetch lost in 2019 a strategic ally in the field: Condé Nast. The publisher of *GQ* and *Vogue* was Farfetch's first high-profile industry backer with a 20 million-dollar investment back in 2013. Without warning, the media group sold through its parent Advance its 5.6 percent stake in Farfetch for an estimated 380 million dollars once the post-IPO six-month lock-up period was over. Jonathan Newhouse, Condé Nast President, resigned from Farfetch's board of directors. Neither Farfetch nor Condé Nast issued a statement about his exit. One will never know whether that move was a sign Condé Nast disagreed with Farfetch's strategy or whether the media group, whose print advertising revenues had declined in recent years, needed the funds and wished to cash in its investment.

In August 2019, Farfetch started a new chapter with the acquisition of New Guards Group, the company that produces clothes under license for Virgil Abloh's brand Off-White—one of Farfetch's best-sellers—and other small brands including Palm Angels, Marcelo Burlon County of Milan and Heron Preston. Farfetch settled the 675 million-dollar-transaction (roughly twice the company's annual sales) partly with its available cash, Farfetch shares and a bridge bank loan facility. Partnering with such a popular label as off-White strengthened the Farfetch brand as well as its presence in streetwear, already significant since its acquisition of sneaker specialist Stadium Goods in December 2018. However, investors reacted negatively to the deal, sending Farfetch shares (already down since its IPO) sharply lower. For them, buying such a big fashion company altered Farfetch's risk profile and raised questions about its future profitability and business model.

Perhaps the biggest challenge for José Neves will be to preserve the company's start-up mentality and corporate culture as staff numbers climbed to more than 3,500 in 2019. Neves controls Farfetch with 78 percent of the company's voting rights. Investors will have to trust the Portuguese entrepreneur can steer the transformation of what was once a small club of online boutiques into a New York-listed Internet fashion and luxury giant. Neves believes he is the best one to run Farfetch and has great ambitions for his company. Farfetch exists "for the love of fashion," he says. In 10 years, perhaps not everybody will love Farfetch, but certainly nobody will be able to ignore it.

Ralph the coach

RALPH TOLEDANO IS THE ONLY FASHION EXECUTIVE I know whose eyes can well up with emotion at the sight of a beautiful dress. This is an unusual and unexpected trait in an industry dominated by financiers. Toledano truly cares about fashion. He lives and breathes it and takes a genuine interest in a designer's inspiration, thought and creative process. Many of his peers, no matter how charismatic or important, look like staid, dry accountants next to him. "When I see a beautiful dress, it gives meaning to everything I do," says Toledano. When he sees an exceptional collection during a catwalk, "it is a rare emotion. It is like a dream you don't want to stop. It is like going into another world."

But the business of fashion is a cruel and harsh one, populated by survivalists with king-size egos. Amid the executive pack, Toledano stands out as the underdog. His name rarely appears in the media and he does not particularly look for publicity. Yet he understands the business of fashion far better than most, particularly its less glamo-

rous aspects such as logistics. On top of all the different brands he has led, which include Karl Lagerfeld, Guy Laroche, Chloé, Jean-Paul Gaultier and Nina Ricci, Toledano is also known for having launched or helped umpteen designers on their career orbits. That list includes designers such as Phoebe Philo, who resuscitated LVHM's Celine, Anthony Vaccarello, who is still driving growth at Saint Laurent and Alber Elbaz, who masterminded Lanvin's successful revamp for 14 years.

"What I love with Ralph is his ability to listen," said Anthony Vaccarello. "Since the beginning, he helped me believe in myself. He told me not listen to anyone as we could not satisfy everybody. This is what I have done. It is anchored in me now." Toledano put his faith in Guillaume Henry to creatively reboot Nina Ricci after having earned his credentials at Carven. Henry is now trying his luck with yet another revival, Jean Patou, a dormant fashion brand LVMH bought in 2018. Ralph Toledano has also been the mentor of Sino-Parisian designer Yiqing Yin, known for her sculpture approach to volumes, who created her own couture house and tried to resuscitate early-1900s designer Paul Poiret with financial backing from Koreans. "Ralph has a sort of animal instinct when it comes to fashion," Yiqing said. "He has the courage to express his convictions and apply them without compromise. I find that heroic in this milieu. Amid a stagnant fashion system, Ralph has deployed a disruptive positive energy, necessary to give movement."

In 2018, Toledano embarked on a new adventure as chairman of Victoria Beckham, a fashion brand that has confounded its early-day sceptics. Launched in 2008 by the former Spice Girl, Victoria Beckham has built a credible vision with simple, well-cut outfits women really do want to buy and wear. Ten years later, it made around 50 million euros in annual sales, grew a promising e-commerce business and branched out into sunglasses and leather goods. With an injection of funds from the private equity firm Neo Investment Partners,[1] Toledano was hired as chairman to help expand sales and put the brand firmly on the path to profitability—his specialty.

Toledano is as demanding of himself as he is of others, as would be any coach worthy of the name. He has little tolerance for those who fall below his standards or betray his trust. The minute a brand's shareholder starts to question his strategy or the way he does things, he answers back and fights tooth and nail for his ideas. But if things get too sour and he loses respect for the shareholder, he prefers to leave than just watch the ship sink. Hence, Ralph Toledano is not the man of one fashion house but of several. Going from brand to brand invariably involved pain and the occasional plunge into the abyss. But working for so many labels has given him a bird's eye view that he exploits as Mr. Paris Fashion Week. Ralph Toledano is chairman of France's Haute Couture and Fashion Federation, the industry's main authority. As such, he gets a say on which brands should be admitted to the official calendar of Paris' runway shows. In that position, he also defends Paris as the world's capital of fashion, where he believes all talented designers should want to present their work and shine, no matter where they come from.

---

[1] Neo Investment Partners has invested in several brands including Valextra, French menswear label AMI Paris and French chocolate maker Pierre Marcolini.

Toledano sees fashion as France's Silicon Valley for innovation, inspiration and job creation. He initiated the merger between two leading Paris fashion schools: Institut Français de la Mode (IFM) and the École de la Chambre Syndicale de la Couture Parisienne (the alma mater of Yves Saint Laurent and Véronique Nichanian). The new institution opened its doors in September 2019. Toledano wants the fashion school to match the prestige and attractivity of rivals such as Central Saint Martin's College of Art and Design in London and Parsons School of Design in New York.

Toledano cuts a slim, discreet and elegant figure. Soft-spoken and slow-moving, he does not have the ebullience of many other luxury executives. Yet he is just as ruthlessly efficient. He can be severe, authoritarian and uncompromising but he carries his power lightly. "When you look at Ralph, you would not say that he is a fashion guy," said Ron Frasch, former president and chief merchandising officer of the U.S. department store Saks Fifth Avenue and who worked many years with Toledano.[1] "Ralph was never a self-promoter. He is reserved, deeply thoughtful. Ralph makes me think of Obi-Wan Kenobi in *Star Wars*. He sees through things."

Toledano is too sincere and candid for his own good. That means he can rub people up the wrong way, which has gotten him into trouble many times. "I am aware that not everybody has embraced him," said Frasch. He is the polar-opposite of Alain-Dominique Perrin's brashness, loudness and generous silhouette. Toledano's tone of voice

---

[1] Frasch, now at U.S. private equity firm Castanea, led its investment in New York fashion brand Proenza Schouler and joined Burberry's non-executive board in 2017.

is at times so feeble, you can barely hear what he says, as if he was about to whisper secrets in your ears. And he actually does that sometimes.

The Toledano clan

Raphaël Toledano was born on September 27, 1951 to an upper-class Sephardic Jewish family from Casablanca, the seaside business capital of Morocco. When he was nine years old, a friend who had just come back from holiday in America called him Ralph and the name stuck. Ralph led a happy and carefree childhood, swimming, playing tennis and hanging out with friends. His father Joseph was a high-profile figure in Casablanca's Jewish community.[1] On Sunday mornings, Ralph would accompany his father for fittings at his tailor or stop by his office. His mother Rose wore dresses by Leonard, Dior and Givenchy, made by local seamstresses based on patterns from Paris. "Sometimes I think of my father, zipping up my mother's dress before going out to dinner," he said. "He would kiss her on the back. It was his love ritual which meant 'you are my wife, you are beautiful and I love you.'"

Family is sacred for Ralph, the source of values, strength and energy. Sidney Toledano, another important figure in the fashion world and in Ralph's life, feels similarly about his family and its heritage. Sidney, Dior Couture's boss for more than two decades, sits on the executive board of Ralph's French Federation of Haute

[1] He was Morocco's representative to the World Jewish Congress.

Couture and Fashion. Despite the common name, the two are not directly related. Their ancestors were banished from the Spanish city of Toledo in 1492 by Isabella, the Catholic Queen of Castile, who with her husband King Ferdinand backed the Inquisition and completed the *Reconquista*.[1] The shared family name comes from the Toledanos, who formed an important Sephardic Jewish community in the city. Sent into exile, they first landed in Salonika in Greece, now Thessaloniki, before settling in Meknes, then Tangiers and later Casablanca. In 1992, 500 years after the eviction, Sidney and Ralph attended a reunion in Toledo at which Spain's Queen Sofia asked the Toledanos for forgiveness and handed each of the 20 invited descendants, including Ralph and Sidney, a key to the city as a symbol of reconciliation. To this day, Ralph and Sidney's families speak Castilian Spanish, a way for them to preserve their Iberian heritage.

"To be a Toledano means you come from a long lineage of rabbis, of erudite and wise men, so I have to live up to my family and live like a Toledano. I think Sidney and I both share this. We know that we must defend and uphold our values and that is much more important than making money," Ralph said.

Ralph and Sidney sat next to each other at school and were inseparable in their late teens. They attended Casablanca's French Lycée Lyautey, passed their baccalaureate exams together and visited Israel after their graduation. Ralph and Sidney's parents had nothing to do with luxury. Ralph's father ran a fish can business and

[1] That same year, in 1492, Ferdinand and Isabella financed Christopher Columbus' voyage to the New World.

worked from the age of 13, while Sidney's father Boris was in carton recycling.[1]

Their paths diverged, but only slightly, when they went to France for higher education. Sidney entered the elite École Centrale engineering school while Ralph went to France's equally prestigious HEC business school. He wanted to be a lawyer, but his parents goaded him into studying business instead. "We both knew that we needed to sort ourselves out on our own," Sidney said.

Starting in fashion in their 20s, the two friends got involved in every aspect of the business, from marketing to opening shops, manufacturing, logistics and supply chains. Ralph and Sidney brought the Toledano clan spirit to the brands they worked for and to the Federation of Haute Couture and Fashion. They have both contributed to turning fashion into one big family that takes years to join but once you are admitted, you never leave.

Sidney worked at Kickers and then at the French handbag maker Lancel before LVMH boss Bernard Arnault hired him to develop Dior's handbags in 1994. Four years later, he became Dior Couture CEO and Chairman, which he would remain until February 2018, making him one of the longest-serving executives in charge of a brand of that size. By 2019, Dior was estimated to generate more than 6 billion euros in annual sales including cosmetics and perfumes.

Ralph forged his own destiny, away from LVMH and his pal Sidney. Neither wanted to be in direct competi-

[1] Boris Toledano, who passed away in 2016, was President of Casablanca's Jewish community. In the early days, he had been counselled by Ralph's father Joseph, who was 16 years older than him and was one of his mentors.

tion with the other. Yet at the very beginning of his career, Ralph worked for a company that would become an LVMH foundation stone. Boussac was one of France's biggest textile and clothes manufacturers. In 1984, Arnault acquired it to get his hands on Dior. Ralph learned a lot about fashion manufacturing while running a Boussac factory that made Ted Lapidus ready-to-wear. Back in the 1970s and 1980s, fashion was mainly about licensing deals. Brands such as Givenchy, Chanel and Yves Saint Laurent would partner with manufacturers like C. Mendes and Boussac to produce their clothes under license. Outfits would then be sold to third-party distributors such as department stores in Europe and in the United States.

Ralph and Sidney are on the same wavelength on many issues, but Sidney is a diplomat while Ralph is anything but. The two men could have been co-presidents somewhere, but one could have never been the boss of the other. "Ralph declares his convictions. He protects himself less than me and has less of an armor than me," said Sidney. "He is also much more sensitive." Ralph's answer to that is that his sensitivity is his strength and is what sets him apart.

Like Ralph, Sidney considers himself a coach. Many of his Dior managers and protégés moved on to run big luxury brands such as Jimmy Choo, Hugo Boss and Robert Clergerie.[1] As the two men worked in the same industry, they established a rule: never poach from the

---

[1] "The School of Sidney Toledano, many luxury CEOs were trained by the Dior Executive," *The New York Times*, Vanessa Friedman, July 6, 2014.

other's teams. "We cannot betray one another as we would not be able to get over it," said Ralph.

Sidney Toledano has witnessed some key moments in Ralph's private life, especially his marriages and re-marriage. Ralph first walked down the aisle with Monique Srolevich in 1974, who made a career at Christian Dior Couture and gave him a daughter named Emmanuelle. Later in 1990, when Ralph was at Karl Lagerfeld, he married Céline Engel, a former professional classical dancer, who was head of collections at KL. The German couturier arrived late at their wedding in a huge Rolls-Royce. Ralph and Céline separated in 1999, divorced in 2005 and remarried a year later. The mayor of the 16th arrondissement said: "I will be happy to re-marry you as many times as shall be necessary." On top of raising their two children, Ilan and Sarah, Céline works as a fashion head-hunter for m-O Conseil, founded by Mathias Ohrel. She is also a consultant for the new design programs of the Institut Français de la Mode following its merger with l'École de la Chambre Syndicale de la Couture Parisienne.

Karl Lagerfeld Inc.

One of the many things Sidney and Ralph agree on is that Karl Lagerfeld was one of the easiest designers they have ever worked with. Ralph collaborated with Lagerfeld when he was chief executive of the German couturier's signature brand from 1985 to 1994. Sidney helped manage LVMH's Fendi in the 1980s, for which Lagerfeld designed as well. "Karl taught me everything I know about human nature," Toledano said of Lagerfeld. "He was like a father to me."

"I have never had any problem with Ralph," Lagerfeld told me in his Parisian studio on rue de Lille. "Ralph — I have always regretted him. We had nice discussions. He let me do what I wanted. Anyway, if one does not let me do what I want, then, I mean, there is nothing to be done. It is the same thing at Fendi and Chanel. Me, I do not do meetings or discuss briefs, etc. I think and then I say, this is what it is going to be. And if someone tells me 'but this, but that,' it is over," he said in his fluent French delivered with a solid German accent. "Me, I was never given a brief. I brief myself. I am self-briefed. Sometimes, I even brief myself beyond the level at which I should have been briefed. No, frankly, I do not believe in such things."

Karl Lagerfeld never risked a penny of his own personal fortune on his eponymous fashion label and its style was always kept distinct from what he did for Fendi, Chloé or Chanel. When Toledano ran his label, silhouettes were graphic with geometric lines. Collections included body-tight dresses, elegant blouses with wide collars and waist-cinched jackets.

The Karl Lagerfeld label flourished most under Toledano's stewardship, according to the German couturier. "There was a wonderful atmosphere. We had offices on the Champs Elysées. It was very cheerful and lighthearted. Ralph brought a joyful spirit. […] I have a lot of affection for Ralph. We spent fantastic years together. It is the others who screwed up afterward. But the years under Ralph were the most pleasant for the Karl Lagerfeld brand. At the time, he wanted to be like the big brands, which was very difficult without investing like the big brands. But Ralph did all that he could. I remember we were the first at Bergdorf Goodman for example. Today, it is another business that has another image."

Rose Marie Bravo, mastermind of Burberry's turnaround in the early 2000s, first worked with Ralph when she was at I. Magnin department store in San Francisco.[1] "Ralph checked everything and was a stickler for detail. He had patience. He understood that building a brand took time. He was one of the most professional people in the industry. He left designs to Karl but managed everything else."

Toledano remained focused on profitability and made timely delivery a priority, particularly in the United States where fashion brands only got six weeks to sell at full price before the November-December sales. The earlier you shipped, the longer you could sell at full price. "The Karl Lagerfeld collections were the first in, so they had one of the best sell-through rates of all," said Bravo. But early delivery also means the designer and manufacturers have to meet their own deadlines. For Toledano, the real barometer of a brand's success is not sales growth or margins, the indicators the stock market focuses on, but what percentage of a collection is sold at full price. He aims for 70 percent while most brands are happy with 40 percent.

After Ralph's departure from the Karl Lagerfeld label in 1994, "people lost interest in the brand," Lagerfeld told me. "The Richemont period [when it owned Karl Lager-

[1] Later, Bravo became President and Chief Merchant officer of the department store Saks Fifth Avenue and rose to bigger fame when she ran Burberry for more than eight years until 2006.

feld from 1992 until it went bankrupt in 1997,] I prefer
to forget, it was only bad decisions."

Designer whisperer

Toledano may descend from a long line of rabbis, but
he has more faith in his instincts than in God. As soon
as someone walks into the room, he senses if things will
work out or not. This is what happened in 1996 when
he was looking for a new creative director after taking
over at Guy Laroche. When Alber Elbaz turned up at his
New York hotel room with his red jacket, red shoes and
no socks for his job interview, Toledano knew he was his
man. Back then, Elbaz had bushy black hair that made
him look like The Cure singer Robert Smith, minus the
messed-up red lipstick. Elbaz had sent him his CV on
red paper with the name Alber without a "t" above his
family name, so that each word would be exactly five
letters long and look graphically well-balanced when
printed one above the other. Such attention to detail
caught Toledano's eye. "I thought this guy knows how
to stand out and be different," he recalled.

Like Toledano, Elbaz was born in Casablanca but left
for Tel Aviv as a child with his family. After Shenkar
design school at Ramat Gan in Israel, he arrived in New
York with a few dollars in his pocket and worked for
nearly eight years alongside American designer Geoffrey
Beene. When he met Toledano, he was in his mid-thir-
ties and ripe for a creative directorship. Toledano thought
Elbaz had the right stuff to put Guy Laroche back on
the fashion map. By the mid-1990s, it had sunk into obli-

vion from a creative point of view. Long gone were the days when French movie stars such as Catherine Deneuve promoted its coat-dresses in the 1970s.

Toledano knew jump-starting Guy Laroche would be an exacting job. The loss-making brand belonged back then to Bic, the maker of razors and ballpoint pens.[1] Toledano told his wife Céline that he had purposefully chosen what was then the world's most difficult fashion brand to get back in business. "It was a way of proving to myself what I was worth," Toledano said. "I have always looked for challenges and I must say that I got what I was looking for at Guy Laroche." He shut down the brand's poorly run factories, got rid of unnecessary high costs and folded the company's loss-making second line Gaston Jaunet.

Elbaz was an ambitious designer who had developed a sensual edge and a practical approach to fashion. When he presented his first collection in 1997, the fashion world took notice. Dawn Mello,[2] president of the U.S. department store Bergdorf Goodman and early mentor of designers such as Donna Karan and Michael Kors, said of the new Guy Laroche designer at the time: "Alber is destined for stardom. His artistic details set him apart from the mainstream. […] We need people like Alber in this industry—new young talent."[3]

Elbaz used mohair wool in original ways for dresses in bright red colors with diamond-studded laced shoes,

---

[1] Today Guy Laroche belongs to Hong Kong group YGM Trading.
[2] Dawn Mello helped Elbaz get his first job at Geoffrey Beene and was instrumental in hiring Tom Ford for Gucci in 1990.
[3] "The new guy at Laroche," *W* magazine, Lisa Arbetter, December 1997.

one of which broke during the runway show and made the designer nearly faint. The collection was well received by buyers and the press, which Toledano took as a sign the brand was on the right track, at least while Elbaz was there. "At that time, Alber built the foundations of what the Lanvin women would become," Toledano said. "There were lots of very feminine Parisian dresses and a few suits, but mainly a lot of dresses. Alber brought the dress back into fashion. And we proved that we could sell a lot of them. He conducts a lot of research in terms of fabrics, textures, colors and cuts. And that requires time. And then he continued at Yves Saint Laurent and Lanvin. He is without a doubt the most gifted designer of his generation."

One day, Elbaz called Toledano to show him a new dress he had just finished. Not many designers would allow themselves such spontaneity with their CEO. "Alber knew that I would be touched that he called me to see this and we stayed a long moment in silence in front of this dress. It was very special," Toledano said. Being able to let himself be moved by the work of a designer explains why the moniker of coach suits him so well. He always tries to give a sincere appreciation of a designer's work and constructive criticism. Designers find that empowering and his feedback encourages them to become even better. "I see myself as a coach. Collaborating with a great creative talent implies working with an exceptional person. An easy-to-get-along-with designer is an oxymoron, it does not exist," Toledano says. "And you can only manage people well if you are at peace with yourself."

Over the years, Toledano has never stopped keeping an eye out for talent. Not only does he peruse the work of every brand shown at Paris Fashion Week and elsewhere, but he also builds relationships with those designers he believes in. "He is someone who gives a designer a lot of assurance in an intelligent manner," said Bouchra Jarrar who, after working with Nicolas Ghesquière at Balenciaga, founded her own brand and designed for two seasons at Lanvin following Elbaz's dramatic exit in 2015. "When Ralph loves the work of a designer, it is very strong. This is why he is a real coach. He is someone who knows how to place creativity at the center of everything."

Elbaz and Toledano communicated more with their eyes than with words. "He was very quiet and observing. He was not the kind of guy who walks into the middle of the room but more the type who speaks on the sidelines," Elbaz said. For Toledano, talent and creativity are important, but intelligence is paramount. He also needs to feel that the designer's soul and sensitivity fits the brand's universe, something one needs peculiar antennas for. When Elbaz first met Toledano, he said: "I saw a person, not a CEO or a system. […] It was heaven working with him. I understood him, he understood me. The hardest moment was when I had to tell him that I was leaving for Yves Saint Laurent."

Toledano saw that coming the minute Pierre Bergé, Yves Saint Laurent's business partner, asked for invitations for Elbaz's third show at Guy Laroche in 1998. Bergé wanted a new designer to boost Yves Saint Laurent's ready-to-wear revenues so he could better sell the brand a few years down the road. The YSL label was worth more with a new vision, a proven track record and a bright future under someone like Alber Elbaz than under Yves Mathieu Saint Laurent, who after four brilliant decades, was nearing the end of his career.

Toledano could not stop his creative director from trying his luck at such a revered *maison*. Elbaz had always dreamt of working with Saint Laurent, whom he regarded as "the ultimate master couturier." The revolutionary designer, known for catch phrases such as "trends pass but style is eternal," [1] freed women by dressing them in thigh-high boots, tuxedo suits, transparent blouses and safari jackets. "Alber will know how to fit in the Saint Laurent style without copying him. He will create something new," Bergé said of his young recruit. [2]

Bergé's unscrupulous poaching of Elbaz put Toledano and Guy Laroche in trouble as the brand was about to sign a major license deal in Asia. Any announcement regarding his departure was not supposed to be done before a certain time, according to his contract. But that did not bother Bergé, who called Toledano to discuss Elbaz's departure. "I am sorry but one simply does not attack an artist!" Bergé told him. Artists were always right, no matter what contracts they had signed. Toledano would understand only later that Bergé was right.

Bergé was bent on announcing Elbaz's appointment as soon as possible to present Yves Saint Laurent with a *fait accompli*. Saint Laurent was not going to take it lightly. But Bergé, the man who had made him king, was lucid

---

[1] In French: "Les modes passent, le style est éternel."

[2] "Alber Elbaz, 37 years-old, couturier. This Israeli-American has just arrived at Yves Saint Laurent ready-to-wear," *Libération*, Anne Boulay, November 4,1998.

about the future. The pair had to cash in while the brand was still on the rise. Saint Laurent was forced to watch as Elbaz put on the white blouse and stepped into his shoes.

Elbaz's work at YSL was applauded by the fashion press and by Bergé himself but his time there would prove short-lived. Right after the second collection, Bergé began talks with potential buyers and sold the brand at the end of 1999 to François Pinault and his PPR group (today called Kering). The following year, Elbaz was booted out after his third collection by Tom Ford, who back then was the new fashion darling who had re-invented Gucci as an all-out glamorous and sexy Italian brand. Ford was in tune with the "bling bling" zeitgeist of the late 1990s. After Gucci, he wanted to get his teeth into YSL, which meant torpedoing Elbaz's dreams and ambitions. When Elbaz was asked to leave, Bergé remarked of Tom Ford: "Well, since he bought the Ferrari, of course now he wants to drive it."

Elbaz did not stay on the job market for very long. In 2001, he was hired by the Taiwanese media magnate Shaw-Lan Wang to revive Lanvin, France's oldest fashion brand still in operation. Wang had acquired the label from the French cosmetics giant L'Oréal. Elbaz turned Lanvin into the go-to label for cocktail dresses, especially its ultra-feminine, silky short dresses adorned with clunky jewels designed by his friend Elie Top, who now runs his own jewelry brand based in Paris. Elbaz stayed for 14 years at Lanvin, spearheading one of the industry's most successful turnarounds.

But a fashion label needs a lot of money to expand and open boutiques around the world and Madame

Wang's fortune proved too small for Elbaz's ambitions. A proud Chinese woman living in Taiwan, Wang refused in 2015 to let in new investors invited by Elbaz, including Qataris interested in betting on the brand's next growth phase. Elbaz set himself on a collision course with Wang. During a board meeting, she accused Elbaz of treason, he insulted her and she promptly sacked him.

Three years after Elbaz's brutal exit, Lanvin was about to go bust in early 2018 when China's Fosun International, a conglomerate with no track record of turning around a luxury brand, acquired most of Wang's controlling stake.[1] Before the debacle that followed Elbaz's ousting, Lanvin had everything to match the success of Saint Laurent and Valentino. Founded in 1889 by Jeanne Lanvin, it is a national treasure. Its story is proof that a name and a heritage sometimes are not enough. The *maison* will need time to get back on its feet and build a new credible creative vision.

The Chloé adventure

After Karl Lagerfeld was bought in 1992 by Dunhill Holdings (what would later become Richemont), Toledano started to have regular meetings with Alain-Dominique Perrin, CEO of its much bigger sister brand Cartier. The two men discussed the strategy of Karl Lagerfeld and that of Chloé as well, which Dunhill Holdings was struggling to make profitable since its acquisition in 1985.

[1] "Why the Chinese bought Lanvin, France's oldest fashion brand," *Fashion Network*, Astrid Wendlandt, February 27, 2018.

Toledano warned Perrin of the many problems he had spotted at Chloé in terms of management, merchandising and supply chain.

By the late 1990s, Perrin realized that Toledano's predictions about Chloé were right. The label continued to lose money and sales were not picking up as much as hoped. In 1999, Perrin became CEO of Richemont and contacted Toledano to talk about the possibility of becoming Chloé's new CEO. After Karl Lagerfeld, Toledano had boldly repositioned Guy Laroche with Alber Elbaz. Perrin loved challenges. Ralph actually wanted to run Lancel or Dunhill, but Perrin told him that if he could turn around Chloé in three years, he would help the group make acquisitions and would get to manage a much bigger fashion brand.

Toledano hit the ground running. He got rid of the handbag and watch lines that did not sell well and closed wholesaling accounts that lost money. He cleaned up the production process, bought only as much fabric as was necessary and obtained better prices from suppliers. Toledano brought Chloé back to profitability in two years rather than three. But Perrin's promise turned out to be wishful thinking. After those two years, Perrin had nothing to offer since Richemont had not made any acquisitions in fashion during that time. And after three years, Perrin told him: "Now Ralph what do you want? A watchmaker in East Germany [referring to A. Lange & Söhne]? You are perfect for Chloé!"

"I love ADP. He is the best leader I have ever worked for, but he is the champion of bad faith," Toledano said of Perrin affectionately. "He had given me an entire program but actually, none of it happened." The two executives are still friends and meet regularly.

Chloé was founded in 1952 by Gaby Aghion, daughter of an Egyptian cigarette factory manager. Aghion's idea was to create a fashion label positioned between affordable ready-to-wear and couture that would distinguish itself from establishment brands such as Christian Dior and Pierre Balmain. "Fashion," Aghion said, "should be as fresh as a salad." Her clothes should feel young and liberating. It was the first fashion label to capture Paris' 'Rive Gauche,' or 'Left Bank' intellectual, literary and irreverent spirit, much before Sonia Rykiel in the late 1960s. Aghion's first collections were presented in writers' haunts on Saint-Germain Boulevard such as the Café de Flore and Brasserie Lipp. Karl Lagerfeld was one of the many talents who earned their stripes and thrived under her well-wishing but demanding command. Lagerfeld designed for Chloé from 1966 to 1984 and later from 1992 to 1997. He only became Chloé's sole creative director in 1975.

Aghion, a petite brunette with pencil eyebrows and an expressive face, helped Lagerfeld become the designer he was, the Kaiser used to say. "I think Karl and my mother got along well because they had great respect and admiration for one another," said her son Philippe Aghion, an economist who lectures at Harvard University and Collège de France in Paris. "Gaby had been close to the Surrealist movement, in particular to Éluard and Aragon, and she appreciated the fact that Karl was so well-read and so much into art. Gaby's idea was that Chloé should dress a working woman, a free and emancipated woman who plays an active role in society. Karl knew how to promote the Chloe spirit and he would play the game with my mother when she would say about his drawings 'this I take,' 'this is a good idea, but I keep it for later,' etc."

Aghion retired after selling Chloé to Dunhill Holdings in 1985 but she continued to play an advisory role for several years. "Gaby Aghion was my friend," said Ralph Toledano. "We would have lunch together nearly every month at her place or at the Bristol hotel. She would never miss a Chloé fashion show and afterwards, she was the first person I would call to ask what she thought about it," Toledano said. "She was the best critic. The DNA of the house, it was her. She talked as if she was still the artistic director and owner of the fashion house. She had an incredible eye. She was a very intelligent, cultivated and very strong woman." Talking about Chloé's best-selling bag, the Paddington, Aghion told Toledano: "I really hate your bags. They are horrible." And Toledano would answer: "If you only knew Madame Aghion how many of them we sell, hundreds of thousands." And she would courteously reply: "Yes, well, I still do not like your bags." Eventually, she bought one for her grand-daughter.

To this day, Chloé continues to be a training ground for young designers. Those who attended the Chloé school include Maxime de la Falaise (mother of Loulou, Yves Saint Laurent's muse and a designer herself), Martine Sitbon, Stella McCartney, Phoebe Philo, Hannah MacGibbon, Clare Waight Keller and since 2017, Natacha Ramsay-Levi who is making her mark at the brand. "I think Ralph was key in placing young female designers in positions of power at an early stage of their career,"

said designer Hannah MacGibbon, who replaced Phoebe
Philo at Chloé in 2008. "It was quite brave at the time.
It was a new theme in the fashion industry, starting with
Stella (who replaced Lagerfeld) and it would have a big
influence on the industry (back then dominated by men).
By putting these young female designers in creative
director positions, it started a whole new wave," said
MacGibbon, who worked with Phoebe Philo.

Together with this new generation of female designers,
Toledano helped redefine the modern Chloé: a tall,
effortlessly elegant woman who wears light and flowing
transparent printed fabrics. The dominant colors are
pastels, beige and sand pink. Less than a year after he
took over Chloé, Ralph noticed that some of Stella
McCartney's jeans and T-Shirts sold particularly well but
did not fit with the rest of the brand's merchandise. So,
he took them out of the main line and built around them
a whole range of ready-to-wear which later would
include bags and shoes. The newly created, more casual
and more affordable line See by Chloé was launched in
2000. It became a major hit, particularly in Japan, one of
its biggest markets. The creation of the second line also
enabled Toledano to move the main Chloé line more
upmarket in terms of price and image.

When Toledano joined Chloé in 1999, *Women's Wear
Daily* published an article that revealed Stella McCartney's plans to launch her own brand. "So, from day one,
I knew how that story was going to end," he said. For a
long time, her design partner Phoebe Philo thought she
was going to be part of the package and leave with her.
But when McCartney negotiated terms, Philo felt left

out and Toledano discretely exploited the rift. McCartney and Philo declined to comment for this book.

McCartney left the French label in 2001 to create her own signature brand, with backing from Gucci Group, which at the time was the name given to the umbrella company that owned the fashion brands controlled by the PPR group.[1] Toledano faced opposition when he put 27-year-old Phoebe Philo in charge of Chloé in 2001. But he was certain of his choice. He had spotted her talent well before McCartney started working on her exit plan. Philo wished to make the brand more sophisticated, which was what he thought himself was needed. "Phoebe Philo's first fashion show for Chloé… It made me cry. It was so magical," Toledano said. "I thought that I had won my bet against all those who said I was crazy when I appointed her after Stella's departure."[2]

In 2005, Philo renewed her four-year contract with Chloé but left six months later to spend more time with her husband and children. Never before had a designer working for such a prestigious name quit her job to look after her family. "It is interesting to note that nobody asked me how it is, that we let Phoebe resign like this only after six months?" remarked Toledano. "I remembered what Pierre Bergé had told me when Elbaz left for Yves Saint Laurent: artists are always right." If a designer no longer wants to work for a brand, there isn't much that can be done about it. Hence, contracts really

---

[1] PPR stands for Pinault-Printemps-La Redoute. Today it is called Kering.

[2] "Ralph Toledano, l'instinct mode," Le Figaro, Marion Dupuis, September 30, 2014.

only bind brands, not designers. Like artists, they only give their best if they do it freely.[1]

In 2006, Toledano won the first Anton Rupert manager of the year prize, named after the father of Johann Rupert, controlling shareholder and chairman of Richemont. During its 2005-2006 fiscal year, Chloé's operating margin was estimated by analysts to have hit a record of around 20 percent. But in spite of his hard work, Toledano did not have only fans among Richemont's upper echelons. Troubles for him began when Johann Rupert appointed someone above Toledano, among several other high-level appointments, who started interfering with his work. Toledano did not have much room for maneuver since that person was close to Rupert. He could not brush that person aside. The individual in question, who cannot be named, convinced Rupert that Toledano was no longer the right CEO for Chloé and had his head in less than a year. Toledano's exit had nothing to do with the brand's performance. He was pushed out simply because that person had decided, for whatever personal reason, that it was better for him to leave. When Toledano joined Chloé in 1999, the brand made an estimated 10 million euros in annual sales and lost around 7 million euros. When he left in 2010, the brand was profitable and analysts estimated it generated more than 250 million euros in sales.

Johann Rupert has many qualities, but he is not a fighter. One of Richemont's most senior executives told

[1] Richemont forced Toledano to get Phoebe Philo to sign a non-compete clause that would prevent her from working for rival brands for some time. Toledano knew there was no point, as she really just wanted to focus on her family.

me of Rupert: "He hates court intrigues and does not like to be under the influence of anyone. The closer one gets to Rupert, the more likely one is to get hit by him. So, best keep your distance. If you made a mistake and he thinks it is a serious one, usually you do not get a second chance." As a case in point, one of Cartier's regional bosses was fired for having put out a campaign Rupert thought was too mass market.

When Toledano left Chloé in 2010, a U.S.-based newspaper wrote that he was fired because the brand had lost money for 10 years, which was not true. But no-one at Richemont asked for a correction. "Ralph is really the man who built Chloé's identity in the fashion world. He laid the foundations for its revival and unfortunately, he left just as the brand was really picking up in terms of momentum and deliver the results of his work," one senior Richemont executive told me.

The way this whole affair was handled left scars. True, Rupert did not give Toledano as much support as he had hoped. But he holds no grudges. He appreciated the fact that the South African billionaire never challenged him on quantitative issues like margins and profits, but rather on qualitative points like strategy and style. Rupert's No.1 preoccupation is preserving the long-term image of all of Richemont's brands. "He does not have a focus on numbers. He even says sometimes: 'do not put this out as it will be too much of a hit,' which would mean too high volumes, which could damage the perceived exclusivity of the brand," another senior Richemont executive told me. In 2010, Ralph Toledano was succeeded by Geoffroy de la Bourdonnaye, former head of London retailer Liberty.

The Puig period

After Toledano left Chloé, the Spanish perfume maker Puig (pronounced *Putch*) approached him to help it develop its fashion businesses. The Barcelona-based group back then focused mainly on fragrances. It ran small fashion operations through its Paco Rabanne, Carolina Herrera, Jean-Paul Gaultier and Nina Ricci brands for which it made perfumes. Puig had its eyes on Valentino, one of the hottest fashion brands in play, for which the group produced fragrances under license. But its informal offer came significantly below that of Qatar's Mayhoola investment company which signed a cheque of 750 million euros.[1] Had Puig won, it would have asked Ralph Toledano to run Valentino.

By 2012, Puig was desperate to stem losses at Nina Ricci and Jean-Paul Gaultier,[2] its two biggest fashion businesses, and asked Toledano to turn around these two brands. Jean-Paul Gaultier's fashion business had been loss-making for years and had survived mainly thanks to perfume royalties. Gaultier was a fantastic designer and showman but he was never really interested in turning his brand into a commercial success. Gaultier declined to comment for this book. In 2014, Toledano ended the

---

[1] Italian fashion mogul Renzo Rosso was also interested in Valentino, banking sources said.

[2] Toledano was hired a year after Puig bought control of Jean-Paul Gaultier in 2011 and acquired a 45 percent stake held by Hermès, an investment that dated back to the designer's friendship with the late Jean-Louis Dumas. Puig had to wait until 2016 to pocket all of the brand's perfume revenues, as the license was until then held by Shiseido's Paris-based perfume unit then called Beauté Prestige International.

brand's ready-to-wear and accessories line and kept Gaultier's couture business and fashion shows, mainly to sustain the image of the perfume brand, which represented a much bigger business.

For Nina Ricci, Toledano had high hopes. It was one of the few historical *maisons* that had kept its original address in Paris, sitting prominently at 29 Avenue Montaigne, opposite Dior and a skip away from Chanel, Louis Vuitton and Gucci. Puig had acquired Nina Ricci in 1998 after having distributed the brand's perfumes for many years. But if Puig kept the Nina Ricci perfume business alive with a few launches, it never made any material investments in its ready-to-wear or accessories lines. It is hard to believe that Nina Ricci still only has a single boutique on Avenue Montaigne. Opening a shop costs a lot money. The priority for the family-controlled perfume group is not to spend vast amounts on fashion but increase profits every year. That objective seems incompatible with the long-term investment horizon required to develop a fashion brand. But Toledano did not know that when he joined Puig in 2012.

When he took over at Nina Ricci, the label had been through several designers in the past decade and Peter Copping's creations were not selling well. Replacing the designer would be a delicate affair. So Toledano worked on what he could while Copping was still in place. He tightened the planning for collections and reviewed supply chains. He put pressure on teams to give manufacturers the right sewing patterns from the start and the right fabrics on time. He made the company win three weeks in delivery terms, which was crucial for selling at full price in the United States and at multi-brand stores.

"You have to be very rigorous in this part of the business. The more rigorous you are in the execution of the plan, the more space and freedom you can have in terms of creativity," explained Toledano. Producing a collection is a race against time and "what you have not been able to do today, you will not be able to catch up tomorrow."

Copping left Nina Ricci in 2014 for Oscar de la Renta, with help from U.S. Vogue editor Anna Wintour, the industry's behind-the-scenes meddler-in-chief who has a special way of letting brands know her opinion about which designer they should hire next. To replace Copping, Toledano had in mind Guillaume Henry, who had successfully revamped Carven. Fashion guru Jean-Jacques Picart, an advisor back then to Bernard Arnault, was the first to tell Toledano about Henry. Picart spoke from experience—he had placed his protégé at Carven to steer the brand's revival there.

When Henry joined Nina Ricci in 2014, there was no genuine fashion heritage left to speak of, other than its distant past as a provider of chic Parisian cocktail dresses in expensive fabrics like organza. Most consumers know Nina Ricci for its best-selling fragrance *l'Air du temps*. Henry would have to define who the Nina Ricci woman was before he could work on her silhouette. As with Elbaz for Guy Laroche, "from the first minutes I met him, I knew he was the man I needed," Toledano said of Guillaume Henry. "And I did not want to meet any other designer." When Henry's lawyer met Toledano to agree terms, Toledano's chief argument was not how big the salary was going to be or what perks he was going to get. His message was that he was going to make sure Henry would be happy at Nina Ricci. "People work better when they are happy," said Toledano. "But that does not mean saying 'yes' to everything."

Toledano would say amen to small requests but he would not hesitate to note if some items were not completely in line with the brand's values and identity. "I am aware that I cannot say 'no' too often, I have to use it sparingly," Toledano said. He also gave Guillaume Henry tight deadlines. Henry's pre-collections for Nina Ricci, which present the styles and mood, had to be ready by a certain date and full collections finished in time as well. "I think fashion is one of the only creative fields in which you have to be really vigilant in terms of deadlines and timing. Some fashion houses do their collections in 10 days and it shows," said Guillaume Henry, who worked at Givenchy under Riccardo Tisci.

After hiring Henry, Toledano spent a year building Nina Ricci's design studio as well as its commercial, communications and production departments. He relied mainly on his own network of contacts. "One of the things that give me the most pleasure is building teams," Toledano said. "I want people who love fashion with an entrepreneur mentality." Team members need time to trust and get to know each other, which is why designers often leave brands with many members of their team. Toledano gives great autonomy and makes clear he wants to be told if there are problems. "Ralph would say 'us' instead of 'I' or 'you.' He was never really my boss so to speak, but rather my referent. I did not work for him, but with him. He was very enthusiastic and trusted me," Henry said.

Henry's 2016-2017 autumn/fall Nina Ricci collection, his third presented at Paris Fashion Week in March

2016, marked a turning point. Toledano could tell it was going to be a success: "I felt the energy and complicity between team members building up. I had faith. This collection was really going to launch the brand," he said. "There were minimalist lines, and I understood that this collection was going to be a synthesis of Guillaume's creativity. This woman was sensual and in love." Notable looks included a sparkling turtleneck flame-red lamé dress, slit open on the chest and between the legs. There were also knitted, tight-fitting dresses with bright, vertical sequined stripes and a few oversized coats worn over laced-satin nightgown looking dresses, outfits that were meant to look like those of women who had slept in their boyfriend's coat. The modern Nina Ricci woman was a 21st century bourgeois with a feminine, sexy edge.

One of those sequined dresses made the cover of *Woman's Wear Daily*, the ultimate accolade for a designer. "This was a subtle collection, but with a sexual pulse and an emotional tug—a step forward for Henry, now getting into the groove after three seasons at the house," Miles Socha wrote in *Women's Wear Daily* about the collection.[1] Ralph sent Guillaume a warm congratulatory note, with his team and Marc Puig copied on the email. Marc Puig declined to comment for this book.

"I told Marc that he needed to do something to make sure Guillaume was going to stay, otherwise big groups were going to come and get him." His foresight proved correct. Henry would leave two years later, in 2018, to work for LVMH as creative designer of Jean Patou,

---

[1] "This quiet collection, with a sexual pulse and an emotional tug, marked a step forward for designer Guillaume Henry," *WWD*, March 5, 2016.

another fashion brand in revival mode. Henry would walk in the footsteps of Toledano who would leave the brand in January 2017. Puig and Toledano did not seem to share the same strategic vision for Nina Ricci. The veteran fashion executive preferred to jump ship than stay at the wheel on the high seas knowing that there wasn't enough fuel to fulfill his ambitions and his dreams.

The lesson of Puig's story is that successful fashion brands are those that are given the money, the teams and the time — as much as eight to 10 years — to take off. But patience is a rare commodity in finance.

Victoria Beckham

In 2018, Toledano started a new adventure. He became non-executive chairman of Victoria Beckham. The strategy, crafted with the brand's private equity backer Neo Investment Partners, was to rely on e-commerce, social media and the former singer's millions of followers on Instagram. "Victoria Beckham is very intelligent, she is a fast learner and knows how to dress women," Toledano said. However, the young brand would have to fight fierce competition from bigger brands, backed by social media heavy weights such as Beyoncé and Kim Kardashian.

Toledano took the job at Victoria Beckham not only because he believed in its future but because he could work again. In December 2014, Toledano suffered from an accident about which the media barely wrote a line. He fell in his bathroom and broke a vertebra in his neck. Since then, he has been living in constant pain. Yet, he continued to work at Puig for two years until January 2017. He left the Spanish group not only because he wanted to move on and pursue other projects but also because he wished to focus on his health. Since his accident, Toledano has been through ups and downs. At times, the pain was so strong and non-stop that he thought of ending it all right there and then. After four years, he started feeling better. He could have a relatively normal life again, even though his movement remained limited.

But his condition did not worry Victoria Beckham. The British designer even agreed to hold board meetings in Paris to spare him trips to London. "Today, I am probably the only chairman who works from his bedroom," said Toledano smiling. "But I am actually quite efficient." Lying horizontally and not moving for long periods of time has sharpened his strategic vision. "I see things more clearly now," he said. Well into his sixties, he lives the life of a recluse, hidden in his cave, like Obi Wan Kanobi. From his elegant flat in the Neuilly suburb of Paris, he is always on the phone, keeping abreast of news and business affairs. But he is now even more removed from the limelight than he was before his accident.

Toledano also takes an active part in the running of the French Haute Couture and Fashion Federation. As its chairman, he continues to coach designers, select new entrants at Paris Fashion Week and defend the city as the world's fashion capital. "Ralph is always available for young designers whose work and talent he defends," says Pascal Morand, executive president of the Federation. Before he became president in 2014, the Federation was run by Didier Grumbach for 16 years.[1] Toledano created an executive board on which Sidney Toledano sits alongside Bruno Pavlovsky, Francesca Bellettini, CEO of Yves Saint Laurent and Guillaume de Seynes. He also set up various committees of CEOs, journalists and designers to oversee the selection process and address current issues and challenges. In November 2018, Toledano became partner at Neo Investment Partners. From then on, he oversaw the private equity firm's portfolio as well as decisions regarding investments and strategy.

Where is fashion going?

For many months, I met with Ralph Toledano on Friday early evenings, just before dinner. Our exchanges helped him focus on other things than the excruciating pain he had to endure. And they helped me understand something about fashion. Aside from listening to his life story and the turpitudes that fashion people (including himself) had to endure, we discussed what was going on in the sector generally. The amount of change it had been through in the past 40 years was mind-boggling. The current business of fashion had nothing to do with the one in which he started his career. Here are a few conclusions I drew from our discussions:

In today's fashion world, designers are no longer in charge. Financial shareholders hold the purse strings.

[1] Prior to 2017, the Federation had a lengthy name: Federation de la couture, du prêt-à-porter des couturiers et des créateurs de mode, or in English the Federation of couture, ready-to-wear of couturiers and fashion designers.

Some designers try to behave like chief executives but that never lasts very long. Actually, designers are no longer called designers (and even less couturiers) but "image and creative directors." They use computers and mood boards, collages of photos and illustrations that give the mood and inspiration of a collection. They no longer draw but tell others what to draw. They will collaborate with other creative and image directors to ensure the brand has something new to say 365 days a year and feeds the beasts of newness and social media.

Since it is all about millennials, consumers born before 1985 no longer interest us, sorry. These people need to be wowed almost every day. No brand will interest them if it does not constantly offer them something new. There used to be two to four collections a year. Now with all the cruise collections, the pre-collections and pre-pre-collections, the collaborations and capsules, there can be easily 10 or 12, if not more.

As a result, designers have become disposable commodities. Some are thrown out, others end up in hospital suffering from exhaustion and depression. If you go to the American Hospital in Paris, you will meet lots of people from the trade. And why do these people put themselves through such ordeals? The focus is no longer on the clothes but on the pictures and films taken of the theatrical decors and extravaganza shows on which brands spend vast amounts to grab attention on social media. And what is left of Paris Fashion Week? Or Milan Fashion Week? Every week is fashion week somewhere in the world. One day it's in Seoul, another it's Moscow, Abidjan or Doha. Nobody cares what journalists think of a fashion show anymore. People want to form their own opinions and publish them on their own social media platforms. The irony is that front-row guests at runway shows barely take the time to look at the clothes. They focus on filming or taking photos instead of enjoying the "here and now" of what is going on.

Men and women models share the podium, sometimes in unisex styles. It can even be difficult at times to see if it is a woman or a man parading on the podium. And their looks need to be ready for purchase right after the show. It's called "see now, buy now," a new concept brands are trialing to stimulate demand. Getting the consumer to open his or her wallet has become increasingly difficult since we are now more into "being" and living experiences than into "owning" stuff. Some people want fewer clothes not more. Hence, there is growing interest in subscription models that allow consumers to rent clothes for a given time-period and spend less money on renewing their wardrobe. The second-hand fashion and accessories market is booming.

In the 1980s, when one flicked through fashion magazines, one could tell from the style who the designer was—Montana, Mugler, Saint Laurent or Jean-Paul Gaultier. Today, it has become much more difficult. Many fashion labels have adopted a rock chic bohemian style. There does not appear to be one silhouette distinctive of our era. It is a hodgepodge of different styles, times and cultures, a "mix and match" of vintage, current and modern trends. Sneakers and street-style at one point were all the rage, but some trend analysts think their popularity is on the wane as they have started to disappear from the podiums. Alber Elbaz sums up well the current state of affairs: "In fashion, you have to constantly impress 300 blasé people. Not easy to get them excited. This is why designers feel they need to push the boundaries all the time," Elbaz said. "I see in fashion a lot of fear and fatigue... What works today is what screams on the screen. But the problem is that screaming does not mean you have ideas."

Jacques the Cossack

COUNT JACQUES VON POLIER, A THIRTY-SOMETHING idealist and French expatriate in Moscow, woke up one day with a huge hangover and 50 percent of Russia's oldest watchmaker. Founded by Peter the Great, Raketa's watch plant is a national symbol of Russian *savoir-faire* and the pride of Saint Petersburg, where it was born and still makes watches. Polier has accomplished what Bernard Arnault did with leather goods maker Moynat and what Tod's Diego Della Valle is trying to do with the Schiaparelli fashion house—resuscitate a dormant brand by leveraging its heritage and giving it a contemporary twist.

Polier nearly lost his sanity trying to return Raketa back to its former glory, with little money but lots of help from A-list friends such as supermodel Natalia Vodianova. "We pretend to be Rolex—without the budget," Polier tells people who have never heard of the brand. Raketa has been riding the country's nationalist streak and new-found love for anything "Made in Russia."

Investors include a descendant of the imperial Romanov family, a member of the Italian industrial Agnelli family and a scion of France's Taittinger champagne-making family. Polier's story speaks volumes about Russia's byzantine, surreal world of business and brings rare insight into the arcane world of watchmaking. Its revival owes much to Polier's wide array of contacts, who range from brothel owners to government ministers. Raketa's revenues are still small compared with major high-end watch brands but Raketa is one of the most impressive turnaround stories in the post-Soviet bloc. Its journey shows that it is possible to convert a Soviet-era factory into a modern high-end facility—with help from a few Swiss machines and engineers.

Back in the 1970s and 1980s, Raketa's size and notoriety within the former Soviet Bloc matched that of Swatch in Europe. It was one of the world's biggest watchmakers, producing several million timepieces a year. Raketa employed more than 8,000 staff. It had its own orchestra, company hymn, hospital, day care center, school, anti-nuclear attack bunker and Black Sea resort. Jobs were for life and every member of a Raketa worker's family was looked after from cradle to grave.

By reviving the factory and brand name, Polier is making the bet that one day, Russia will be known for producing things other than oil, gas, tanks, Kalashnikovs, fighter jets and shabby cars. The name itself evokes fond Soviet memories for the average Russian. Raketa, which means "rocket" in Russian, was adopted by the watch factory after Russian cosmonaut Yuri Gagarin became the first man to travel into space in 1961. The company still boasts in Soviet style on its website: "We supply the Russian army, cosmonauts and civilian population."

Polier will never regret embarking on the Raketa adventure even if the obstacles he had to overcome were far greater than what he ever imagined. When he first visited the Raketa factory in 2009, he noticed people were making screws and other metallic parts too big to fit in a watch. In the company's financial accounts, he spotted mysterious inflows of revenues from unidentified sources. It took a while for staff to tell him the truth: Raketa had been surviving for years on military orders. It turns out that Raketa was also one of the country's leading specialists in micro-mechanical measurement systems. Russian war planes are equipped with fallback mechanical systems that function without electricity should they fly through a radioactive zone. "A Mig-29 fighter jet cannot fly without us," Polier told me. He would not divulge any further detail.

Polier bought Raketa at the tail-end of the financial crisis of 2007 and 2008. At that time, people gave the company six months. The roof leaked, few machines actually worked and salaries had not been paid for months. Only a skeleton team remained. It took determination, enthusiasm and faith in Russians' ability to make do with little to get the factory back on its feet. Today, the company employs 150 people, including a dozen in Moscow. It sends young recruits to Switzerland for training, buys machines from Swatch Group and employs Swiss watch engineers. In addition to the more than 250 tiny parts it manufactures for its mechanical movements, Raketa is also one of the only watch plants in the world that makes its own intricate balance springs. Several times thinner than a hair, the balance spring is the heart of a mechanical timepiece. It is what gives the watch its beat. Without it, nothing moves. Like an old shamanic recipe, only a handful of people know how to produce it, and they transmit this secret orally from generation to generation. Raketa could be producing hair springs for Swiss watchmakers and sell them at competitive prices, but the fact that it is based in Russia, spooks big brands. They prefer working with European producers such as Swatch Group's Nivarox.

Polier has been living in Moscow since 1996. A self-declared fan of Vladimir Putin and a Russophile, he cultivates an irrepressible penchant for provocation. When asked why he lives in Moscow, he answers that he is a "French cultural refugee." When one mentions corruption in Russia, he says that there is just as much in France, only people talk less openly about it. Raised in Paris, Polier is a refined man with a trim beard, deep hazelnut eyes and gracious manners. Now that he has dedicated his life to Raketa, he wears a watch on each wrist to complement his customary initialed white shirt.

Polier has family roots going back to aristocratic Huguenots who fled from France to Germany in the 17th century. He also has ties to Russia. His great-grandmother was born in Crimea at a time when it was unequivocally Russian. One of his ancestors fought alongside Napoleon in Russia and fell in love with a Russian girl. After the *Grande Armée* was defeated and humiliated in 1812, he went back to Russia, married the girl and started a family.

Polier, whose father and three brothers all run their own companies, is a natural-born entrepreneur. "Developing a brand allows me to express my creativity. I am excellent at improvisation," says Polier. "I am not good at learning things by heart and repeating them."

In Moscow, Polier is known as much for his Raketa venture as for the raucous parties he organizes in his gigantic flat opposite the statue of Russian bard Vladimir Visotsky. He occupies the entire top floor of one of the few pre-revolutionary buildings that survived the war against Napoleon. Until his arrival in the late 1990s, it was a communal flat shared by several families. The parquet-floored living room, as big as a ballroom, is adorned with crimson red theater curtains and imposing portraits of Tolstoy, Lenin and Pasternak hung on grass-green walls. At one end of the room stands a cabaret-style black piano with white candles, surrounded by guitars and balalaikas waiting for musicians to start playing and for the party to begin.

"The first time you come to Jacques' flat, you expect to land in the salon of the earl of Burgundy and then you realize that you are actually in some Kusturica film,"[1] says French travel writer Sylvain Tesson, one of Jacques' oldest friends. His personality, soirées and closeness to high-profile figures such as Ekaterina Peskova, ex-wife of Dmitry Peskov, Putin's spokesman since 2000, inspired a *Financial Times* correspondent to write a portrait of Polier in 2015.[2]

"I don't how he does it, but when he is around, there cannot be such a thing as a routine," Tesson said. One

---

[1] The Serbian filmmaker is known for his off-the-wall films such as *White Cat, Black Cat* and *Underground*.

[2] "French count Jacques von Polier and his wild nights in Moscow," *Financial Times*, Courtney Weaver, April 17, 2015.

morning, the French writer and his photographer showed up at Polier's house after one of their many long-haul trips in Siberia. Polier welcomed them with a breakfast that consisted of beer and a pot of paint filled with beluga caviar. "You see what I mean," said Tesson.

A few weeks later, Tesson was back in Paris and got a message from Polier on his answer phone. "Hi Sylvain, it's Jacques. We are off to space. There is one seat left. Call me back," it said. Polier went flying with friends, but without Tesson, in an Ilyushin training jet based at the Moscow Space Centre. It was one of those only-in-Russia moments. Back in the 1990s, flying in an Ilyushin or a MiG fighter jet cost only a few thousand dollars.

Polier studied economics in Paris, Hamburg and Moscow. Three months after graduating from the Plekhanov Russian University of Economics in Moscow in 1996, he set up a recruitment agency for foreign staff and a real estate agency. "We rented out apartments from babushkas[1] on Tverskaya," he said, referring to Moscow's Champs-Elysées. "We got them another place to live, repainted the flats white, got Tajik workers to re-lacquer the floors and rented them out for a fortune to expats." Within two years, Polier, who was not even 30, had made his first million dollars. But by the summer of 1998, when the ruble collapsed and Russia defaulted on its debt, he lost everything. It was time for a break from Moscow. He returned to Paris thinking he should try to land some sort of real, respectable job. "It was the first and last time I wrote a CV," he told me. During a job interview to work in marketing at a big consumer goods brand, a

[1] Old ladies. *Babushka* first means grandmother in Russian.

young stiff-upper-lip type asked him what were his three main qualities and weaknesses. Polier snapped: "I had created two businesses, travelled all around Russia and Europe, seen the war in Yugoslavia. If those were the best questions this guy could come up with, I was out of there."

Having enjoyed so much freedom in Russia, Polier could not lock himself up in the French system again, so he decided to move on. He bought a Niva 4×4 and went on a year-long trip from Paris to China via central Asia and Mongolia with his friend Julien Delpech, another entrepreneur. The voyage was sponsored by France Telecom, the retailer Fnac and the celebrity magazine Paris-Match, which published several of their reportages. The pair compiled their stories in a book called *Davaï!*, or 'let's go' in Russian.[1] Bright moments include drinking tea in Afghanistan with commander Ahmad Shah Massoud, the Talibans' No.1 enemy who was killed by a suicide bomb — organized most probably by al-Qaeda — two days before the September 11, 2001 attacks that would trigger NATO's assault on Afghanistan. Once deep in the Gobi Desert, the companions' car broke down. There were only two options: die of thirst or try to repair the car. They painstakingly got the car moving again, but only in reverse gear. The two men crossed the Gobi Desert for more than 400 km in reverse gear, replacing each other every 25 km to literally save their necks.

Eventually, Jacques went back to Moscow and landed a job without any prior experience as a trader at the Troïka Dialog brokerage. Later, he managed a fund for a

[1] *Davaï, sur les chemins de l'Eurasie*, Julien Delpech, Jacques von Polier, Robert Laffont, 2002.

major French financier he did not wish to name but is known to have invested in Russia on behalf of Bernard Arnault. Within a few years, having topped up his bank account, Polier started to think about what else he could do that would give a bigger meaning to his life than finance. At first, he considered investing in the Russian cigarette brand BelomorKanal, known for its long carton filters and Soviet-era packet, but it did not work out.

The first foreign owner of the Raketa watch brand and factory in the post-Soviet era was David Henderson-Stewart, an English lawyer and adviser to Sergey Pugachev, a Russian banker who fought against Putin for years and tried in vain to get back his state-seized billions after falling out with the Russian president. Henderson-Stewart acquired Raketa in 2008 from a Russian steel conglomerate. For months and months afterwards, he pestered Polier to chip in. One evening, the two men got drunk and Polier ended up owning half of Raketa when he woke up. He vaguely remembered that he wrote the contract himself. In it, he inserted the rule that if the two men were ever to get into a major argument, which could easily happen between equal co-owners, they would have to spend a whole night drinking together. If by morning they could not resolve their differences, only then could they call their respective lawyers. "Since David was a lawyer and knew all the tricks, I thought that it should be me who writes the contract between us," Polier said.

Polier put the entire value of his investments in the company's coffers as working capital. The partners hesitated for a long time about keeping the plant as consultants warned them that a proper reboot would require huge capital investments. But in the end, they managed to resuscitate the factory at a fraction of what it would have cost them in Switzerland. The two split the workload. Henderson-Stewart oversees production at the factory in Saint Petersburg while Polier looks after design and communications in Moscow. "David is the back office, I am the front office," says Polier.

The watch factory

On a long rainy weekend in November 2017, I travelled to Saint Petersburg and Polier gave me a tour of the Raketa plant. It is located some 30 kilometers from central Saint Petersburg in the suburban town of Peterhof, where Tsar Peter the Great erected his fairy tale yellow Summer Palace, Russia's answer to Versailles. The palace is topped with golden cupolas, surrounded by fountains and stunning views of the Bay of Finland. Right next to it, Putin and his oligarch friends have built oversize pastel-colored mansions protected by huge walls and CCTV cameras. A few blocks away stands what was once the Raketa factory, a huge castle-like complex in red brick with square towers and a clock over the company's black and red logo. But once in the compound, my taxi driver could only find a Chinese restaurant, a hairdresser, a massage center and a few offices. "Drive further," Polier barked over the phone when I called for directions. "Stop at the last puddle." There he was, standing under the rain in a damp white Raketa-embossed blouse outside a soot-covered Brezhnev-era building. Above the front door, a nailed tarpaulin read "Peterdvorstovy (Peter's Palace) Watch Factory", the only visible sign that watchmaking was going on inside. It might not stay there forever, Polier reassured me, as he was in talks to have the factory transferred to one of the city's historic buildings.

The factory's vast machine room reeks of burnt metal and burning oil, like in some Soviet plant from the 1960s. Lines of workers are bent silently over dark green mechanical monsters that pound away incessantly. Many of them are engraved *CCCP* (USSR). On the walls, propaganda posters from the communist era show joyful employees in white blouses lifting their arms in the air like the young Pioneers and saying *svegda gotov*—always ready! There are also old photos of staff smiling serenely as they assemble watches. It's difficult to figure out what all these bulky machines do. Some spit out microscopic parts, measuring a few dozen microns. Hefty Russian ladies with over-plucked eyebrows and impeccably manicured nails polish minuscule watch parts. Two ashen-faced men with watchmaker's eyepieces strapped around their foreheads sit making holes in brass dials.

Down a light pink corridor, Polier ushers me through a succession of rooms, each dedicated to different steps in the production process. In one room stand giant aluminum basins for mixing metallic alloys. Watch parts are washed in another room. Further down, there is a huge neon-lit open space where people painstakingly assemble watch movements, alternating between a microscope and a magnifying lens. Not a sound other than resounding rounds of tick tocks. In one corner, there are rows of machines turning watches around to test the movements and check how they react to being worn. In clear plastic boxes, they rotate as if they were roasting chickens.

Some of the watchmakers were in their 20s, others in their 60s, 70s and even 80s. Polier introduced a rule that each senior Raketa employee must train at least two or three juniors. The veteran's year-end bonus would depend on the performance of his or her protégés. One young recruit was named Sasha, a 24-year-old from Vladivostok at the eastern end of Russia's eleven time zones. Sasha used to repair Omega, Patek Philippe and Zenith watches in a tiny shop out there. He had read about Raketa in a newspaper article, clicked on the company's website and learned it had new owners and was hiring. He travelled to Saint Petersburg, got an interview and was hired on the spot. "I love my profession because there are so few of us who really know how to make and repair watches," says Sasha. "It makes me feel special." At home, Sasha spends his free time dismantling and repairing old timepieces. Polier wished he had more enthusiasts like him. Attracting young talent is not easy. "Most young Russian men these days are only interested in girls and money. They're light years away from the world of watchmaking," he said.

Down a corridor, Polier stops to point toward another room. "You see, behind this door is where we make balance springs and escapements—the very heart of a watch," he said. "People at Richemont and LVMH would kill their grandmother to see what we do here." An elderly man, Raketa's top spring specialist, greets us. Next to him three similarly old ladies, sitting at their desk, assemble escapements made up of no less than 26 parts.

From Rolex, Polier hired the Swiss hairspring specialist Jean-Claude Quenet to oversee the factory's modernization. Quenet said the first thing he did was to "teach people how to wash the floors and fight dust." The big difference with most Swiss watchmakers, he said, was that "in Switzerland, if you need something, a screw, a machine, a small part, you drive 20 minutes and you get it, as all the watch-makers and parts providers are concentrated in one area. In Russia, you have to make do with what you have, and solve problems yourself." Quenet was impressed by how inventive and simple Raketa's Soviet-era watchmaking machines were, some several times smaller than those in Switzerland that did exactly the same job. "The Russian mind works like a chess player, it will review all the options, take its time and then choose the optimal solution." he said.

Quenet's remarks recalled the famous NASA pen from the 1990s that worked with zero gravity. Russians would laugh at the expensive pen while their astronauts took off simply with pencils in their pockets. In a similar vein, the precise time and rhythm of every passing second is set by the Swiss government's atomic watch that most watchmakers are aligned with. They also use fancy instruments to measure the regularity of seconds and a watch's overall long-term precision. At Raketa, watches are connected to a microphone that listens to the beats and translates them into dots on a screen or a piece of paper. There are also a few fat ladies with a metronome in one ear and a watch in the other, checking a beat's regularity.

The Raketa story

Raketa originally started as a workshop founded by Peter the Great to cut stones of all sorts, from emeralds to marble. A copy of the workshop's original founding decree, stamped with the double-crowned Russian imperial eagle seal, hangs in the one-room museum near the factory's entrance. Peter Alexeyevich, Tsar of All Russia, ordered workmen to set up the atelier in 1721 next to his Summer Palace. It was almost two decades after he founded Saint Petersburg, following a protracted war against the Swedes that gave Russia access to the Baltic Sea. The tsar's plan was to move the epicenter of power there from Moscow and give Russia a window onto Europe. The stonecutters' mission was to provide the city's mansions with marble floors, staircases and sleek granite pillars. The Peterhof plant also produced the malachite room of the Winter Palace, the mosaics of Saint Isaac cathedral in Saint Petersburg and giant vases in lapis-lazuli now on display at the Louvre museum in Paris. In the late 19th and early 20th centuries, its artisans supplied famous jewelers such as Peter Carl Fabergé, known for his Easter eggs popular among Russian and European royals.

The workmen also cut rubies for watch movements. The plant began producing timepieces in earnest in the second half of the 19th century. Between the 1870s and the revolution of 1917, its watchmakers also repaired the clocks of every palace in Saint Petersburg, a huge task considering there were dozens of them in and around the imperial city. Before the Bolsheviks seized power, the factory was led by three generations of Frenchmen, all bearing the family name Morin.

Once the country adopted Lenin's communist ideas, jewelry and watchmaking were considered bourgeois and the plant's activities were widened to include military precision instruments, in particular in-flight measurement devices. When Hitler's forces crushed the Baltic States in 1941 and reached the Gulf of Finland, the factory found itself right on the front line. Thousands of workers perished in the fighting. Many also died of hunger. After months of heavy battle, the factory was reduced to rubble. Vladimir, Raketa's oldest worker and one of the only men who knows how to repair all of the plant's Soviet-era machines, remembers the horrors of the Leningrad blockade. For more than 900 days, the Germans cut off the city's supplies and more than one million people died of hunger. Some tried to survive feeding on cats, rats and corpses. "I saw so many people die of cold and hunger, the horror was indescribable. To this day, I still have nightmares about it," says the 81-year-old man who has worked for Raketa all his life. Vladimir told me proudly that he had trained more than 30 people since Polier's arrival and hoped to continue doing so for as long as he could.

The factory was rebuilt stone by stone by women who survived the war. The museum has black and white photos of that time showing the bombarded buildings and fallen Raketa workers. A glass cabinet displays shrapnel and artillery found in the vicinity. It took several years to bring the factory back to life. By the 1950s, it expanded into mass watch production and by the 1970s, it ranked as one of the biggest manufacturers in the world, producing six million units a year.

One of Raketa's most popular models featured a zero instead of the number 12 at the top of its dial. In the 1980s, Mikhail Gorbatchev famously pointed to the zero of his Raketa watch when speaking to foreign journalists, saying it symbolized perestroika and the country's historic reboot. Today, one of the brand's best-sellers is inspired by that model with a "0" instead of a 12 on the dial.

After the collapse of the Soviet Union in 1991, state orders dried up, salaries stopped being paid but workers continued to make watches. They had nothing else to do and hoped one day they would be paid for their work. Many also stayed on because it gave them a sense of purpose after the overwhelming loss they felt when communism ended and they were told that it was a 75-year-long mistake.

To survive the dire 1990s, workers were paid in Raketa watches that they could sell directly to their friends, relatives and passers-by on the street. The factory's real estate empire of more than 30 buildings was sold off piece by piece by opportunists who did not care about its precious know-how or place in Russia's history. In the late 1990s, factory director Anatoly Cherdantsev gathered a small group of workers to rescue all the best machines before they were thrown out and destroyed. They hauled them into the building where the plant is located today, on the fringes of where the great Raketa factory used to be. "It was an epic and tragic moment as the lifts did not work," recalled Cherdantsev, who is still in charge of the plant. "Actually, had I known how difficult it was going to be, I would never have done it."

The workers gathered enough machines to continue making a few movements and models. Lyudmila Yakovlevna, 75, saved all the paper maps and archives, which were later digitalized. "We had production maps not only for watches but for many different things," said the veteran head of production, her grey hair pulled into a bun. She has been working for Raketa since she was 19. Back in the 1960s and 1970s, the plant produced more than 40 million different timepieces, including alarm clocks, and provided specialized parts for blood pressure monitors.

Somehow, the factory miraculously retained some staff and was able to call back many former employees. Some of them were way past retirement age but preferred being useful to just getting old, watching TV at home. Raketa may no longer have an orchestra but it still has a hockey team that regularly plays against local army teams and rival squads from other cities. It also has a choir composed of cheery old ladies. Every November 3, the day Peter the Great signed the plant's founding *ukaz*, or decree, they don traditional bright green satin costumes and sing Raketa's anthem. The hymn relates how Peter the Great created a factory of stonecutters and Yuri Gagarin brought back the Raketa name from space for eternity.

Raketa has no marketing department. Polier calls advertising propaganda. "What I really hate about luxury is marketing," he said. "It is really about taking people for complete idiots." Raketa's head of retail is a doctor in nuclear physics who used to work in a bar frequented by loose women and rich men. His business card identifies him as the "head of nuclear physics." Polier said the term head of retail "was just too depressing."

Miss World

After supermodel Natalia Vodianova, Jacques von Polier recruited as the new face of Raketa a former Miss World, a leggy sapphire-blue eyed goddess we will call Maria to avoid anybody getting into trouble. Like Vodianova, who loved the brand and its patriotic streak, Maria gave Polier photos of herself for free. There was no money involved, but the Frenchman got saddled with a strange debt. One morning, he received a phone call from a man with an imperious voice: "Hello, I am the husband of Maria. You see, my wife would like to meet Mario Testino (the famous fashion photographer), so you will organize that for her, won't you Jacques?" Polier sensed the man was no lightweight and he had to oblige.

Polier had a theory. For him, the worlds of fashion and supermodels were completely closed off to the circuits of Miss World and Miss Universe contests. Even if they wanted to, these women could never become supermodels. His politically incorrect explanation was that fashion was, by and large, dominated by gay photographers and designers who were into skinny, androgynous-looking women. But beauty pageants were selected by straight men. "As a result, women were exciting, they had breasts and asses, unlike most models you see in the fashion world," Polier explained. This particular Miss World thought she had what it took to make it in fashion and Testino was going to help her.[1]

---

[1] That was of course before 2018 and the whole #metoo movement, Harvey Weinstein scandal and allegations of sexual harassment levelled at Mario Testino.

The only problem was the friend who had introduced Polier to Maria had oversold his friendship with
Testino. She had convinced the beauty queen that Polier
knew everybody in fashion personally, including Testino.
In reality, the two had only partied together a few times.
"That did not necessarily make us friends," said Polier.
He knew he had to think fast. A direct request to Testino
to meet a former Miss World would never work, since
the guy could meet any drop-dead gorgeous woman he
wished at the click of a mouse. So, sitting in his boxer
shorts and white blouse on his red couch in his Moscow
flat, he sent Testino an SMS saying: "Hi Mario, I am in
London, do you want to meet for drinks." To which
Testino promptly replied: "Yes! Come by to my studio
tomorrow at 5 p.m."

Jacques promptly called Maria to tell her the good
news. Within two hours, "there was a 'black train' in front
of my front door," Polier recalls, using a Russian expression that means a convoy of Mercedes sedans with black-
tainted windows. It took off for Sheremetyevo airport,
speeding at 200 km an hour in the middle lane, avoiding
cars in both directions. Sitting with him was this intri-
guing beauty and her broad-shouldered husband, who at
one point remembered that Russians needed a separate
visa for Great Britain. "So, I guess this means that you,
young man, will be travelling alone with my wife?" he
asked sternly. Polier nodded and promptly reassured him
of his honorable intentions. The Frenchman and cat-lady
flew off to London in a private jet, indulging in Dom
Pérignon champagne and Russian caviar on the way.

After spending the night in their respective suites at
the Ritz, the pair made their way the next day to Testi-

no's studio in London and a miracle happened. Not only did Testino shoot Maria, but she took part in his legendary white towel series, the Holy Grail of fashion photography. She was on cloud nine and Polier felt immensely relieved. Back in Moscow, he got another phone call, again from Maria's scary husband: "Jacques, listen, I want to thank you for what you did, so you are going to give this person a call on my behalf, OK?" Polier did not know who the man in question was. Out of curiosity, he dialed the number. A lady answered and said: "One minute please, I pass you the minister." Polier was on the line with Russia's industry minister, who invited him to come see him the next day.

Polier walked out of that meeting with a fantastic government order. Raketa was commissioned to build the world's biggest mechanical clock inside the cathedral-like atrium of Moscow's giant Detsky Mir toy shop, opposite the Lubyanka headquarters of the Federal Security Service, formerly known as the KGB. The Raketa clock would be 13 meters high, eight meters wide, composed of some 5 thousand parts and weigh nearly five tons. It was conceived and built in only five months.

BRIC luxury

For Polier, the future of luxury is no longer in Europe, its main hub today, but in fast developing countries such as Brazil, Russia, India and China—the BRICs. "The Louis Vuitton of the future will be Chinese, Indian or Russian. These countries are endowed with significant cultural heritage, which is essential for a luxury brand to thrive, and we are already seeing new labels emerging," he said. He argues that brands such as France's Dior and Chanel stand a chance because they have so much history behind them and are so closely associated with fashion. However, he is not sure about many others, which he declined to name.

In the 1990s, Russians rejected their culture and their roots and were only interested in foreign brands. Back then, more than 90 percent of fashion magazines such as Russia's *Vogue* and *Cosmopolitan* were about foreign brands. Today, bling from abroad occupies significantly fewer pages. When Polier bought Raketa in 2009, he noticed that Russians, flooded with imports since the collapse of the Soviet Union, were starting to yearn for home-made goods. Foreign restaurants in Moscow were not as popular as they had been a decade before. "After having been to Saint-Tropez and Courchevel, Russians finally understood that their culture was just as rich and wonderful as that of other countries and Tchaikovsky actually was cool," Polier said. With its famous composers, painters and writers, Russia was in the top five countries in terms of cultural importance and heritage, he argued. Yet it did not have a single major global consumer goods brand. He aimed to remedy that anomaly with Raketa. For him, a luxury brand could be successful if it had three things money could not buy: history, know-how and brand awareness. And that awareness had to exist without advertising. Raketa had all these three assets, which was why Polier believed in it.

Polier said he took all possible legal precautions to make it nearly impossible for anybody, including the Russian government, to take over his company. For all its faults and strange business practices, he found that Russia was actually a relatively easy place to raise money, particularly for such a well-known brand. When he needed extra funds in 2012, he persuaded wealthy Russian friends to inject cash into the company, after having held informal talks with two major French luxury groups he did not wish to name. Polier wanted investors from outside luxury and watchmaking, fearing they might meddle too much otherwise. "The day I have to give accounts to financers, the adventure will be over, I will no longer get a hard-on. And Raketa will no longer interest me," he said. Polier's ambition for Rateka is not to turn it into a provider of fancy watches with complications—the additional features in a mechanical timepiece beyond the simple display of hours, minutes and seconds. "We want to be the Kalashnikov of watches," he says. His focus is on resistant, "made in Russia" retro-style watches inspired by Soviet designs from the 1960s and 1970s. His mechanical watches cost from 1,000 to 14,000 euros. Models include a sparkling red-star model created by Vodianova and a Polar watch featuring light green ovoid lines on the dial.

Polier says a third of the brand's sales come from special orders, private individuals and government bodies such as the Moscow police celebrating an anniversary or special occasion. At the factory, workers can customize dials with any inscription, from honoring a division of parachutists to declaring "Vladimir Vladimirovich (Putin), I love you." Raketa watches are sold in upmarket Moscow shopping malls such as TsUM and GUM and dozens of boutiques across Russia. Polier says one of his biggest achievements is to have convinced Russian multi-brand retailers to sell Raketa watches next to high-end brands such as Omega and Audemars Piguet. In 2011, it resumed major exports for the first time since going private in the 1990s. Five years later, it opened a Paris office on the apt rue de Saint-Pétersbourg near Gare Saint-Lazare. The office now serves as a base to oversee exports. Raketa is sold in many places in Europe, including at the watch specialist Fréret-Roy near Place Vendôme.

Polier has also persuaded an impressive number of well-known people and sports events in Russia to team up with Raketa for free. It is associated with Saint Petersburg's Zenith football club. It is also the official timekeeper of the national tank-biathlon, a popular race on sand tracks in the Urals where participants shoot at a series of targets while maneuvering their tanks as quickly as possible. "People think Raketa has a lot of money. When I tell them we have none, they are surprised. I explain that we actually need their help to develop Raketa, a factory founded by Peter the Great where survivors of WWII still work, and they accept," said Polier. His audacity no doubt helped the brand's revival and as did his talent for provocation. In 2014, after the US and Europe imposed sanctions on Russia after the annexation of Crimea, Polier half-seriously announced that Raketa would stop selling watches to the West in retaliation. It was a smart publicity stunt that cost him nothing, since Raketa sold very little abroad back then. After the January 2015 attacks on French satirical weekly *Charlie Hebdo*, Raketa put out a T-shirt with "Je suis Rossiya" on it. Polier had by then turned into an even more fervent patriot than the Cossacks themselves.

Will Raketa become a global brand? "Everybody at the company thinks it will and they are all very motivated," said Jean-Claude Quenet, the Swiss engineer who joined from Rolex. "Me personally, I think they will succeed. You know why? Because they do not know that it is impossible."

Origins and spirituality of luxury

OUR PIONEERS REVEALED THE SECRETS OF SOME OF THE world's biggest luxury brands with behind-the-scenes accounts of how they became genuine powerhouses. Through their life adventures, we discovered some of the virtuous and some of the more somber aspects of the luxury business. This industry is caught in constant tension between light and darkness. It reveals the best and the worst in us, our egotism and magnanimity. But what has become of the very idea of luxury these pioneers explored and promoted? What does luxury mean in the 21st century? When deciding where to go next, it is always good to know where you came from.

Luxury has always been a way for humans to affirm their non-animal state and their power of transcendence, defined as the ability to project themselves onto something greater and more fundamental than themselves. It is their natural response to the metaphysical angst of knowing that their days are numbered. Ever since man became man, he has felt that he could assuage his spiritual needs with material things. Once upon a time, humans made sacrifices and offered precious objects, food, virgins and children to communicate in some way with higher orders, spirits and gods. Today, one empties one's bank account to live a special moment or acquire a luxury object.

Professor Henry de Lumley, who is head of the Human Paleontological Institute in Paris, thinks one cannot talk about luxury without discussing man's quest for beauty. Every civilization seeks beauty, he says, whether they are African bushmen or Bolivian coffee growers, pushy New Yorkers or snob *Parisiennes*. In an office filled with dusty skulls and piles of files, this tiny man's eyes light up when he spins out his ideas about prehistoric luxury. In Tanzania a few decades ago, he pointed out, archaeologists dug up rock balls that were perfectly round and smooth. These balls, only about the size of a hand, served no apparent purpose. They were clearly carved solely for their beauty, he said, just so they could be admired. They dated back more than two million years, from an era when man made his first tools and walked upright on two feet. Looking up to the sky, he speculated, the first humans must have started to ask deeper questions about life and develop symbolic thinking. For him, these stone balls were a clear manifestation of an inner quest for beauty that linked them to what they saw above. Since they had no function other than to fulfill an irrational need, they were the first luxury items for prehistoric man.

Another important step in the evolution of man's symbolic thinking was the biface hand axe, an almond-shape tool with a rounded base and pointed end. It marked the first time humans made an object that reflected their own symmetrical self. To watch such a tool come out of a stone was a magical moment, said Lumley. Once this hand axe emerged from rough stone, it was imbued with a new power that didn't exist in the animal world. It could be used to cut wood for fuel, hunt animals to eat and dress game for food. With the human imagination going beyond what animals could perceive, it was a short leap to making other objects that responded to man's burgeoning spiritual needs.

Archeologists have found biface hand axes thrown in sepulchral sinkholes and graves, perhaps as tools for the afterlife. An impressive sample was found in a pit at Sima de Los Huesos in Atapuerca, in northern Spain, in the first decade of this century. It was carved in pink quartzite with splashes of mustard yellow and seemed to have never been used. The finding provided evidence that man performed funeral rites more than 350,000 years ago and practiced some early form of spiritual life. The question of when exactly man started to believe in the divine is one of history's unanswered riddles. Many are still scratching their heads, from paleontologists to anthropologists and anyone reflecting on the theory of evolution itself.

Archaeologist Jean-Marie Le Tensorer, a colleague of Lumley, noticed that the most beautiful hand axes were generally the oldest. The more recent ones—a few dozen thousand years old—were carved more roughly, with less attention to detail and to the object's overall shape and harmony. It is possible that over time, man realized that his biface did not need to be beautiful to work well and its symbolic power eroded.

Humley argues that the manual power and skills of 21st century *Homo sapiens* are significantly weaker than those our ancestors had many centuries, if not many millennia, ago. People make fewer things with their hands than they did in the past, outsourcing a growing number of tasks to robots and machines. Those involved in manual work do not have the strength, resistance and talent of their forebears. Lumley's students, equipped with much bigger brains than the *Homo erectus* who carved the biface, are incapable of making a hand axe quickly. They require months and months of training and hard work to replicate the quality and beauty of the original object. However, their survival does not depend on the hand axe, which might also explain why they cannot carve with the same determination as their distant forebears.

Man's mental capabilities have also grown weaker, due to distractions introduced by the devices of the modern age. Like manual work, many cerebral tasks are fulfilled by computers. Who can claim to be able to make elaborate mental calculations and master arithmetic? Videos have reduced the need to read books. The Internet search engine answers nearly every question. Our brain no longer needs to retain information since it is at the tip of our fingers on a computer screen.

The notion of beauty, essential to understand what luxury means, comes from the interaction of the human spirit with the living universe. It is a natural, unexplainable sense of harmony. Beauty is a living being, ephemeral, mysterious and vulnerable. If beauty were a human being, it would have a pure soul, one that shines and warms all around as a beacon of light in one's private garden. In his *Ode on a Grecian urn,* John Keats writes:

"Beauty is truth, truth beauty—that is all ye know on Earth, and all ye need to know."

Beauty is a personal experience that one feels with the heart more than with the mind. The German philosopher Immanuel Kant wrote that beauty was a combination of the product of our imagination and our reading of the world in "free play" with one another. It is disinterested, which is to say that it is not linked to our needs. Kant wrote in his *Critique of Judgment,* published in 1790, that "beauty is not a quality inherent to things, it only exists in the mind that contemplates it and each mind perceives a different beauty." His irreverent contemporary Voltaire added: "To a toad, what is beauty? A female with pop eyes, a large, wide mouth, a yellow belly and a spotted back."

Like luxury, beauty is in many ways tied to our spiritual self. Capturing and feeling true beauty is a form of transcendence. It reflects the urge to project oneself unto another world and feel connected to something greater. Beauty makes us enter into a dialogue with our inner self. This is where luxury objects invite themselves into our consciousness. Luxury and fashion thrive on our inner quest for beauty. They develop an interpretation of beauty that expresses an ideal through colors, forms and patterns. Luxury brands project images of a beautiful and simple life, detached from mundane anxieties and marked by a taste of freedom, daring and glamour.

In the modern age, brands exploit these complex emotions to tell consumers "buy this product and you will become a member of our wonderful community." They use carefully calibrated key words that press magic buttons in our subliminal selves. To enhance the authority of their image, Dior, Chanel, Gucci and the others at times behave like idols, or terrestrial expressions of divinities. And the unthinking reaction of many average people is to treat them unconsciously as idols in return.

Fashion and luxury brands have always borrowed words from the lexicons of the sacred and the religious. Every brand, for example, has its "iconic" products, borrowing from the Greek word for religious paintings. For Chanel, it will be the 2.55 flap bag, for Louis Vuitton the Never Full bag, for Prada the Galleria bag. In watches, it will be the Oyster Perpetual for Rolex, the Royal Oak for Audemars Piguet, and the Alhambra pendants with their recognizable four-leaf clovers for the jeweler Van Cleef & Arpels. Even young luxury brands use the word "iconic" to describe what they think will become their best-seller, even though few people have yet heard of it.

Words like "guru" and "gospel" pepper the fashion and luxury vocabulary, as do terms such as "temple" and "altar." That last word has come a long way from its original meaning in ancient times as a surface for ritual animal slaughter. Anna Wintour is known as the high priestess of fashion and some designers, such as Hedi Slimane, ex-Dior, ex-Saint Laurent and now at Celine, are said to have cult status. As noted earlier, luxury king Bernard Arnault is called "God" internally at LVMH, and a meeting of his top assistants can be described as a congregation. Arnault usually only gives two public speeches a year, at the LVMH annual general meeting and the group's annual results presentation, and his words are awaited like those of a modern prophet.

In 2016, Gucci and Alexander Wang gave fashion's proximity to religion a new twist by staging their show in a church. Wang's racy, punkish silhouettes jarred with Byzantine mosaics of the Saint Bartholomew Episcopal Church in midtown Manhattan. A few months later, Gucci's garish "geek chic" cruise collection clashed with the austerity of Westminster Abbey's Gothic cloisters. Reverend Peter Owen-Jones, an Anglican priest and author, said the show sent a confusing message about what a church stood for. He saw it as part of a "Disneyfication" of England's "traditional sacred spaces" and said Gucci's show was "selling our soul for a pair of trousers."[1] In 2013, the German documentary *Mode als Religion* (Fashion as Religion) starring "fashion missionary" Karl Lagerfeld, explored that relationship between faith and style. It argued that trend followers were religious devotees, fashion magazines were the modern Bible and models were angels sent from high above.

Owning luxury can be an obsessive end in and of itself. On a winter afternoon in 2015, I gave a lecture in the library of a high-security prison in northern France to 12 inmates. One of them, a tall man from Ivory Coast, said something very telling. "You know, it is actually because of luxury goods that I am here, I mean in this prison," he confessed. The lure of luxury, in the form of expensive cars, jewelry and watches, had made him steal money and end up in prison. Now freedom had for him become the greatest luxury.

Luxury can be a never-ending illusion of happiness, an intense moment of satisfaction that once consumed, no longer brings that sense of fulfillment for which one was longing. And the quest starts again and never ends.

---

[1] "Westminster Abbey's Gucci show is like 'selling our soul for trousers," *Daily Telegraph*, Patrick Sawer, May 28, 2016.

Jean-Paul Agon, CEO of the French cosmetics giant L'Oréal, understands better than most the constant renewal of one's quest for beauty and the importance of newness. It's the name of the game in his business. "Beauty is an ideal, a permanent quest, so consumers always want to try new products," he said.[1]

A few years ago, I saw someone offering to sell his soul on eBay for $80. With the death of God in the 20th century, money has become a new religion for many. This seems to be especially pronounced in Asia, where societies inspired by Confucius believe that there is a ritual and social conformity aspect to luxury that should be publicly displayed.[2] To better grasp Asians' relationship to luxury, one needs to first understand the notion of "face" or *mianzi* in Chinese. Nothing is more important than preserving face, which in essence means cultivating and preserving the respect of others. According to this way of life, it is forbidden to shout at someone in public, whether colleagues, friends or family, because it is humiliating. If you lose face, you lose your place in society. This belief rests on a deeply communitarian view of the world in which each individual is part of a whole and interconnected with others. These relationships are fundamental for success and prosperity. To remind others that you exist, it is important to display your status symbols and make others envy you.

[1] Agon spoke at L'Oréal's annual results on February 8, 2019. That year, he was preparing himself to pass the baton to his deputy Nicolas Hieronimus, who had a stellar track-record at L'Oréal, lastly as head of the group's luxury products division.

[2] *Les religions et le luxe, l'éthique et la richesse d'orient en occident*, Pascal Morand, IFM/regard, 2008, p.198.

When successful Chinese businessmen started wearing Rolex and Omega watches two decades ago, legions followed suit. The concept of "face" explains why back then Chinese mainly bought big Western brands. Small brands had a hard time elbowing their way into that "winner-takes-all" market. Today, China's traditional communitarian view is challenged by exposure to Western values and individualism. Young Chinese want to develop their own identity distinct from that of their parents. They are into megabrands, but also into cool niche labels.

With the atomization of societies, the break-up of families and general loss of faith in established religions, the individual has become king. The primary focus has moved away from God and the community to the self. The very idea of luxury has evolved from being something spiritual and sacred to a celebration of self-indulgence in the form of rare delights and expensive objects.

Canadian philosopher Charles Taylor argues that "the dark side of individualism is a centering on the self, which both flattens and narrows our lives, makes them poorer in meaning, and less concerned with others and society."[1] Since the individual comes first, society's welfare is no longer a priority. The main focus is on one's own personal material comfort and that of close friends and family. Taylor highlights a loss of a heroic dimension to life. He says people no longer have a sense of higher purpose or something worth dying for. He cites the French philosopher and traveler Alexis de Tocqueville's evocation of the constant search for "small and vulgar pleasures" in

---

[1] *The Malaise of Modernity*, Charles Taylor, House of Anansi Press, 2003, p.4. *De la Démocratie en Amérique,* volume 2, Alexis de Tocqueville, Garnier-Flammarion, 1981, p. 385.

the democratic age. That democratic equality draws the individual towards himself, he argues, and as Tocqueville wrote, threatens to leave him "enclosed in the solitude of his own heart."[1]

The latest manifestation of our culture of narcissism is our "selfie mania," which involves taking photos of ourselves non-stop and posting them on social networks. What is the Facebook or Instagram potential of what I am doing has become an obsession. What is the point of going on a beautiful trip or acquiring a beautiful object if it is not to show it to everyone? It is no surprise that the iPhone is a best-seller. The first letter "i" subconsciously expresses the idea of "me, myself and I."

Symbolism

A luxury object is by definition a symbol. Such images include as much as they exclude, because they draw their strength from the beliefs people invest in them. If a Martian landed on Earth tomorrow, Professor Lumley said, he would no more grasp the meaning of a Christian cross than did the Iroquois Indians, who were baffled at the sight of explorer Jacques Cartier planting so many of them along the shores of the Saint Lawrence River. Each culture develops its own symbols. A *Birkin* bag means nothing to a Saami reindeer herder in Lapland just like the Saamis' zoomorphic protective amulets signify little to a Chinese businessman from Guangzhou. Some symbols may be positive for one culture and negative for

---

[1] *The Malaise of Modernity*, *op. cit*, p.4.

others. A Richard Mille watch costing more than 100,000 euros is a symbol of success for a Russian oligarch, but a retired French entrepreneur from a leafy Paris suburb might sniff at it as a watch for "New Russians" foolish enough to spend such vast amounts on a timepiece. Rings remain symbols of beliefs and status which couples still exchange at their wedding. Other rings bear the symbol of an alma mater or a family crest, which centuries ago served as an identity marker and were used to seal letters with melted wax.

Luxury would not exist without symbolic thinking. New symbols emerge while older ones disappear. What will be the symbols of success in fifty or one hundred years from now? They could be objects using materials from meteorites that fell from outer space on a specific day. They could be made with newly invented fabrics or connected textiles capable of reading and interpreting our moods. For city dwellers, one popular symbol of success has long been a house in the countryside with a verdant garden. Bracing themselves for the much-expected apocalypse and annihilation of our civilization, some Silicon Valley billionaires have gone much further, buying up large chunks of New Zealand. Those with more modest means have downshifted and tried to live off the grid, on the margins of society. Who knows how to live a happier life? Nobody has figured out yet how to survive solely on love and fresh air.

The future of luxury

AS PEOPLE FOCUS EVER MORE ON THEMSELVES, hedonism has become a way of life. That does not mean indulging in orgies and drinking wine all day on a couch à la romaine. These days, it involves quite the contrary—exercising regularly, eating organic food and getting massages. Health is the new wealth, and wellness the new *Must*. Far gone are the hippy 1970s, when people smoked lots of cigarettes and grass and paid little attention to their health.

For Italian fashion mogul Renzo Rosso,[1] eating well is the luxury of the future. Rosso has invested vast sums in organic farms as well as in his own Diesel Farm, an organic ecosystem spanning several hills in northern Italy on which his livestock roam freely. It produces fruit, vegetables, olive oil and wine.

---

[1] Renzo Rosso founded the denim brand Diesel. His group Only the Brave owns brands Maison Martin Margiela, Marni, Viktor & Rolf as well as Paula Cademartori.

Young people no longer want to toil day and night to afford luxury goods. They want free time to enjoy life. Values have changed. We are no longer into "having" but rather into "being." This trend raises serious questions about the future demand for luxury goods. In 2015, for the first time, the rate of increase in spending on luxury experiences such as hotels, trips and fancy restaurants was higher than that of spending on luxury items such as fashion accessories, watches and jewelry, according to consultancy Bain & Co. Newly rich people are still interested in status symbols, especially in Asia. But even there, people are starting to spend more money on experiences than on luxury "stuff." LVMH and many other luxury players have recently stepped up their investments in fancy hotels, restaurants and cafés to tap into that growing high-spending market.

As for beauty, there are as many definitions of luxury as there are people living on this planet. Luxury is what is precious, rare and carries symbolic value. As with beauty, luxury can be material or immaterial. Beauty can be seen, it can be felt, it can be imagined—just as luxury can be enjoying a rare bottle of wine, watching the sun rise from a mountain refuge or getting a custom-made suit. French philosopher Yves Michaud sees the idea of luxury "as a quest of intensity and emotion and a continuation of dreamed life."

As there are many kinds of luxury, it is useful to place them on a linear spectrum. It starts with the ostentatious, baroque, flamboyant and flashy, and ends with the all-natural, Zen and minimalist. At that latter end, it's what is left after all unnecessary layers have been removed. Small artisans, who make simple and beautiful objects, figure somewhere toward this end of the spectrum. Their products have the brightest future in my view.

The term "luxury industry," even though we all use it, is an oxymoron. There cannot be an industry of a genuine luxury product for the sophisticated consumer, since it is supposed to be something that is commissioned by one person and produced by another. It cannot be on a mass industrial scale.

At Geneva's annual watch fair, the Salon International de la Haute Horlogerie founded by Alain-Dominique Perrin, a forty-something Belgian entrepreneur and watch connoisseur named Henry told me an interesting story. Since childhood, he had been fascinated by how hundreds of microscopic parts could fit into a small object that gives the time, date and moon phases. He had amassed a collection of more than 100 watches from the biggest brands including Patek Philippe, Rolex, Audemars Piguet and Vacheron Constantin. One day, he decided to sell them all. He was tired of being treated badly by big watchmakers and had grown exasperated by their excessive price increases. Rolex's Daytona watch was worth 5,400 Swiss francs in 2009, 9,000 francs in 2010 and more than 10,000 francs in 2012.[1] Henry also thought that after-service repairs were very costly and said he was even refused the right to acquire certain rare models. "One day, you are their best client, and the next day, you are nobody," he said. Henry now only buys timepieces from small watchmakers he gets to know personally and with whom he develops a relationship. Some of his favorite watch brands are small producers such as De Bethune

[1] *Qui a tué le luxe? La face cachée d'un univers opaque*, Fabio Bonavita, Slatkine, 2016.

and Kari Voutilainen. "For me, real luxury is much more than owning a beautiful object. It is about knowing the person who made it," he said.

His philosophy extends beyond watches. Henry wears only custom-made glasses by Bonnet, which boasts former clients such as Yves Saint Laurent and Jacques Chirac. He carries umbrellas made by Michel Heurtault in Paris, wears boots by Northampton-based shoemaker Edward Green and eats his steak with knives designed by Antoine Van Loocke. He is a stickler for quality and no longer buys anything from big brands if he can avoid it.

The powerful attraction of a hand-made object, whether it is a table, a dress or a handbag, stems in part from the fact that it carries the energy transmitted by the person who made it. Consumers have grown tired of the over-abundance of cheap and soulless machine-made objects and are concerned by the damage they inflict on the environment. Many now are willing to pay extra for the lasting quality, comfort and warmth brought by a hand-made item. It used to be that we preferred to spend a lot of money on things that lasted, instead of small amounts on things that had to be replaced quickly. "I am too poor to buy cheap," say those who remember the privations of war. Years ago, an expensive pair of shoes or a dress lasted much longer than they do today. They were made with higher quality materials and involved more hand-made steps. Luxury brands will vehemently deny that, but customers know best.

There is hardly a luxury brand today that does not claim that its products are hand-made. However, that much-vaunted description usually applies to one element or just a few steps in the production process, such as polishing watch parts or hand-waxing the seams of a handbag. Hand-made is crucial to give the impression of quality and image that luxury brands need to survive.

There is a lot of discussion about new technologies and their impact on craftsmanship. Many fear robots will replace workers and artisans will become a thing of the past. But actually, technology can be a craftsman's ally. It can feed creativity and give more space to things men are better at than robots. Computer software helps fashion designers create dresses, bags, shoes and other items. 3D printers produce prototypes and help speed up the creation process. Computers have not replaced designers. In fact, they execute their orders. In the same vein, one should not be afraid of artificial intelligence. Thanks to AI-powered search engines, brands can spot fashion trends better they can could ever before. They can produce useful interpretations of their data, accumulated online and elsewhere. AI has freed time for other tasks. The future will belong to brands with the confidence and energy to pursue those other tasks and with the ingenuity to build new bridges between technology and craftsmanship.

Undoubtedly, the biggest challenge for those working in fashion and luxury will be the preservation of the environment. Tall trees and clean seas may be the last things one thinks about at a fashion show, but the dirty secret is that the fashion industry is one of the most polluting in the world. Something will eventually have to be done about this.

H&M is a fashion company that sells looks that are inspired from catwalks but which are cheaper and available before those produced by big brands. H&M admitted in 2018 that it had more than 4 billion euros worth of unsold clothes and accessories. That represents an enormous amount of wasted energy and resources. H&M is not the only brand plagued by unsold stock; every brand has some. When Burberry said in its 2018 annual report that it had destroyed tens of millions of pounds sterling worth of stock, people were shocked. Yet every brand destroys its stock. It is too expensive to keep. Publishers pulp unsold books for the same reason. Some governments in Europe are introducing bans on the destruction of unsold items, marking the first time public policy interferes with private companies' use of inventory.

Stella McCartney, one of the most militant pro-environment fashion brands, was the first to promote fake leathers and furs in the early 2000s. The brand has a bright future ahead of it. Bernard Arnault also thinks so, which is why LVMH bought a minority stake in Stella McCartney in 2019. Today, brands are having a hard time justifying their use of calf, pony, ostrich and crocodiles, in spite of the charts they sign about animal welfare. Many have announced bans on furs and exotic skins but have been keeping mum on calf leather. This depends on a slight difference between a calf and a mink. A calf is taken away from its mother at birth, lives a miserable and lonely life in a box and makes its first and last steps on its way to the slaughterhouse. Its skin goes to make leather and meat gets sold as veal. A mink lives a similarly grim existence locked up in a cage and will be killed when it has grown big enough. But we do not eat mink meat. If concern for animal welfare continues to grow, this distinction may disappear and slaughter of both mink and calves may become unacceptable.

The future of luxury and fashion will belong to those who can produce on demand—not easy to put in place on an industrial scale[1]—or to those that can recycle goods or rent out items through subscription services. The popularity of second-hand websites such as The RealReal and Vestiaire Collective and of subscription sites will continue to rise. After years of marketing and rhetoric on the subject, LVMH, Kering, Richemont, Chanel and other groups and brands are finally starting to make genuine efforts to minimize the impact of their operations on the planet. But the scale and complexity of the changes needed to make a difference is so daunting that one can only wonder if their initiatives, no matter how laudable, are not just a way of giving themselves a good conscience while continuing to pollute and deplete natural resources. Many brands fund non-governmental organizations (NGOs) that try to change things, but they do not know or want to know what is really going on.

I gathered evidence of this when I travelled to Madhya Pradesh in India in 2018 to write a story about organic cotton. It turned out that organic cotton was a promise that brands could not keep. Much was being done to help but there were so many steps involved between the harvest and the production of a shirt that it was simply impossible to make sure that the cotton purchased was 100 percent organic, i.e. without genetically modified seeds and pesticides. To uphold their promise, fashion brands would need to control every step, from checking the quality of the land on which the cotton grows to the ginning, the manufacturing of the yarns and the finished product. NGOs work hard to promote organic agri-

[1] Lectra is a French company that is trying to do just that.

culture, but the reality is that they cannot guarantee that the organic cotton that fashion brands purchase is not mixed with non-organic cotton. Fashion labels want to stamp "organic cotton" and "sustainable development" on their items but they are not interested in knowing what happens on the ground. And they do not want their customers to know either.

The luxury of tomorrow will have to be about preserving the environment. Luxury goods displayed in fancy shops will take on a new meaning when the resources they use become scarce. The most important luxury for our children will be fresh air, clean water and soil. Hopefully, their values will be different from ours, more focused on the essential. All the money in the world will not buy them a new planet and no-one can afford the "luxury" of ignoring that.

Bibliography

To find out more about:

The notion of beauty and what is luxury

Fabrice Aghassian, *Beautés sacrées, les soins du corps dans les trois Livres : Bible hébraïque, Nouveau Testament, Coran*, Cerf, 2016.

Jean Castarède, *Le Luxe*, "Que sais-je?" Puf, 1992.

Lucien Jerphagnon, *Histoire de la pensée, d'Homère à Jeanne d'Arc*, "Pluriel", Tallandier, 2009.

Emmanuel Kant, *Critique de la raison pure*, "Quadrige", Puf, 2015.

Gilles Lipovetsky, Elyette Roux, *Le Luxe éternel, de l'âge du sacré au temps des marques*, Gallimard, "Folio", 2003.

Henry de Lumley, *Le Beau, l'art et l'homme : Émergence du sens de l'esthétique*, CNRS Éditions 2014.
—, *Sur le chemin de l'Humanité*, CNRS Éditions, 2015.

Patrick Mathieu, Frédéric Monneyron, *L'Imaginaire du Luxe*, Imago, 2015.

Yves Michaud, *Critères esthétiques et jugement de goût*, Jacqueline Chambon, 1999.
—, *L'Art à l'état gazeux, essai sur le triomphe de l'esthétique*, Stock, 2003.

—, *Le Nouveau Luxe, expériences, arrogances, authenticité*, Stock, 2013.

Pascal Morand, *Les Religions et le luxe, l'éthique de la richesse d'Orient en Occident*, IFM Regard, 2012.

Charles Taylor, *Sources of the self, the making of the modern identity*, Harvard University Press, 1989.

—, *The Malaise of modernity*, House of Anansi Press, 2003.

Georges Vigarello, *Histoire de la beauté, Le Corps et l'art de l'embellir de la Renaissance à nos jours*, Seuil, 2004.

History of fashion, designers and luxury

Raphaëlle Bacqué, *Kaiser Karl*, Albin Michel, 2019.

Jean-Claude Biver, Gérard Lelarge, *Jean-Claude Biver, l'Homme qui a sauvé la montre mécanique*, Eyrolles, 2015.

Jean Castarède, *Le Grand Livre du luxe*, Eyrolles, 2014.

Alicia Drake, *The beautiful Fall, Fashion, genius and glorious excess in 1970s Paris*, Bloomsbury, 2007.

Rhonda K. Garelick, *Mademoiselle Coco Chanel and the pulse of history*, Random House New York, 2014.

Lauren Goldstein Crowe and Sagra Maceira de Rosen, *The Jimmy Choo Story: Power, profits and the pursuit of the perfect shoe*, Bloomsbury, 2009.

Didier Grumbach, *History of International Fashion*, Interlink Books, 2014.

Émilie Hammen et Benjamin Simmenauer (commented by), *Les Grands Textes de la mode*, Éditions IFM-Regard, 2017.

Yann Kerlau, *Les Dynasties du luxe*, Perrin, 2010.

Paul Poiret, *En habillant l'époque*, Grasset, 1930.

Dana Thomas, *Gods and Kings, the rise and fall of Alexander McQueen and John Galliano*, Penguin Random House, 2015.

Yseult Williams, *Impératrices de la mode*, Éditions de la Martinière, 2015.

The fashion and luxury industry

Teri Agins, *The End of Fashion, how marketing changed the clothing business forever*, Harper, 2000.

Vincent Bastien, Jean-Noël Kapferer, *Luxe oblige*, Eyrolles, 2008.

Christian Blanckaert, *Luxe*, Cherche Midi, 2007.

—, *Luxe Trotteur*, Cherche Midi, 2012.

—, with Ashok Som, *The Road to luxury, the evolution, markets and strategies of luxury brand management*, Wiley, 2015.

Fabio Bonavita, *Qui a tué le luxe? La face cachée d'un univers opaque*, Slatkine, 2016.

Michael Boroian, Alix de Poix, *India by design: The pursuit of luxury and fashion*, Wiley, 2010.

Elizabeth L. Cline, *Over-dressed: The shockingly high cost of cheap fashion*, Portfolio/Penguin 2012.

Frances Corner, *Why Fashion matters*, Thames & Hudson, 2015.

Sophie George, *Les Univers de la mode,* Les Éditions Falbalas, 2016.

Valérie Haie, *Donnez-nous notre luxe quotidien*, Institut supérieur du marketing de luxe, Gualino Éditeur, 2002.

Stéphanie Le Bail, *Le Luxe : entre "business" et culture*, France-Empire Monde, 2011.

Giulia Mensitieri, "*Le plus beau métier du monde*", *dans les coulisses de l'industrie de la mode*, Éditions de la Découverte, 2018.

Guénolée Milleret, Élodie de Boissieu, préface Anne-Sophie Pic, *Les Vitrines du luxe*, Eyrolles, 2016.

Misha Pinkhasov, Rachna Joshi Nair, *Real luxury: How luxury brands create value for the long term,* Palgrave Macmillan, 2014.

Erwan Rambourg, *The Bling dynasty: Why the reign of Chinese luxury shoppers has only just begun*, Wiley, 2014.

Jean Révis, Delphine Vitry, *Mad about Luxe, "Il faut que tout change pour que rien ne change…"*, Amazon Fulfillment, 2018.

Marie-Claude Sicard, *Luxe, mensonges et marketing*, Pearson Éducation France, 2010.

Lucy Sykes, Jo Piazza, *The Knockoff*, Anchor Books, Random House, 2015.

Dana Thomas, *Deluxe: How luxury lost its luster*, Penguin, 2007.

Index

A

AGHION, Gaby: 229.
AGON, Jean-Paul: 278.
ALAÏA, Azzedine: 27, 133.
ALIBABA: 171, 180, 192, 198.
AMAZON: 20, 40, 43, 171, 176, 178, 180, 185, 193, 197, 199, 200, 205.
ARNAULT, Antoine: 134, 145.
ARNAULT, Bernard: 20, 22, 23, 46, 49, 111, 112, 115, 117, 118, 119, 125, 126, 127, 128, 129, 134, 135, 136, 140, 141, 142, 143, 144, 146, 147, 155, 156, 162, 216, 217, 237, 247, 255, 276, 288.
ARNAULT, Delphine: 23, 146, 162.
AUDEMARS PIGUET: 55, 269, 276, 285.

B

BAIN & CO: 284.
BALMAIN: 30, 42, 229.
BAMBERGER, Arnaud: 53, 66, 67.
BARRÈRE, Hubert: 39.
BARRET, Agnès: 136, 147.
BAZELAIRE, Menehould de: 86, 97.

BAZIRE, Nicolas: 141.
BEENE, Geoffrey: 221, 222.
BELLONI, Antonio: 141.
BENSIMON, Pacha: 105, 106.
BERGDORF GOODMAN: 220, 222.
BERGÉ, Pierre: 23, 224, 225, 226, 232.
BEZOS, Jeff: 20, 40.
BIVER, Jean-Claude: 156, 157.
BLANCKAERT, Christian: 82, 93, 96, 97, 102, 107.
BOS, Nicolas: 71.
BOTTOLI, Marcello: 142.
BOURDONNAYE, Geoffroy de la: 234.
BOUSSAC: 125, 141, 217.
BRAVO, Rose Marie: 220.
BRETON, Thierry: 112.
BROZZETTI, Gianluca: 142.
BURBERRY: 48, 166, 213, 220, 288.
BURKE, Michael: 127, 129, 141, 144, 146.
BUSQUETS, Carmen: 201.

C

CECILIO, Daniela: 201.
CESARE, Paolo de: 120.

CHALHOUB, Patrick: 121, 173.

CHANEL: 15, 18, 19, 20, 22, 24, 27, 29, 31, 36, 37, 38, 39, 43, 48, 63, 72, 88, 99, 100, 120, 123, 129, 160, 180, 198, 217, 219, 236, 267, 276, 289.

CHAPELLE, Anne: 188.

CHEVALIER, Alain: 128.

CHLOÉ: 24, 29, 47, 61, 165, 211, 219, 227, 228, 229, 230, 231, 232, 233, 234, 235.

CHRISTIAN DIOR: 18, 29, 82, 93, 96, 99, 102, 112, 123, 125, 129, 141, 146, 147, 150, 153, 165, 204, 214, 216, 217, 218, 229, 236, 267, 276, 280.

C. MENDES: 217.

COLBERT (Comité): 53, 119, 121.

CONDÉ NAST: 179, 180, 190, 198, 207.

COURT, Frédéric: 189, 190, 201.

D

DE BEERS: 140.

DELAGE, François: 140.

DELLA VALLE, Diego: 32, 48, 247.

DELLIÈRE, Anne: 69, 71.

DELPECH, Julien: 254.

DEMIRI, Ben: 203.

DUMAS, Axel: 45, 90, 99, 100, 110, 111.

DUMAS, Pierre-Alexis: 83, 91, 98, 99.

DUMAS, Robert: 85, 87, 88, 101.

E

ELBAZ, Alber: 100, 211, 221, 222, 223, 224, 225, 226, 227, 228, 232, 237, 244.

F

FALAISE, Maxime de la: 230.

FENDI: 18, 23, 27, 29, 38, 141, 147, 173, 188, 204, 218, 219.

FENIOU, Laurent: 67.

FERRAGAMO: 151, 160.

FORD, Tom: 222, 226.

FOSUN INTERNATIONAL: 227.

FRASCH, Ron: 213.

FRENCH FEDERATION OF HAUTE COUTURE AND FASHION: 18, 47, 212, 214, 216, 241, 242.

FRITSCH, Thierry: 68, 130.

G

GAEMPERLE, Chantal: 144.

GAULTIER, Jean-Paul: 27, 89, 211, 235, 244.

GHESQUIÈRE, Nicolas: 133, 162, 163, 165, 167, 224.

GODÉ, Pierre: 141.

GREGORIADÈS, Rena: 86, 97, 98, 101, 103.

GRIMAL, Anne-Catherine: 130.

GUCCI: 20, 29, 99, 111, 120, 127, 203, 222, 226, 232, 236, 276, 277.

GUIONY, Jean-Jacques: 205.

GUTEN, Michel: 57.

GUY LAROCHE: 35, 211, 221, 222, 224, 225, 228, 237.

H

HENDERSON-STEWART, David: 255, 256.

HENRY, Guillaume: 211, 237, 238, 239.

HIERONIMUS, Nicolas: 278.

HOCQ, Robert: 56, 57, 59, 60, 61.

I

INSTITUT FRANÇAIS DE LA MODE: 213, 218.

J

JACOBS, Marc: 135, 136, 137, 165.
JACOT, Jean-Marc: 62.
JARRAR, Bouchra: 224.
JD.COM: 173, 191, 192, 198.
JONES, Kim: 165, 277.

K

KANOUI, Joseph: 60.
KELLY, Grace: 86.
KERING: 20, 21, 22, 23, 113, 147, 160, 203, 226, 232, 289.
KESSEL, Joseph: 75.
KORS, Michael: 135, 143, 222.

L

LACROIX, Christian: 126, 150.
LANCEL: 216, 228.
LANCIAUX, Concetta: 125, 135.
LANG, Helmut: 133, 186.
LANVIN: 99, 211, 223, 224, 226, 227.
LARIVIÈRE, Jean: 133.
LECTRA: 289.
LEIBOVITZ, Annie: 134.
L'ORÉAL: 43, 84, 124, 160, 226, 278.
LOUBIER, Jean-Marc: 125, 131, 133.
LUISAVIAROMA: 206.
LUKOFF, Frederick: 188.
LUMLEY, Henry de: 272, 273, 274, 280.

M

MACGIBBON, Hannah: 231.
MAISON MARTIN MARGIELA: 89, 186, 283.
MARIA LUISA: 186, 187, 188.
MASSENET, Natalie: 49, 176, 192, 206.
MATCHESFASHION: 191, 206.
MAYHOOLA: 235.

McCARTNEY, Stella: 188, 230, 231, 232, 288.
MELLO, Dawn: 222.
MENCHARI, Leila: 99, 100, 101, 102.
MILLE, Richard: 55, 281.
MOLTENI, Andrea: 175.
MORAND, Pascal: 241, 278.
MUSSARD, Pascale: 91, 92, 96, 113, 114.

N

NEO INVESTMENT PARTNERS: 212, 240, 242.
NET-A-PORTER: 49, 151.
NICHANIAN, Véronique: 88, 90, 94, 213.
NINA RICCI: 211, 235, 236, 237, 238, 240.
NOUVEL, Jean: 73.

O

OMEGA: 55, 258, 269, 279.

P

PAVLOVSKY, Bruno: 36, 48, 123, 180, 242.
PHILO, Phoebe: 31, 211, 230, 231, 232, 233.
PICART, Jean-Jacques: 237.
PINAULT, François-Henri: 20, 21, 22, 23, 49, 111, 155, 226, 232.
PISTONO, Federico: 158, 159.
PRADA: 22, 48, 99, 107, 120, 128, 160, 163, 276.
PRIGENT, Loïc: 136, 137.
PUIFORCAT: 90, 94.
PUIG: 235, 236, 239, 240, 241.

Q

QUENET, Jean-Claude: 259, 270.
QUERCIZE, Stanislas de: 75.

R

RACAMIER, Henry: 53, 126, 127, 128, 131.
RAMSAY-LEVI, Natacha: 165, 230.
RICHEMONT: 23, 49, 54, 55, 57, 60, 61, 62, 69, 70, 71, 73, 74, 113, 117, 147, 160, 161, 176, 220, 227, 228, 233, 234, 258, 289.
ROGERS, Holli: 151.
ROLEX: 247, 259, 270, 276, 279, 285.
ROSSO, Renzo: 235, 283.
RUPERT, Anton: 60, 61, 70, 233.
RUPERT, Johann: 49, 61, 69, 70, 76, 158, 233.

S

SAKS FIFTH AVENUE: 213, 220.
SEYNES, Guillaume de: 108, 242.
SHANG XIA: 109.
SITBON, Martine: 230.
SOLZHENITSYN, Alexander: 149.
SOUSA, Cipriano: 183, 196, 197.
SROLEVICH, Monique: 218.
STOCKER, Marie-Aude: 161.
SWATCH: 55, 156, 249, 250.

T

TAITTINGER: 249.
TESSON, Sylvain: 16, 252, 253.
TESTINO, Mario: 264, 265, 266.
THOMAS, Patrick: 44, 94, 108, 109, 110, 111, 179.

TIDE-FRATER, Susanne: 188, 200.
TISCI, Riccardo: 166, 238.
TOLEDANO, Boris: 216.
TOLEDANO, Céline: 218, 222.
TOLEDANO, Joseph: 214, 216.
TOLEDANO, Sidney: 123, 141, 146, 147, 153, 214, 215, 216, 217, 218, 242.

V

VACCARELLO, Anthony: 211.
VALENTINO: 147, 166, 188, 227, 235.
VAN CLEEF & ARPELS: 24, 53, 71, 99, 161, 162, 276.
VAUTRIN, Catherine: 139.
VICTORIA BECKHAM: 47, 211, 240, 241.
VIGNERON, Cyrille: 77.
VODIANOVA, Natalia: 247, 264, 268.

W

WAIGHT KELLER, Clare: 230.
WANG, Shaw-Lan: 226.
WARGNIER, Stéphane: 109.
WINTOUR, Anna: 237, 276.

Y

YIQING, Yin: 211.
YOOX: 189, 202.
YVES SAINT LAURENT: 23, 38, 40, 173, 213, 217, 223, 224, 225, 230, 232, 242, 286.

Corlet Imprimeur
(Condé-en-Normandie).
October 2019.
No. : 19090480.

Printed in France.